GREAT AMERICAN HOTELIERS
Pioneers of the Hotel Industry

STANLEY TURKEL

authorHOUSE®

AuthorHouse™
1663 Liberty Drive
Bloomington, IN 47403
www.authorhouse.com
Phone: 1-800-839-8640

First published by AuthorHouse 9/14/2009

ISBN: 978-1-4490-0754-6 (e)
ISBN: 978-1-4490-0753-9 (sc)
ISBN: 978-1-4490-0752-2 (hc)

Library of Congress Control Number: 2009907588

Printed in the United States of America
Bloomington, Indiana

This book is printed on acid-free paper.

On the cover (from left clockwise):
- *A.M Sonnabend*
- *Bill and J.W. Marriott*
- *Frederick Henry Harvey*
- *Henry Morrison Flagler*
- *Henry Bradley Plant*
- *Carl Graham Fisher*

Antique postcards from the author's collection

TABLE OF CONTENTS

DEDICATION

To four men who influenced my business career in significant ways:

1. Nathan Turkel- my immigrant/entrepreneur father who successfully operated the Manhattan-based New York Laundry for forty-five years.

2. Victor Kramer- founder of the Victor Kramer Laundry Consulting Co. who taught me how to be a consultant.

3. Preston Robert Tisch- co-founder of the Loews Hotels Corporation who gave me my first hotel job as the resident manager of the 1840-room Americana Hotel of New York.

4. Harold S. Geneen- chairman of the International Telephone & Telegraph Co. whose fact-based management methods were a revelation to me when I served as the product line manager helping to oversee the Sheraton Corporation of America.

FOREWORD

By Stephen Rushmore, President, HVS International

What better way to learn about the hotel industry than to experience it through the eyes of some of the world's greatest hoteliers. Stanley Turkel's book, <u>Great American Hoteliers: Pioneers of the Hotel Industry</u>, takes an upfront and personal view of 16 leaders who shaped the American hotel industry over the past century. Familiar names such as J. Willard Marriott, Howard Johnson and Conrad Hilton are mixed with some obscure players such as Henry Bradley Plant, Carl Graham Fisher and Henry Morrison Flagler to provide a unique insight into the intricacies of hotel development, operations and investment.

Drawing from more than 40 years of industry experience including managing some of the largest New York City hotels, Turkel captures the spirit of each of these pioneers and relates their achievements to important lessons that we can all learn from.

John Q. Hammons, still going strong developing hotels in tertiary cities at the age of 90, shows us the need to give back to the local community. While he might negotiate to buy a hotel site for only $1. his huge convention hotel developments have brought new prosperity to many decaying cities.

Juan Trippe, founder of Pan American World Airlines and InterContinental Hotels, created one of the first global hotel companies. Trippe was one of the few hoteliers who were able to create synergy through the direct ownership of hotels and airplanes. He also helped countries economically by providing state-of-the art hotel accommodations for tourist and business travelers.

Kanjibhai Manchhubhai Patel, one of the first Asian American hoteliers came to the United States in 1923 and started operating a small residential hotel in San Francisco. Over the years thousands of Patels and other immigrants followed- they became American citizens, they purchased hotels, and they realized the American dream of owning your own business.

Turkel's book is not just a biography detailing the lives of important hoteliers but an informative text covering a number of important industry issues. For example, the Asian American hotel community through the Asian American Hotel Owners Association (AAHOA), have over the years battled the large hotel franchise companies to obtain fairer franchise terms and provisions. Turkel not only vividly describes how this war has evolved, but includes all 12 points of AAHOA's Fair Franchising Policy. Great reference material for both newcomers to the hotel industry and seasoned professionals.

Stan Turkel has written more than 200 articles on hospitality related topics. He never shies away from taking a controversial point of view and relentlessly prods industry players to do better. The titles of his articles certainly demonstrate his push for perfection; "Reinventing Hotel Franchising," "Accounting Guide Needs Revision," "Imbalance of Equity in Contracts," and the one that gives me pain- "Little Reality in a Typical Feasibility Study." Ugh! Readers of his book will see that Stan has pin-pointed many of the important issues facing the hospitality industry today and using his usual straight-forward approach- offers relevant solutions. What Stan also brings out is that many of the issues we face today are the same issues faced by the hotelier pioneers of yesteryear- how to motivate and retain staff, how to grow your company and how to fight the big guys.

Thank you to Stanley Turkel for giving the hospitality industry your unique perspective on its pioneers, its issues and most importantly its solutions.

Stephen Rushmore is President and Founder of HVS International, a global hospitality consulting organization with offices in New York, San Francisco, Miami, Boulder, Dallas, Vancouver, Toronto, Sao Paulo, Buenos Aires, London, New Delhi, Singapore, Madrid, and Sydney. He directs the worldwide operation of this firm and is responsible for future office expansion and new product development. Mr. Rushmore has provided consultation services for more than 12,000 hotels throughout the world during his 35-year career and specializes in complex issues involving hotel feasibility, valuations, and financing.

PREFACE

How lucky can you get? For the past thirty years, I have made a good living doing what I love to do. I am one of the most widely- published hotel consultants in the United States. Yet my entry into the hotel business was a random series of unexpected opportunities. My very first job in a hotel was as the Resident Manager of the Americana of New York. The general manager was Tom Troy, whose forbearance, patience and training enabled me to learn the craft of hotel keeping. Tom had trained earlier in the Statler Hotel Company. His stories about the genius of the Statler systems were stored in my memory bank until I started to write this book.

Those unexpected opportunities started after my graduation from New York University with a BS in Business Management when I went to work for my father in the New York Laundry on the east side of Manhattan. When he sold the business some three years later, I joined the Victor Kramer Company, a laundry management consulting firm. Their clients were mostly hospitals and some hotels with problems in their laundry operations and linen control systems. During the next seven years, as I served my clients (individual hospitals and state and county institutions), I schooled myself in housekeeping methods, engineering and maintenance, water and steam science, kitchen equipment and food and beverage operations. In short, I became a back-of-the-house expert. One of the clients I served was the Tisch Hotel Company, owned by Laurence and Preston R. Tisch. They owned and operated the Laurel-in-the-Pines, Lakewood, N.J.; the Grand Hotel, Highmount, N.Y.; the Traymore and Ambassador Hotels, Atlantic City, N.J.; and the Belmont Plaza and the McAlpin Hotel in New York City. When the Tisch brothers acquired Loews Theatres, they created the Loews Hotel Corporation and began an extensive new hotel construction program including the Summit Hotel, the Americana Hotel and the Regency in New York City; the Americana in San Juan, Puerto Rico; the Americana in Bal Harbour, Florida. With this expansion, I joined the Loews Corporation and helped to design, staff and operate the back-of-the-house departments of all the Loews Hotels. Then, I was selected to be the Resident

Manager of the Americana Hotel (now the Sheraton New York) on 53rd Street and Seventh Avenue (1840 rooms, 125,000 square feet of meeting, banquet and exhibition space, 3 restaurants and the Royal Box Night Club). After ten months in this concentrated on-the-job training position, I was named the General Manager of the 680-room Drake Hotel on 56th Street and Park Ave. After two and a half years at the luxurious Drake Hotel, I became the General Manager of the 762 room Summit Hotel at 51st Street and Lexington Avenue. When the Summit was built in 1969, the first new hotel in New York in 30 years, it was designed by the famous Florida architect, Morris Lapidus, In a critical comment about its design, a critic said that "it was too far from the beach".

After three years at the Summit Hotel, I was recruited by the International Telephone & Telegraph Corporation who had recently acquired the Sheraton Corporation of America. After a year as assistant to the ITT Vice President of Consumer Services, I was promoted to Product Line Manager for Worldwide Hotel Services. In the next seven years, I traveled all over the United States, Canada, South America, Europe, the Mideast, Hawaii, the Far East on ITT/ Sheraton business negotiating new hotel developments and reviewing Sheraton Hotel budgets and performances.

During those years, the Dunfey Hotel Company in New Hampshire was Sheraton's largest franchisee. When Dunfey was acquired by the Aetna Life and Casualty, Jack Dunfey asked me to serve as his consultant. This year-long consulting contract enabled me to establish my own hotel consulting practice.

During the past thirty years, I realized that a knowledge of the history of the hotel business is essential for anyone interested in a career in the lodging industry. As Confucius wrote, "Study the past if you would divine the future." With the rapid technological changes taking place, it is more than ever important to know where we have been in order to predict where we are going.

I am an emeritus member of the Board of Advisors of the New York University Preston Robert Tisch Center for Hospitality, Tourism, and Sports Management. I consider myself fortunate to have been present at the birth of the NYU "hotel" school back in 1997. On the many occasions that I have lectured at the school and elsewhere, I have been struck by the lack of knowledge of the students about the history of the American hotel industry. This book is my contribution to the essential effort to teach this important subject.

INTRODUCTION

Americans invented the urban luxury hotel at the beginning of the 19th century. Anthony Trollope, the famous British novelist wrote in 1862 that one of the striking features of American life in the mid-nineteenth century was that "everybody travels in the States." He observed that "the first sign of an incipient settlement (was) a hotel five stories high, with an office, a bar, a cloak room, three gentlemen's parlors, two ladies' parlors, and a ladies entrance and two hundred bedrooms." Hotel buildings defined the central business districts like the taverns and inns before them. They provided drawing rooms and parlors, sleeping accommodations, communal eating places, bars, and by the early twentieth century, private and lockable bedrooms and bathrooms.

The Eastern Hotel, Whitehall Street, New York, N.Y. in 1906 (with awnings and fire escapes). It was built by Captain Coles in 1822 and it was first called the Eagle Hotel. When the first successful Atlantic Cable was laid in 1858, the hotel was renamed the Great Eastern, after the ship that laid the cable. It survived for 98 years until Prohibition sealed its doom in 1920.

Do students know that when Ellsworth M. Statler opened the first modern hotel in Buffalo, N.Y. in 1908, the following practices were commonplace?

- Some hotels embarrassed nonpaying male guests by cutting off their trousers at the knees and making them parade in the lobby with sandwich signs that proclaimed them as "deadbeats."

- One hotel specifically forbade guests from spitting on the carpets, lying in bed with their boots on, or driving nails into the furniture.

- Even the better hotels had shared bathroom facilities. Bathtubs were usually built on a platform, and hot water cost 25 cents extra.

- About 90 percent of hotels were American plan, with cheap, unlimited food included in the room rate.

- Smoking was usually not permitted in dining rooms, bars barred women and wine and beer sold better than hard liquor.

- Rooms were heated with stoves or open fireplaces. Signs reminded guests to not blow out the gas jets.

- No hotel owner called his house full until all double beds were fully occupied, often by complete strangers. Talk about yield management.

The development of America's 19th century hotels was the result of many things; the restlessness of the U.S. population; the increasing wealth of the commercial and industrial classes; the relative classlessness of American society; the growth of the trans continental railroad system which made long-distance travel possible (and in time luxurious); and the growth of great urban centers.

During the thirty years prior to the Civil War, Americans built hotels larger and more ostentatious than any in the rest of the world. These hotels were inextricably intertwined with American culture and customs but were accessible to average citizens. As Jefferson Williamson wrote in *The American Hotel* (1930), hotels were perhaps "the most distinctively American of all our institutions, for they were nourished and brought to flower solely in American soil and borrowed practically nothing from abroad."

As in the past, development of hotels was stimulated by the confluence of travel, tourism and transportation. In 1869, the transcontinental railroad engendered hotel development by Henry Morrison Flagler, Fred Harvey, George Mortimer Pullman and Henry Bradley Plant. The Lincoln Highway and the Interstate Highway System triggered hotel development by Ellsworth Statler, Kemmons Wilson, Howard D. Johnson and Carl Graham Fisher. The airplane encouraged Juan Trippe, Conrad M. Hilton, J. Willard Marriott, John McEntee Bowman, Ernest Henderson, Sr., A.M. Sonnabend and John Q. Hammons.

Because the class system was not firmly rooted in America, hotels were seen as public buildings which were business and meeting-oriented and a place where all classes and people mingled together, the wealthy along with workingmen and frontiersmen.

Donald Albrecht, in his preface to *New Hotels for Global Nomads* writes,

> Hotels are buildings that have been reinvented and reimagined for two hundred years- now more so than ever. Since the nineteenth century, hotels, whether in cities or remote oases, have evolved from simple places to sleep while on the road into elaborate destinations that combine private guestrooms, with restaurants, lounges, gyms, spas, meeting facilities and ballrooms. Architecture has become experience.

Long before hotel franchising, segmentation and branding, there were taverns with hotel rooms catering to the 19th century road warrior. But, like today there were also sharp-eyed critics of hotel amenities and services. One of the best known was a humorist named Josh Billings who wrote the following hilarious critique in the New Albany Weekly Ledger, New Albany, Indiana, March 22, 1871:

I don't know of any business more flattersome than the tavern business. There don't seem to be anything to do but to stand in front of the register with a pen behind the ear, and see that the guests enter the house, then tell John to show the gentlemen to 976, and then take four dollars and fifty cents next morning from the devil of a traveler.

Your room is 13 foot 5 inches, by 9 foot 7 inches, parallelogramly. The carpet is ingrained with the dust, kerosene oil, and ink spots of four generations. There is two pegs in the room to hitch coats onto; one of them broke off, and the other pulled out and missing.

There is no curtain to the window, and there don't want to be any; you can't see out, and who can see in? The bed is a modern slat-bottom, with two mattresses – one cotton and one husk, and both harder and about as thick as a sea biscuit. You enter the beds sideways, and can feel every slat at once as is you could the ribs of a gridiron. The bed is inhabited. You sleep some, but roll over a good deal.

Just because America is a nation of travelers, travel has not always been an exercise of comfort. In fact, the tavern/hotel described by Josh Billings above was more the likely lodging accommodation during the eighteenth and early nineteenth century. It was not until 1794 that the first American hotel was created when a lodging property was built on the site of the old Burns Coffee House on "the Broad-way" in New York City. The proprietor called it The City Hotel. The unknown builders claimed it was the first structure erected solely for "hotel purposes" in America. The City Hotel had seventy three rooms, large enough for visitors to call it "an immense establishment". Shortly thereafter, real hotels were built in other cities: Boston's Exchange Coffee House (1804), Philadelphia's Mansion House (1807), Baltimore's City Hotel (1826) and New Orleans' St. Charles (1837). New York's first skyscraper- for so it was regarded at the time- was the six-story Adelphi Hotel which opened in 1827.

In those days, sharing beds with strangers was common practice. It was an early manifestation of revenue maximization. Apparently, it made no difference if guests were of different sexes. This apocryphal story reveals the practice:

> A man traveling in Connecticut in about 1820 was reproached by a matron of his acquaintance who accused him of living a dissipated life. The man protested that he was not so different from anyone else, that most people would act as he did when put in similar circumstances. The matron asked him to name one situation in which she would act as he did. "Suppose, then, madam," the man said, "that in traveling you came to an inn, where all of the beds were full except two, and in one of these was a man, and in the other a woman, which would you take?" "Why the woman's to be sure", the matron answered. "Well, madam", said the man, "so would I."

Charles Dickens wrote in his 1842 travel journal that Boston's Tremont House "has more galleries, colonnades, piazzas, and passages than I can remember or the reader would believe." The Tremont had 170 rooms, many more than the typical inn. Designed by Isaiah Rogers, a well-known architect, the Tremont had a neo-classical white granite façade and filled an entire block on Tremont Street. The Tremont contained a long list of innovative installations and features, including "electro-magnetic anunciator" that guests used to communicate with the front ("One ring for ice-water, two for bellboy, three for porter, four for chambermaid, and not a darned one of them will come," quipped a wit of the day.); public spaces with high ceilings and marble mosaic floors; washbowls and free soap in rooms; bellhops on duty to carry guest luggage upstairs; eight bathrooms in the courtyard; and a la carte food service.

George Augustus Sala, a popular London journalist, was one of the most enthusiastic admirers of America's hotels. He wrote in the Temple Bar Magazine in 1861: "The American hotel is to an English hotel what an elephant is to a periwinkle.... An American hotel is (in the chief cities) as roomy as Buckingham Palace, and is not much inferior to a palace in its internal fittings. It has ranges of drawing rooms, suites of private rooms, vast staircases and interminable layers of bedchambers." American hotels were the wonder of the Old World. Their size, luxurious furnishings, and the excellence of their table were constant subjects of admiration in European newspapers. In fact, the belief was widespread in England that all Americans lived in hotels.

Perhaps the most super-elegant and grandest hotel of the time was the St. Nicholas which opened January 6, 1853 in New York City. The St. Nicholas was six-story 500-room, white marble treasure-house of fine, expensive things, such as window-curtains costing $700 apiece, gold embroidered draperies costing $1,000, a grand piano valued at $1,500. On all sides in the public rooms, with their twenty-two-foot ceilings, there was paneled mahogany and walnut, carved richly in scroll and figure designs. Every room, public or private, was crowded with rosewood and mahogany furniture, and the chairs and sofas were upholstered in Flemish tapestry. Turkish rugs and thick Brussels carpets were installed in hallways and rooms, and window-hangings of damask and figured silks hung at windows and between beveled French pier-glasses in ornate gilt frames. Mirrors were everywhere, in public and private rooms, in vestibules and halls, with the gaslight from huge fancy chandeliers blazing down through a riot of colored prisms on their highly polished surfaces. And everywhere, it seemed, there was gold paint. The St. Nicholas laid its gold-leaf on with lavishness that it gave rise to a popular joke of the day. It is related that an English comedian declined to put his shoes outside the door to be shined, for fear the management would gild them. The St. Nicholas lasted only thirty years until 1884, a victim of rapid mechanical and structural advancements.

Hotel pioneers went beyond electric lights, steam-powered heating, grand public spaces and private bathrooms to attract guests. They created two types of food service: the American plan in 1830, where guests paid for a days' or weeks' worth of meals along with the room—whether or not they ventured into the dining room. The European plan whereby the guest paid only for his room and took his meals wherever he pleased, originated in France and spread slowly in the U.S. after 1870.

The Parker House in Boston was one of the first hotels to deviate from the American plan and embrace the more flexible European plan. As such, it claims status as the oldest continuously operating hotel in America, along with the first passenger elevator in the city. Hotelier Harvey Parker was also the first to offer meals continuously throughout the day, rather than at fixed intervals, and the second floor became a popular choice for the dining clubs of the time. Twentieth century Americans resisted the European plan as an affront to democratic ideals. Today, the American plan exists only on cruise ships and certain inclusive resorts, like Club Med. The Parker House had little culinary competition in Boston, but its great contribution to the nation's menu is its namesake roll. The ideal Parker House roll "should be delicate, soft and rather sweet, typical of American rolls in the 19th century," said food critic James Beard, "and consume butter by the tons."

A few other hotels are known for their kitchen's creations. Swiss immigrant Oscar Tschirky was a busboy at New York's Hoffman House and waited tables at Delmonico's before joining the newly opened Waldorf-Astoria on the site of the Empire State Building in 1893 as maitre d' hotel. As Oscar of the Waldorf, he is credited with simplifying menus in general, but specifically for writing the 907- page "The Cook Book by Oscar of the Waldorf" in 1896, one of the great American guides to luxurious dining.

The Brown Hotel in Louisville Kentucky, built in 1922 by lumberman J. Graham Brown, is known for its namesake dish "Hot Brown". Created in the hotel's early years by chef Fred K. Schmidt as a brand new enticement for late-night dance business, this hearty dish layers toast and sliced turkey and is slathered with Mornay sauce and topped with parmesan cheese and two strips of bacon for good taste.

The Brown Palace Hotel in Denver opened in 1892 with an eight-story atrium designed by architect Frank E. Edbrooke. More than 400 wrought iron grill work panels ring the lobby from the third through the seventh floor. Two of them are upside down, one to serve the tradition that man is imperfect; the other sneaked in by a disgruntled workman. Finding these bits of history still intrigues visitors to the 115-year old Brown Palace Hotel. Architect John Portman gave new life to the hotel atrium with his design for the Hyatt Regency Hotel in

Atlanta in 1967. Incidentally, all the major hotel companies including Hilton, Sheraton and Loews turned Portman down. Only the fledging Hyatt Houses (operator of airport inns) had the foresight to imagine this new version of a historic design.

The famous novelist Sinclair Lewis who worked in a hotel and knew the business well had a traveling salesman describe it in his 1934 novel "*Work of Art*":

> Look here, son! Somebody been ribbing you about hotel keeping not being a dignified and highfalutin' line of business? You tell 'em to go soak their head! Dignified! I tell you, way I figure it, some day there's going to be even bigger and sweller hotels than the Waldorf, and then, as the hotels get bigger, the hotelmen are going to be more important.
>
> Go to it, boy! You've got to learn a lot. You'll have to learn accounting and purchasing; deal with big supply houses for maybe a thousand knives and forks, a hundred turkeys and five kegs of oysters. You'll have to know all about china and silver and glass and linen and brocade and the best woods for flooring and furniture. A hotel manager has to be a combination of a housefrau, a chef, a barroom bouncer, a doctor for emergencies, a wet nurse, an upholsterer, a walking directory that knows right off hand, without looking it up, just where the Hardshell Baptist Church is and what time the marriage license bureau opens and what time the local starts for Hick Junction. He's got to be a certified public accountant, a professor of languages, a quick-action laundryman, a plumber, a heating engineer, a carpenter, a swell speechmaker, an authority on the importance of every tinhorn state senator or one-night stand lecturer that blows in and expects to have the red carpet already hauled out for him. He's got to know more about wine and cigars than the fellows that make 'em- they can fool around and try experiments, but he's got to sell 'em. If you can do all this, you'll have a good time. Go to it.

My research into the lives of great American hoteliers reveals one continuous strand: the presence of a unique entrepreneur who created a singular hotel company one hotel at a time. Most of these men did not grow up in the hospitality business but became successful through their intense on-the-job training experiences. Their tradition-breaking vision and single-minded ambition led them to heights they could not have imagined. My investigation has uncovered remarkable and startling true stories about these pioneers, some of whom are well-known and others whose accomplishments are lost in the dustbin of history.

SOURCE MATERIAL

1. Donald Albrecht, *New Hotels For Global Nomads*, Cooper-Hewitt, National Design Museum, New York, 2002

2. Carolyn Bancroft, *The Brown Palace in Denver*, Denver 1955

3. Charles Dickens, *American Notes for General Circulation*, Penguin Classics, New York, 1842

4. New Albany Weekly Ledger, New Albany, Indiana, March 22, 1871

5. Sinclair Lewis, *Work of Art,* Doubleday, New York, 1934

6. Brian McGinty, *The Palace Inns: A Connoisseur's Guide to Historic American Hotels*, Stackpole Books, Harrisburg, 1978

7. The New York Times, New York, December 12, 2004.

8. James W. Spring, *Boston and The Parker House*, Boston, 1927

9. Arthur White, *Palaces of the People: A Social History of Commercial Hospitality*, Taplinger Publishing company, New York, 1970

10. Jefferson Williamson, *The American Hotel: An Anecdotal History*, Alfred A. Knopf, New York, 1930

John McEntee Bowman (1875-1931):

INTERNATIONAL SPORTSMAN AND EXTRAORDINARY DEVELOPER OF BILTMORE HOTELS

John McEntee Bowman, president of the Bowman-Biltmore Hotel Corporation had no easy boyhood. Born in 1875 in Toronto to Irish-Scottish immigrants, Bowman came to New York in 1892- he was then seventeen- with the traditional lack of funds. He carried a letter of introduction to the manager of the old Manhattan Hotel at Madison Avenue and Forty-second Street. After waiting hours for an interview, he left without seeing the manager. He subsequently mailed the letter, asking for an appointment but received no reply and no returned letter. He got his first experience in the hotel business when an employment agency sent him as a front desk clerk to a summer hotel in the Adirondacks and the following winter to a hotel in the south. He later landed a job as riding- master at the Durland Riding Academy in Manhattan, a skill he learned in Canada working for a stable of race-horses on the county fair circuit. When Durland's passed a rule that the riding masters had to wear uniforms, Bowman rebelled, resigned and set up his own small riding academy. He had few horses and little cash but the venture was profitable enough when he left it to take charge of wines and cigars in the old Holland House on Fifth Avenue then operated by Gustave Baumann. Baumann served as his teacher and mentor and ultimately appointed him as his assistant and secretary. When Baumann opened the New York Biltmore Hotel on New Year's Eve in 1913, he appointed Bowman as vice president and managing director. In the summer of 1914, when Baumann in a fit of depression leaped from an upper-story window of the Biltmore, Bowman succeeded to the presidency. The Biltmore was designed by Warren & Wetmore in the popular Beaux-Arts style. Whitney Warren (1864-1943) studied at the Ecole des Beaux-Arts in Paris and with his partner Charles Delavan Wetmore (1866-1941) specialized in the design of hotels, office buildings and railroad stations. Architect Leonard Schultze (1877-1951) was a lead designer for Warren & Wetmore and later designed some of the most famous U.S. hotels (Pierre, Sherry-Netherland, Waldorf-Astoria, Lexington, Breakers) in his own firm, Schultze and Weaver. The Biltmore opened near Grand Central Station with twenty-seven stories, and one thousand guestrooms.

At the turn of the twentieth century, railroads provided the genesis for the development of hotels. No invention up until then transformed modern life like the railroad which fostered development of new hotels near city railroad terminals. The ultimate development was the Grand Central Terminal in New York City, the Beaux-Arts centerpiece of an extraordinary complex of hotels, office buildings and apartment buildings. Railroad engineer William Wilgus conceived a way "to make the land pay more." Prior to the construction of Grand Central, land was viewed as having value on and below the surface including rights to mineral resources. But Wilgus realized that the space over the tracks was valuable as well and invented the concept of "commercial air rights". To pay for the enormous costs of excavating this area, Wilgus proposed selling the rights to real estate developers who were eager to build skyscrapers over the tracks. Throughout the 1910s and 1920s Wilgus's concept of air rights was realized. The Commodore, Biltmore, Park Lane, Roosevelt and Waldorf-Astoria were all developed in keeping with Wilgus's brilliant innovation.

The Hotel Commodore in New York City was opened in December 1917 as the world's largest hotel with 2000 rooms adjacent to the Grand Central Terminal Station. It is now the Grand Hyatt Hotel.

The Hotel Monthly ("The Biltmore, New York's Newest Hotel Creation," January 1914) praised the operating benefits of the Biltmore's regular, square-shaped plan, including symmetrical layout of corridors with very few turns, easing the circulation of guests. The U-shaped light well of the guestroom floors allowed better light and ventilation, creating a large number of desirable rooms. The interior design located the public spaces in a logical and well-established division with the lower-level public rooms and upper-floor ballroom.

When Prohibition during the 1920s removed the economic cushion of liquor profits, John Bowman and the Warren & Wetmore firm applied a more rigorous cost analysis for the new Commodore Hotel in New York (1918-1919). They intended that the Commodore, built over Grand Central Station, would have two thousand rooms at lesser rates than the Biltmore. John Bowman wrote in <u>Hotel Management</u> (April 1923):

> This large number of people includes many who are not used to complete personal service such as the attendance of a valet, and who do not like to be waited upon too much. So the degree of our service which corresponded with the reduced cost as compared with the Biltmore, also corresponded with fair exactness to the desires and business demands of the guests. This great volume as compared with the overhead makes it possible to give say roughly eighty percent of the Biltmore service at sixty percent of the prices.

<u>Hotel World</u> magazine apparently agreed with Bowman. In an article titled "Hotel Commodore, New York City Now Heads Bowman Chain of Caravansaries" (February 1919), they wrote,

> No other hotel in the world offers so much at any price. In the construction of the building the thought has been kept constantly in mind to produce a great hotel that could be operated at very low cost… This the architects have been able to accomplish.

From the Bowman flair for the spectacular comes many a story. Example: a delegation of foreign hotel men visited the Commodore. Why not, thought Mr. Bowman, show them a typical U.S. spectacle? So he put up a tent in the Grand Ballroom of the Commodore, covered the floor with sawdust, secured sideshow acts and wild animals from his circus friend John Ringling. When the delegation arrived, it walked into a genuine circus, complete even to an elephant which the Commodore's freight elevator had safely transported.

Open the night stand drawer in almost any hotel room in the world and you will find a bible place there by the Gideon's International. The oldest Christian business professional men's association in the United

States, the Gideons have been around for more than 100 years and have been placing Bibles in hotels rooms for almost that long.

The Association began in a hotel room on September 14, 1898, in Boscobel, Wisconsin. The manager of the Central Hotel there asked traveling salesmen John H. Nicholson of Janesville, Wis., and Samuel E. Hill of Beloit, Wis., to share a room in a crowded hotel, which was hosting a lumbermen's convention. In Room 19, above the saloon, the men discovered that they were both Christians. They prayed and read the Bible together before settling down for the night. They talked about starting a Christian traveling men's association but parted ways the next morning without any definite plans. A chance meeting the following May rekindled the idea, and on July 1, 1899, the two salesmen, joined by a third, William J. Knights, met in Janesville and founded the Gideons. The name comes from the Old Testament book of Judges. Today, the Boscobel Hotel, where the two founders met, is listed on the National Historical Register, and Room 19, where the idea of the Gideons was conceived, is marked with a special plaque.

The Gideons primary purpose has always been personal evangelization conducted by Christian business and professional men. As early as 1900, the organization considered putting Bibles at the front desk of the hotels its members stayed in, but it was not until 1908 that the association voted to place Bibles in all hotel rooms. Within 20 years of the first placement of a Gideon Bible in the hotel room, the association distributed one million Bibles. Because the Gideons so quickly became associated with hotel room bibles, the association has, at times, had to remind its members that the Bibles are but a means to an end, not an end in themselves. The sole purpose for the group is to win men, women, boys and girls to a saving knowledge of the Lord, Jesus Christ through personal witnessing and the distribution of Bibles.

John McEntee Bowman took the initiative to new heights. On the third floor of the Hotel Biltmore in New York, a mediation chapel was opened for guests and employees alike. It contained benches, a small altar and fresh flowers. Over the altar was the inscription, "Come unto me all ye that labor and are heavy laden and I will give you rest." (Matthew 11:28). Similar meditation chapels were installed in other hotels operated by the Bowman Biltmore Hotel Corporation. John Bowman said, "The presence of one spot in the hotel disassociated from the worldly things of life and dedicated to the God we profess to serve, is now recognized as a spiritual necessity."

By 1919 Bowman had bought and sold two major New York hotels, had acquired the Hotel Ansonia and had taken over the operation of the Murray Hill Hotel and the Belmont Hotel. By the time he opened the Commodore, his New York properties totaled nearly eight thousand guestrooms and, according to a headline in the New York Times (May 6, 1918) "encircled" Grand Central Terminal. Meanwhile, Bowman was expanding his Biltmore hotel empire across the United States and into Cuba.

"The Biltmore Hotel" was the name adopted by Bowman for his chain of hotels. The name evokes the Vanderbilt family's Biltmore estate whose buildings and gardens are privately-owned historical landmarks in Asheville, North Carolina.

- Los Angeles Biltmore Hotel- in the early 1920s Southern California had a great surge in population, business creation and real estate development. Bowman commissioned Schultze and Weaver to design the Los Angeles Biltmore. The 11-story 1,112 room hotel opened in 1923 and became known as the "host of the coast". Composed of three huge towers, the Biltmore quickly became a Los Angeles icon with its grand ballroom seating 650. The main lobby is three stories high with deep barrel vaulting, a gilded, coffered ceiling and features a dramatic staircase derived from an early sixteenth- century staircase in the Spanish Burgos Cathedral. The hotel has served as the backdrop setting for more than 50 major motion pictures including *Ghostbusters*, *The Nutty Professor*, *Independence Day*, *True Lies*, *Dave* and *Beverly Hills Cop*.

- Sevilla- Biltmore Hotel, Havana, Cuba- During the 1920s, Havana was a favorite winter vacation destination for well-to-do Americans. In 1919, John Bowman and Charles Francis Flynn bought the four-story Sevilla Hotel which was built in 1908 by the architects Arellano y Mendoza. On January 28, 1923, the <u>New York Times</u> reported that Bowman would build a ten-story addition with Schultze and Weaver designs. Set at a right angle to the original Sevilla, the new building added two hundred guestrooms and bathrooms, the 300-seat Roof Garden restaurant with spectacular views of the Presidential Palace, the Capitol Building and Morro Castle. The expanded Sevilla Biltmore Hotel opened on January 30, 1924. Bowman and Flynn timed their expansion just right. The Sevilla-Biltmore opened five years after Prohibition was imposed in the United States.

The hotel was featured in Graham Greene's novel, *Our Man In Havana*.

- <u>Atlanta Biltmore Hotel</u>, Atlanta, Georgia- John McEntee Bowman and Holland Ball Judkins partnered with Coca-Cola heir William Candler to develop the $6 million Atlanta Biltmore in 1924 with eleven floors, 600 guestrooms, extensive convention facilities and an adjacent ten-story apartment building. The Atlanta Biltmore was designed by Bowman's favorite architectural firm of Schultze and Weaver.

The Atlanta Biltmore was built close to the downtown area but separated from the business district. The hotel opened with great fanfare with a chartered train from New York City to bring wealthy and famous guests to Atlanta for the grand opening. The opening festivities were broadcast nationally over the radio. According to one reporter, hotels like the Atlanta Biltmore provided "the background for a ceaseless pageant of human life, and even of human romance, and architecturally it is at its best when it dramatizes the people beneath its roof, when it makes the life and spirit within its walls transcend the routine and ordinary everyday trend of existence."

The Atlanta Biltmore, once known as the South's supreme hotel, staged galas, tea dances, debutante balls, and recitals by visiting Metropolitan Opera stars. It served celebrities such as Franklin D. Roosevelt, Dwight D. Eisenhower, Mary Pickford, Bette Davis, and Charles Lindbergh. For more than 30 years, WSB, the South's first radio station, broadcasted from its studios within the hotel and the radio tower on the hotel roof which became a landmark on the city skyline. Facing increased competition from Atlanta's modern downtown hotels, it was sold to a series of owners beginning in the 1960s and closed its doors in 1982. In Spring 1999 after extensive renovations, the former Biltmore Hotel reopened for the first time in almost 20 years and won an Honorable Mention in the Best Mixed-Use Deal of the Year category in the Atlanta Business Chronicle.

- The Westchester Biltmore Country Club, Rye, N.Y.- In May 1922, Bowman opened the luxurious Westchester-Biltmore Country Club in Rye, New York. The $5 million hotel and country club was located on 680 acres purchased from three different sellers. In the summer of 1919, an eight-story building was built from designs by the New York architects Warren & Wetmore. In it Bowman combined what were to become signature elements of all his great hotels; a total environment that would include amenities well beyond that of an ordinary country club. Members and guests were able to participate in golf, tennis, squash, trap shooting, and swimming at a private bathing beach on Long Island Sound. Bowman, who was a fan of amateur horse racing, built a polo field designed for horse shows and other equestrian entertainment. The two 18-hole golf courses were designed by Walter J. Travis, the great British and American golf champion-turned-golf course architect. Bowman had a special interest in fox hunting. He belonged to the Westchester Country Beagles Club, the Fairfield County Fox Hounds Club and the United Hunts Racing Association. On May 15, 1922, John McEntee Bowman formally opened the Westchester County Club with almost 1,500 members.

- **The Arizona Biltmore Hotel**, Phoenix, Arizona- Warren McArthur, his brother Charles and John McEntee Bowman opened the Arizona Biltmore on February 23, 1929. The Biltmore's architect of record is Albert Chase McArthur but it is often referred to as a Frank Lloyd Wright design. This attribution is refuted by Wright himself who wrote in the Architectural Record:

> All I have done in connection with the building of the Arizona Biltmore near Phoenix, I have done for Albert McArthur himself at his sole request, and for none other. Albert McArthur is the architect of that building- all attempts to take the credit for that performance from him are gratuitous and beside the point. But for him, Phoenix would have had nothing like the Biltmore, and it is my hope that he may be enabled to give Phoenix many more beautiful buildings as I believe him entirely capable of doing.

McArthur did utilize one of Wright's signature design elements: the textile block system. In 1930, the McArthurs lost control of the resort to one of their primary investors, William Wrigley, Jr. Ten years later, the Wrigley family sold the hotel to the Talley family. In 1973, after a large fire destroyed most of the property, it was promptly rebuilt better than ever. After a series of ownership changes, CNL Hotels and Resorts acquired it in 2004 and gave the management contract to KSL Recreation, Inc.

Many celebrities have stayed at the Arizona Biltmore including every president since 1929. Other celebrity guests include Marilyn Monroe, Fred Astaire, Irving Berlin, James Cagney, Bing Crosby, Walter Cronkite, Michael J. Fox, Ava Gardner, Barry Goldwater, Bob Hope, Evander Holyfield,

Edward G. Robinson, Spencer Tracy, the New York Mets baseball team, etc.

The Hotel Nacional de Cuba in Havana was built in 1930 with 550 rooms with a casino operated by Meyer Lansky. Today, it is maintained and operated as a five-star hotel by the Cuban Government with two outdoor swimming pools, dining rooms, museum and business center.

- The Hotel DuPont, Wilmington, Delaware- At its opening in 1913, the Hotel DuPont was designed to rival the finest hotels of Europe. The new hotel contained 150 guest rooms, a main dining room, rathskeller, men's café/bar, ballroom, club room, ladies' sitting room and more.

During the first week alone, after its gala opening, 25,000 visitors toured the new hotel, where no expense was spared. In the ornate public spaces, nearly two dozen French and Italian craftsmen carved, gilded and painted for over two and a half years. Suites with large sitting rooms all featured cozy fireplaces. Polished brass beds were made up with imported linen, while sterling silver comb, brush and mirror sets were placed on the dressing tables. In the main Dining Room, now known as the Green Room, fumed oak paneling soared two and a half stories from the mosaic and terrazzo floors below. Rich forest greens, browns and ivories, embellished with gold, decorated the room. Six handcrafted chandeliers and a musicians' gallery overlooked the opulence. After dinner, many guests enjoyed professional performances at the Hotel's own Playhouse Theatre, now known as the DuPont Theatre. Built in only 150 days in late 1913, its stage is larger than all but three of the New York City's theatres.

During the early days of the DuPont's Brandywine and Christina Rooms, the hotel showed its commitment to struggling local artists by displaying their works. Today, they highlight one of the foremost collections of Brandywine art, including three generations of original Wyeth masterpieces. Through the years, the Hotel DuPont continued to evolve with the times. In 1918, 118 guest rooms were added and the beautiful Rose Room- the French salon reserved for women- became the new lobby. Wooden inlaid floors became marble, mirrored walls were replaced with imported travertine stone, and the ceiling was sculptured with carved rosettes and scrolls.

In the 1920's the hotel was managed by the Bowman-Biltmore Hotel Company and named the DuPont-Biltmore Hotel. Through the years, the Hotel has been host to presidents, politicians, Kings, Queens, sports figures, corporate giants and celebrities including: Charles Lindbergh, Amelia Earhart, Ingrid Bergman, Prince Rainier of Monaco, Joe DiMaggio, John F. Kennedy, Jacques Cousteau, Eleanor Roosevelt, Elizabeth Taylor, Katherine Hepburn, Duke Ellington, King Carl XVI Gustaf and Prince Bertil of Sweden, Norman Rockwell, Henry Kissinger, Kathleen Turner, Bob Hope, Lucille Ball, and many more. More recent celebrities include Barry Manilow, Reese Witherspoon, Ryan Phillipe, Warren Buffet, Joe Gibbs, Jeff Gordon and Whoopi Goldberg.

- The Providence Biltmore Hotel, Providence, Rhode Island- In 1922, the Providence Biltmore was designed by the famous architectural firm of Warren & Wetmore (who also designed Grand Central Station in New York) in a unique V-shape. Its developers were John McEntee Bowman and Louis Wallick. For 71 years (until the Westin was built in 1993), at 18 floors it was the tallest hotel in Providence. The Biltmore's Garden Room featured Benny Goodman, Louis Armstrong and Jimmy Dorsey, among other popular musicians. The dance floor was transformed into an ice-skating rink for Olympic star Sonja Henie and into an aquarium for the movie swimming star Esther Williams.

In Rhode Island, the opening of the Providence Biltmore Hotel was described in a front-page story in the June 6, 1922 edition of the Providence Journal predicting that it would be "the most elaborate social event ever to be held in the city." Over 1,000 people attended the party, including local officials and several prominent New York City hoteliers. For the occasion, the building was illuminated from top to bottom with more than 25,000 lights.

The 600-room Biltmore hotel was a self-sufficient city within a city with its own laundry, chicken coops, printing shop, carpentry and upholstery shop, and photo lab. Since Bowman planned the Providence Biltmore as a state-of-the-art hotel, guests were offered a choice of six different restaurants.

The waitresses in the Biltmore's Bacchante Room were known throughout the country for their beauty and poise. The dining area featured dimmed lights, mirrored walls and banquettes for seating. To be served customers pushed a button to summon a Bacchante Girl. She would appear in her costume, which featured a diaphanous, see-through skirt. The bar area had a glass floor which was lit from below with pink lighting to dramatize the waitresses' beautiful legs.

The hotel has survived the worst of the notorious New England weather and the devastating hurricanes of 1938 and 1954. The 1954 hurricane flooded the building, with water pouring down into the elevator shafts. Couches floated through the lobby and were stopped by the revolving doors. A plaque mounted atop a column in the lobby commemorates the high water mark.

In 2006, the Biltmore received a $14 million renovation including a Red Door Spa by Elizabeth Arden, and a McCormick & Schmick's Seafood Restaurant. The Providence Biltmore Hotel has been placed on the National Preservation Register as one of the country's cherished architectural treasures and remains the Grand Dame of Providence.

- The Belleview Biltmore Hotel, Bellaire, Florida- When "The White Queen of the Gulf" was built in 1897 by Henry Bradley Plant, the prominent railroad tycoon and hotel developer, it was the largest occupied wooden structure in the world. The Belleview Hotel opened with 145 rooms, Georgia-pine construction, swiss-style design, golf course and race track. By 1924 the hotel had expanded to 425 rooms. It became a retreat for the wealthy (the Fords, the duPonts and the Vanderbilts) whose private railroad cars were often parked at the railroad siding built to the south of the hotel. Guests enjoyed the amenities of regal rustic living; yachting and sailing on Clearwater Bay; horseback riding in the woods south of the hotel, golfing, tennis, skeet shooting and bicycling. In keeping with the national craze for bicycling at the turn of the century, Bellaire was the scene of six-day bicycle races as well as other national and international cycling events.

In 1920, the hotel was acquired by John McEntee Bowman who added it to his chain of Biltmore hotels hence the name change to the Belleview Biltmore Hotel. Just north of the hotel, a casino was built and operated until World War II. During the war, the hotel became an Army Air

Corps training facility. The Biltmore was listed on the National Register of Historic Places in 1979 and the National Trust for Historic Preservation in 2005. This spectacular property was under threat of demolition in recent years. However, as this chapter is being written, the Legg Mason Real Estate Investors Inc. of Los Angeles has acquired the Biltmore (for $30.3 million) and will embark on an historic restoration to make the hotel a four to five star property.

The Belleview Biltmore includes 22 acres, an 18-hole Donald Ross-designed golf course, a 200,000 gallon swimming pool with waterfalls, 40,000 square-feet of meeting space, the 13,000 square foot Tiffany Ballroom (the ceiling is made of Tiffany stained glass), the 4,400 square foot Starlight Ballroom, Bellaire Amphitheater, a 14,000 square foot Eclipse Day Spa, 4 clay tennis courts, a new $3 million clubhouse and the Beach Club on Sand Key. The hotel presently has 247 guestrooms with the possibility of 400+ total with the opening of the upper floors. The restoration plan, which is estimated to cost $100 million will include underground parking for 700 cars, service tunnels, a new one-story 18,900 square foot spa, renovation of the Magnolia, Palm and Sunset Cottages and construction of a new five-story 174 room hotel annex.

- The Biltmore Hotel, Santa Barbara, California- In 1925, the Bowman Biltmore Corporation purchased the site and Los Angeles architect Reginald Johnson began drawing plans for a grand Spanish Colonial Revival hotel to be called the Santa Barbara Biltmore. In exclusive Montecito, this Spanish colonial-style 207 room resort has been a glamorous Santa Barbara beachfront institution since opening as the Biltmore in 1927. Golden Age movie stars like Greta Garbo, Lana Turner, Bing Crosby and Errol Flynn enjoyed Butterfly beach and croquet on the great lawn. The Biltmore featured sweeping archways, heavy carved woodwork. Now a Four Seasons hotel, it has recently been renovated with a 10,000 square foot spa, Mission- style antiques, local art, decorative ironwork, rain showers and deep soaking tubs, 42-inch plasma screen TVs with surround sound, DVD players and broadband internet access. A botanical guide to the 44 exotic and rare plants in the resort's 22 acres of tropical and subtropical gardens is available at the concierge desk. In the summer of 2007, guests were allowed access to the Coral Casino Beach and Cabana Club next door.

• The Miami-Biltmore Hotel, Coral Gables, Florida- Six months before the announcement of the building of the Miami-Biltmore Hotel in February 1924, John McEntee Bowman created the Bowman-Biltmore Hotel Corporation. Board directors Percy A. Rockefeller, William Wrigley, Jr., Joseph Harriman (president of Harriman National Bank) and Lee A. Phillips (vice president of the Pacific-Mutual Life Insurance Company) combined their interests in nine hotels representing $29 million in assets. Their plan called for the acquisition of 80 percent of the capital stock of the hotels in the Bowman group: the Commodore, Biltmore, Belmont, Murray Hill and Ansonia in New York City; the Griswold Hotel in New London, Connecticut; the Belleview Biltmore in Bellaire, Florida; the Los Angeles Biltmore in Los Angeles, California and the Sevilla-Biltmore in Havana, Cuba.

In February 1924, George Merrick was able to convince John McEntee Bowman to join him in developing, financing and building the Miami-Biltmore Hotel in Coral Gables. In order to create a one-of-a kind resort hotel, Bowman selected the architectural firm of Schultze and Weaver once again. As Bowman wrote in a 1923 issue of *Architectural Forum*, "Any well constructed building will provide adequate shelter and good management bears the responsibility of food and services but for atmosphere- that's intangible to the well-being and satisfaction of the hotel guest- we must look primarily to the architect." Schulze and Weaver had Miami experience as the designers of the *Miami Daily News*

Tower (1925) and Miami Beach's Nautilus Hotel (for Carl Graham Fisher) and Roney Plaza Hotel (for E.B.T. Roney).

In a burst of hyperbole, an early Biltmore sales brochure said,

> The Miami-Biltmore Hotel and the Miami-Biltmore Country Club represent... the last word in the evolution of civilization. This Hotel and Country Club will attract the right kind of people to the land. People with money are no better than people without it. But there is no question that they do more good to the country they live in. They employ labor and increase the value of property. The Miami-Biltmore Hotel and Miami-Country Club, by attracting this kind of people, draws the South to the attention of the moneyed men of the country. It attracts, by its sports, its arts, its climate, and its atmosphere of romance. All these constitute an ideal vacation, and the Miami-Biltmore Hotel is the ideal home in which to spend it.

At the gala opening dinner on January 14, 1926, John McEntee Bowman, clearly pleased with the new hotel, said,

> There has since come a demand for Biltmores throughout the country, and the demand has been met in the North, South and West. The call came to me from Coral Gables, when the picture of the city beautiful had been completed.
>
> I was at first attracted, than fascinated by the outlook. It did not require much to convince me that Coral Gables was the home for the next Biltmore Country Club... The seed of a Biltmore was planted here less than two years ago and after two years of cultivation. Tonight we present you with the finished product, for which we have to thank the Almighty, then the architect and the artisans.

Bowman displayed his broad knowledge of hotel operations when he introduced his guests to the latest state-of-the-art equipment in the "back of the house". He personally toured the enormous in-house laundry, the ice-making machinery, the modern kitchen with ranges, ovens, steam tables, refrigerators and walk-in boxes.

Hundreds of guests arrived from New York on two special trains on the Atlantic Coastline Railroad and the Seaboard Air Line Railway. Earlier, Architect Leonard Schultze had purchased genuine Italian gondolas and hired real gondoliers from Venetian canals and lagoons. The beautiful gondolas were richly furnished with silken tapestries, rugs and cushions.

The grand opening party was an extraordinary display of jewelry, furs and clothing by the 1500 guests. Famous band leader Paul Whiteman conducted one of three orchestras that entertained the guests. Although the 18th amendment to the Constitution (January 1920) prohibited the sale and manufacture and sale of intoxicating liquor, it did not spoil the party since, it was said, champagne was flowing.

The 1939 "W.P.A. Guide to Florida" describes Coral Gables as "a boom-time city, blue-printed to the last detail before a palmetto was grubbed from the site." Contiguous to Miami, Coral Gables lies a scant 15-minute drive from Miami International Airport, downtown Miami and the beaches, but it is, by design, a world apart from city and sand. Set within the fairways and canals, the Biltmore Hotel and Country Club with its 18-hole Donald Ross- designed golf course surpasses normal expectations.

The hotel's 300-foot-high belfry is visible from just about any spot in Coral Gables's low-zoned residential area. Lighted by day by the subtropical sun and at night by powerful spotlights, the orange Mediterranean-Moorish belltower, modeled after the Giralda tower in Seville, rises between two seven-story wings. Guests enter into a large impressive space with marble under foot and more than two dozen 25 foot-tall Corinthian columns supporting a ceiling coffered in the center and groin vaulted at either end. The room, with a fireplace in one wall, is decorated with new and antique furnishings and carpets chosen to evoke the grandeur and elegance of an earlier era.

The 275-room hotel's history is as improbable as its setting. The Biltmore was built in 1925. The resort flourished under the patronage of wealthy and celebrated travelers drawn by the mild weather, the golf course, the big bands and the poolside shows. Only months after it opened, however, the worst hurricane in Florida history struck, leaving the hotel intact but destroying its reputation for a hospitable climate, and the hotel's occupancy declined. The 1929 crash succeeded where the storm had failed and the hotel declared bankruptcy.

The hotel changed hands a couple of times and continued to operate until 1942 when the Federal Government took it over for a military hospital during the World War II. After the war ended, the hotel became a Veterans Administration hospital, and in the 50's and 60's it was the site of the University of Miami Medical School. In 1968 the building was abandoned and left in derelict condition. The Federal Government gave the Biltmore to the city of Coral Gables in 1973 as part of the Historic Monuments Acts and Legacy of Parks program, although it was another 10 years before the city decided what to do with it. Finally in 1983, the city selected a developer to renovate the building as a hotel.

During 1986 the Biltmore underwent a $47 million restoration to correct damage from government use and nearly two decades of disuse. The hotel, listed on the National Register of Historic Places, has been restored to the original design. Government- issue linoleum was removed from the marble floors, windows that had been filled with concrete were reopened. Three dozen painters from Mexico were brought in to repaint the frescoes on the lobby's ceilings. The project was completed in less than a year so the investors could qualify for Federal tax credits for historic restoration. The hotel, which continues to be owned by the city of Coral Gables, is operated under a 99-year lease by the Seaway Group.

The original and restored architectural features include a red tile roof, a loggia and an immense lobby-level terrace behind the hotel, which surrounds a courtyard. In the courtyard are a fountain and an outdoor cafe. From the far end of the terrace visitors often get their first look at what is believed to be the largest hotel pool in the country. The irregularly shaped pool measures 150 by 228 feet. It is said to exceed the size of Roman emperor Diocletian's pool, the largest man-made swimming pool ever recorded.

The Coral Gables Biltmore is a Cecil B. DeMille production. Photographers regularly bring models to the terraces and the pool for advertising and fashion shoots. Which isn't to suggest that the Biltmore is glitzy, rather that it is a workable combination of various styles: Mediterranean, Moorish, Spanish-Revival, Beaux Arts, Gothic Renaissance. Ultimately, though, the hotel is an evocation of its own period, the Jazz Age.

The Biltmore's amenities are not only architectural. There is 24-hour room service, restaurants and ballrooms. The 10 tennis courts are lighted at night, and the golf course has 18 holes. The guestrooms are comfortable and airy, and a few have terraces with view of either Miami or the golf course. Of the hotel's original 350-guestrooms, 240 and 35 suites (including a duplex in the tower) have been remodeled with air-conditioning, television and a safe in the closet. The bedrooms, no two of which are alike, are done in subdued earth tones that seem to shift from sand to pink or beige to green as the light changes. Draperies and upholstery are grand but subtle and complement the hand-painted and carved headboards and armoires done in a style prevalent in the 20's. The bathrooms are sleek and well-lighted and contain baskets and soap, shampoo and other toiletries.

It is without difficulty that the guest imagines the Biltmore's first opening day, in January 1926. when, as today's hotel brochure recalls, "Venetian gondolas glided through canals, while hounds bayed among the pines, tracking red foxes imported for the hunt. The Paul 'Pops' Whiteman Orchestra played 'Moon Over Miami' and smoky-eyed maidens swooned on cut velvet settees".

It was John McEntee Bowman's crowning achievement.

- The Shenecossett Country Club & Griswold Hotel, Groton, Connecticut- Henry B. Plant's son, Morton, was heir to the railroad and steamship empires and became an active member of the New York and Larchmont Yacht Clubs. He was a sophisticated businessman with homes in New York City, Florida and Groton, Connecticut. He built his thirty-one room Branford House at Avery Point on Long Island Sound designed in the grand style of Newport, Rhode Island mansions. Plant purchased the Fort Griswold House at the end of the 1905 summer season and replaced it with an imposing four-story, four-hundred room wooden structure, the Griswold Hotel designed in classical style. Amenities included a barbershop, beauty salon and an ice cream parlor. Rooms were furnished in mahogany, lighted with electricity and provided with long distance telephone service. So highly successful was the first season that a new wing was added; annexes were built in 1909 and in 1916, making it one of the largest summer resort hotels on the east coast of the United States. Plant set out "to cater to a class that demands the best." To this end, he supplied guests with fresh vegetables, dairy products and poultry from his own Bradford Farm. Under Plant's guidance, the Griswold became the social center of the summer colony and attracted some of America's wealthiest families such as the Astors, Vanderbilts and Rockefellers. The Griswold shared managers, staff and orchestra in addition to golf professionals with the Hotel Belleview in Bellaire, Florida. In 1913, Plant acquired the Shenecossett Country Club and golf course and joined it with parcels of adjacent land which he had purchased between 1903 and 1912. Plant hired the well-known Donald J. Ross to lay out eighteen holes on one hundred and twenty nine acres. Ross, a Scottish immigrant, had earned a national reputation from his earlier design for the Pinehurst golf course in Pinehurst, North Carolina. His design at Shenecossett produced a golf course 6,029 yards in length that played to a par of 71. Plant, in his characteristic pursuit of excellence, had soil shipped from Virginia and New Jersey for use in shaping bunkers as well as fairways that were remembered as the best between Boston and New York.

Opened under the Griswold management in 1914, the Club was advertised as "the finest in New England".

In 1919, John McEntee Bowman acquired the Griswold Hotel from Morton Plant's estate. The Shenecossett golf course gained national recognition as site of the Griswold Cup, a women's invitational golf tournament played from 1919 to 1940. Whereas only twenty-four women competed in 1920, one hundred eighty six did so in 1925. In 1929, two hundred forty two women played, a record number of entries for a women's tournament.

SOURCE MATERIALS

1. Karl P. Abbott, *Open For The Season*, Doubleday & Company, Garden City, 1950

2. Susan R. Braden, *The Architecture of Leisure: The Florida Resorts Hotels of Henry Flagler and Henry Plant*, University Press of Florida, Gainesville, 2002

3. Leslie Dorsey and Janice Devine, *Fare Thee Well: A Backward Look at Two Centuries of Historic American Hostelries, Fashionable Spas & Seaside Resorts*, Crown Publishers, Inc., New York, 1964.

4. Marianne Lamonaca and Jonathan Mogul, Editors, *Grand Hotels of The Jazz Age*, Princeton Architectural Press, New York 2005.

5. Samuel D. Laroue, Jr. and Ellen J. Uguccioni, *The Biltmore Hotel: An Enduring Legacy*, Arva Parks & Company and Centennial Press, Miami, 2002

6. Brian McGinty, *The Palace Inns: A Connoisseur's Guide to Historic American Hotels*, Stackpole Books, Harrisburg, 1978.

7. The American Hotel: The Journal of Decorative and Propaganda Arts, The Wolfsonian- Florida International University Miami Beach, Issue 25, 2005.

8. Jefferson Williamson, *The American Hotel: An Anecdotal History*, Alfred A. Knopf, New York, 1930.

Carl Graham Fisher (1874-1939):

MR. MIAMI BEACH, MR. MONTAUK AND MUCH MORE

In 1915 a real-estate developer stood on the corner of Lincoln Road and Washington Avenue watched the jungle of mangrove trees being chopped down and said, "Gentlemen, Lincoln Road will become one of the most beautiful shopping areas in the world."

That developer was Carl Graham Fisher, and the legacy of his accomplishments lives on to this very day, as indicated by the following list of developments and projects that he envisioned and then created.

- Miami Beach.

- Fisher Island.

- Montauk, Long Island.

- The Indianapolis Speedway was built by Fisher, and the Indianapolis 500 is regarded by many as the world's premier automobile-racing event.

- The Lincoln and Dixie highways. Fisher raised private funds for these two road projects, which were forerunners of the U.S. Interstate Highway System.

Despite Fisher's extraordinary accomplishments, however, no beach, no highway, no hotels, and no race track is named for Carl Graham Fisher. Only Fisher Island bears his name. Fisher bought the island in 1919 from Dana A. Dorsey, a prominent black businessman in Miami who had given up on an effort to build a resort for blacks (who were barred from segregated Miami's beaches). The island itself was created in 1905 when the federal government sliced off the southern tip of Miami Beach to make a shipping channel from Miami to Atlantic Ocean. At that time it was an alligator-inhabited mangrove swamp. That lack of recognition would probably have been okay with Fisher since he always considered the project to be more important than his particular role in it. Dreaming, planning, working, and building were his most important values.

Carl Fisher was one of America's large-scale land developers who envisioned entire new cities springing out of the ground. Born into poverty January 12, 1874, in Greensburg, Indiana, Fisher left school at the age of twelve to help support his family. Carl's failures in school were probably the result of his poor eyesight. With a case of severe astigmatism, Carl was almost half-blind. It was not until he was thirty-one that the problem was diagnosed and corrected. However, his poor vision did not hamper his well-coordinated physical activities, such as running backwards. He often challenged and beat his friends who ran forward. A gifted athlete, Carl excelled at ice skating, swimming, diving, roller skating and bicycle riding. He set out into the world determined to make a mark for himself taking as his heroes Lincoln and Napoleon. The Civil War had ended only twenty years earlier with President Abraham Lincoln as a national martyr and former Indiana resident. From his earliest years Fisher was blessed with an uncanny ability for sales and promotion.

Competitive bicycling was all the rage at the turn of the century. Endurance races captured the imagination of the public, and were promoted by the fledging bike industry. Fisher joined one of the best-known bike clubs in the midwest, the Zig-Zag Cycling Club and made quite a name for himself on the racing circuit. Realizing the money to be made in selling bikes, rather than riding bikes, he opened his first bike shop when he was only seventeen years old. Within a few years he had done well enough to transform his bike shop into an automobile dealership, the first of its kind in Indianapolis. There he sold Packards, Stoddard-Daytons, Stutz cars, as well as REO trucks, and the Fisher garage became one of the leading auto dealerships in the country. Carl's success was the result of a series of extraordinary promotional stunts and hard work.

Fisher's involvement in the early automobile industry led to an investment that brought his first fortune. In 1904 Percy Avery walked into Fisher's shop, and together he and the younger Fisher changed the automobile industry. Avery had bought the patent to a promising French device which consisted of a compressed gas cylinder filled with acetylene gas which was then used for lighthouses and buoys. It gave off an intense light far superior to anything in the car market. (Among the many challenges of early motoring was the poor quality of auto headlights.) A problem, however, was that acetylene gas is extremely flammable, and no auto manufacturer would touch it.

Fisher was a risk taker, however, and he put up the money to begin manufacturing this new, compressed-gas automobile headlight. The 1904 Packard was the first car to feature the new headlamps. Despite the light's popularity, a significant manufacturing problem existed, which was that the product's unstable chemicals frequently caused the factories to blow up. When the Omaha factory exploded, for instance, a wire was sent reading, simply, "Omaha left at 4:30." Eventually the chemical tanks were made safer when they were lined with asbestos. With that change, Fisher's profits from the company soared. By 1913 the use of Prest-O-Lite headlights became standard equipment and caught the attention of the Union Carbide Company. Nine years after Fisher started the company, Prest-O-Lite was sold for $9 million, of which Fisher's share was $6 million. With that bankroll in hand, the 43-year old Fisher began to look for even bigger, and more exciting projects on which to lavish his considerable skills.

Next he pursued his dream of building a major American automobile racetrack. On a 1905 trip overseas to compete in France's James Gordon Bennett Cup Races, Fisher was stunned by the European cars superiority over the U.S. models, noting that they could "go uphill faster than the American cars can come down." Fisher wrote to Ray C. Thompson, sports editor of the Indianapolis News in May 1937 that.... "we had two very fast cars, but there was no place in America to test them over a continuous drive of more than two miles, and in order to test them even the two miles in Toledo, we had to hire special guards to do the work at daylight; and even this testing was stopped because the cars made so much noise on the boulevard. So, we went to Europe with cars that were very fast but with no place to test them at high speed for a continuous run of 100 miles or so... As a result, the French beat the tar out of us; in fact, we didn't have either car finish, and I could see that it was a lack of being able to test the cars over a continuous speed run; and I made up my mind then to build a speedway where cars could be run 1,000 miles in a test, if necessary."

When he returned to America, Fisher set out to convince auto manufacturers that a testing track was essential to improve American-made automobiles and that Indianapolis was the logical location for such a track. Incredibly, of the more than one hundred different cars manufactured in Indiana, only sixteen survived fifteen years: American, Apperson, Auburn, Cole, Davis, Duesenberg, Elcar, Empire, Haynes, Lexington, Marmon, Maxwell, McFarlan, Studebaker, Stutz and Waverley Electric.

Fisher gained the support of Tom Taggert, three-time mayor of Indianapolis who proposed that the track be built at French Lick Springs, Indiana where he was building a new hotel and spa. Unfortunately, there was insufficient land available for the racetrack.

Finally, in 1909 on the old Pressley farm, five miles northwest of Indianapolis, Fisher and his partners, Arthur C. Newby of the National Motor Vehicle Company, Frank H. Wheeler of the Wheeler-Schebler Carburetor Company and Jim Allison invested $250,000 and built a two-and-a-half-mile oval track for automobile racing: the Indianapolis Speedway.

Cars, however, were not the first machines to race at the Speedway, which was originally paved with crushed stone. Instead, motorcycles tested the new track's fitness. The motorcyclists didn't know what to make of the facility when they came to Indianapolis in August 1909. The two-wheel daredevils were used to small board tracks, and seemed intimidated by the Indianapolis raceway's long straightaways and monstrous curves. On August 19, 1909, a week after the motorcyclists had tried their luck, the first automobile races were run at the Speedway. The results were immediately deadly; six people were killed, including three drivers. Fisher stopped the race after 235 miles of the scheduled 300 miles had been completed.

The crushed stone track proved unsuitable for racing, so Fisher returned to the drawing board. He convinced his associate, Arthur C. Newby, to pay for repaving the track with 3,200,000 ten-pound bricks and "The Brickyard" was born. The new surface stood up well during the 1910 racing season, and Fisher promised bigger things to come for the next year. On Memorial Day in 1911, the Speedway hosted the first in its long tradition of 500-mile races. Ray Harroun, driving an Indianapolis-made Marmon Wasp, won the race with an average speed of 74.59 miles per hour. Fisher had helped inaugurate an event that became known as "the greatest spectacle in racing," and he drove the first Indianapolis 500 pace car- a Stoddard Dayton.

Fisher next turned his restless energy to a problem that had plagued the automobile industry for years, namely, bad roads. Driving an automobile in those days was a real adventure as motorists not only had to deal with inadequate roads but also a lack of directional signs. Drake Hokanson, in his history of the Lincoln Highway, pointed out that the 180,000 registered motor vehicles in the United States in 1910 had only 2.5 million miles of road to drive on (with only 7 percent of those miles improved in any manner).

"The highways of America," Fisher wrote his writer friend Elbert Hubbard, "are built chiefly of politics, whereas the proper material is crushed rock or concrete." Fisher met the road problem like he did any other problem- head on. At a September 1912 dinner party for automobile manufacturers at the Deutsches Haus in Indianapolis, Fisher unveiled his plan for a highway spanning the country from New York City to California, "A road across the United States! Let's build it before we're too old to enjoy it!" Fisher urged the auto executives. His idea was to build a coast-to-coast highway in time for the May 1915 Panama-Pacific International Exposition in San Francisco. Fisher estimated that a transcontinental highway would cost $10 million, and he sought pledges from the automobile executives present at the dinner. Just 30 minutes after his talk, Fisher received $300,000 from Frank A. Seiberling, of the Goodyear Company, who pledged the amount even without first checking with his board of directors.

A few months after the Indianapolis dinner, Fisher received a letter from Henry Joy, Packard Motor Company president, pledging $150,000 for the proposed roadway. Joy, a leading force behind getting the coast-to-coast highway built, suggested that the road be named for Abraham Lincoln. On July 1, 1913, the Lincoln Highway Association was created with Joy as president and Fisher as vice president. The association's goal was to:

> ... procure the establishment of a continuous improved highway from the Atlantic to the Pacific, open to lawful traffic of all description without toll charges: such highway to be known in memory of Abraham Lincoln, as "The Lincoln Highway."

Fisher, as he had for his other ventures, employed a direct method for raising money. He wrote one Lincoln Highway Association official that it was easy to get contributions from people. "You should first give them a good dinner, then a good cussing, whenever you want money," Fisher explained. Although this technique worked with most people, it did not work with one of America's leading automobile manufacturers-Henry Ford. Despite help from U.S. Senator Albert Beveridge, Thomas Edison, and Hubbard, all close Ford friends, and a personal appeal from Fisher, Ford refused to give any financial assistance to the Lincoln Highway. He declared it was the government's responsibility, not industrialists', to build better roads. The association announced the Lincoln Highway's intended route at the annual governors' conference in Colorado in late August 1913. The planned route ran for 3,389 miles, from Times Square in New York to Lincoln Park in San Francisco and passed through New Jersey, Pennsylvania, Ohio, Indiana, Illinois, Iowa, Nebraska, Wyoming, Utah, Nevada, and California. As work progressed on the first U.S. transcontinental highway, Fisher turned his sights elsewhere, especially to improving a jungle of swamps to be known as Miami Beach.

Although Fisher had big dreams for the Miami area, his wife, Jane, was not impressed with the area on their first trip in 1912. Mosquitoes blackened the couple's clothing and Jane "refused to find any charm in this deserted strip of ugly land rimmed with a sandy beach." Carl, however, had a grander vision: "Look, honey," he told his wife, "I'm going to build a city here! A city like magic, like romantic places you read and dream about, but never see."

Florida, as Fisher envisioned the state, could be the perfect vacation spot for Midwestern automobile executives and their families who wished to escape harsh winter weather. To get vacationers to his resort, Fisher, the "father of the Lincoln Highway," had to use his promotional talents once again to nurture another highway's birth. On December 4, 1914, he wrote to Indiana Governor Samuel Ralston and suggested that the Dixie Highway would "do more good for the South than if they should get ten cents for their cotton." The highway could also "mean hundreds of millions of dollars to Indiana in the next 25 years." Fisher also offered his promotional skills on the road's behalf, leading 15 cars from Indianapolis to Miami on a Dixie Highway Pathfinding Tour. In September 1916 Fisher and Ralston attended a celebration in Martinsville that marked the opening of the roadway from Indianapolis to Miami.

Throughout Fisher's early years he showed a keen eye for identifying potentially valuable real estate. He also appreciated the importance of using quality materials and the best construction techniques, and so his showrooms, offices, plants and homes were showplaces. In 1913 he applied his appreciation for real estate and construction to a project that thrust him into the ranks of the country's leading real estate czars.

While vacationing in south Florida, Fisher couldn't help but notice the barrier island that paralleled the city of Miami. Miami Beach, as it was called, comprised 3,500 acres of dense mangrove swamps and beach. In 1912, Miami Beach was just a remote peninsula. Three different companies were selling land for homesites without much success. In northern Miami Beach, Quaker John Collins and his son-in-law Thomas Pancoast were trying to promote a hotel site: "Facing 600 feet along the Atlantic Ocean. Special inducements and liberal terms to parties who will erect the class of hotel desired." (Advertisement in the Miami Metropolis, March 21, 1914).

After Henry Flagler's Florida East Coast Railroad was extended through Miami to Key West, it is not surprising that the Collins and Pancoast families created the Miami Beach Improvement Company. Patriarch John Collins realized that if Miami Beach was to become a popular vacation resort, access from the mainland by automobile was a necessity. After overcoming opposition by the Biscayne Navigation Company which provided ferry service across the bay, Collins finally received permission to build the bridge in May 1912. However, the actual building costs far exceeded estimates and the Collins family ran out of money less than a half mile short of Miami Beach: the longest wooden bridge in the world going nowhere. Collins' savior was Carl Fisher who had just sold Prest-O-Lite for $9 million. Fisher gave a $50,000 loan to John Collins which was secured by title to 200 acres of land which became Fisher's first development on Miami Beach. Earlier, Fisher had purchased a lovely winter house on Miami's Brickell Avenue from Alonso Bliss who made his fortune manufacturing herbal medicines. Collins bridge later became the Venetian Causeway.

In a relatively short time, Fisher single-handedly transformed Miami Beach into one of the most stylish resorts in the world. He cut down the mangroves and, to the astonishment of most observers, he dredged sand from Biscayne Bay to fill the swampland, and shipped in hundreds of tons of topsoil from the Everglades. He then built streets and sidewalks and laid out the city of Miami Beach. Fisher also bought an additional 60 acres from the brothers J. N. and J. E. Lummus, who both headed local banks. While the Lummus brothers already carefully screened the purchasers of their land (lawbreakers were excluded, as well as African Americans), Fisher aimed to attract an even more-exclusive crowd. He wanted other newly-rich industrial magnates to vacation in Miami Beach. Several of them did, including Harvey Firestone and Alfred duPont. (Working in Fisher's favor was the factor that new-money industrialists generally were shunned by Palm Beach's upper crust).

Fisher built the spectacular Flamingo Hotel in 1921. He named the hotel after the flamboyant birds he saw on a visit to Andros Island in the Bahamas. The hotel featured an 11-story tower with a glass dome. At night, multi-colored spotlights shone far out over the ocean, and were visible for seven miles. Fisher did not believe in locating hotels on the ocean side, and therefore, he built the Flamingo facing Biscayne Bay at Fifteenth Street on Miami Beach.

Flamingo Hotel, Miami Beach, Florida 68

The spectacular Flamingo Hotel, Miami Beach was opened in 1921 with an 11-story tower, a glass dome and multi-colored spotlights visible for seven miles. The Flamingo had private docks on Biscayne Bay, bath houses and gondolas steered by Bahamians wearing brass earrings.

Segregation attitudes prevented African Americans from staying in Florida hotels and anti-semitism kept Jews out. Flamingo general manager Charles S. Krom wrote Fisher, "All convention people are naturally noisy.... I have never yet seen a convention that didn't have some Jews in the crowd and I don't believe a bunch of Realtors are going to be different from any other." Fisher agreed with this policy since his later hotels would not admit Jews, although he sometimes made exceptions for his wealthy jewish associates. This "gentiles only" policy was common among Miami Beach hotels and apartment buildings through the 1950s.

To provide guests with the fresh dairy products, Fisher brought 40 Guernsey cows from Wisconsin. In the winter of 1922, people slogging through the snow and cold of New York City were brought up short by a large, new illuminated sign on the corner of Fifth Avenue and 42nd Street flashing this message: "It's June in Miami." Among its many features, the Flamingo had private docks, bath houses, and gondolas steered by Bahamians wearing brass earrings. There were also a men's club, broker's office, laundry, exclusive shops, and many other diversions. Among the first of the Flamingo's celebrity guests was president-elect Warren

G. Harding in January 1921. While in Miami Beach, Harding's golf caddie was one of Fisher's imported circus elephants. Fisher employed a number of gimmicks to attract attention, including importing a polo team from England, dressing young women in risqué bathing suits, and widely distributing publicity photographs taken at the hotel.

"The national press just ate that stuff up," says Howard Kleinberg, a columnist for the Miami Herald. "You couldn't pick up a paper in the United States without seeking a picture of either the elephant or some group of bathing beauties standing by the beach... Miami Beach all of a sudden became the place to go."

In 1923 Fisher expanded the Flamingo, adding sixty more rooms. He also built the Nautilus Hotel, the King Cole and the Boulevard Hotel. At a cost of $870,000, the Nautilus, offered the ultimate for wealthy guests: posh rooms, and swimming pool with cabanas, beautiful stairways and chandeliers, a gourmet dining room, and, of course, the adjoining polo fields.

The increasing demand for rooms lengthened the tourist season and sparked a hotel building boom. The Lincoln Hotel opened on November 1 during the 1923-24 season, and the Wofford Hotel opened on December 6, 1923. Land sales and values escalated. In 1923, the Fisher-Collins interests sold a total of $6 million in real estate; in 1924, it was $8 million; and in 1925, sales almost tripled to $23 million.

By the mid-1920s, other developers began new projects. George Merrick and John McEntee Bowman were building in the Coral Gables community with the Miami-Biltmore Hotel as its centerpiece. Further north, Addison Mizner designed and built the fabulous Boca Raton Resort and community. J. Perry Stoltz built the luxurious Fleetwood Hotel during the 1924-25 season and Newton Baker Taylor (N.B.T.) Roney built the largest hotel, the $2 million Roney Plaza on Miami Beach at 23rd Street.

By 1925 Miami Beach had 58 hotels with 4,500 available rooms. There were also new casinos and bathing pavilions, polo fields, golf courses, movie theaters, an elementary school, a high school, churches, and radio stations.

The dredges continued to pump sand, creating more land. Islands were created in the bay and sold to the wealthy. All of south Florida was booming. "Miami was transformed from a sleepy little town on the edge of Biscayne Bay into a Magic City of modest skyscrapers and legendary real estate profits" wrote Kenneth Ballinger in *Miami Millions*. Before long enough celebrities lived in Miami Beach to create a market for sightseeing buses. Guides used megaphones to identify the homes of the rich and famous. They could point out the estates of Harvey Firestone, Julius Fleischmann (Fleischmann's Yeast), Gar Wood, Albert Champion, Harry Stutz (Stutz Bearcat), Roy Chapin and C.F. Kettering (Delco). J.C. Penney owned a mansion on Belle Isle, and he brought pianist Artur Rubinstein and violinist Paul Kochanski to entertain his guests there. The Fishers hosted Jascha Heifitz, Irving Berlin, Will Rogers, and George Ade.

Fisher himself was called the "Prest-O-Lite King," and he and his wife, Jane, were referred to as the "king and queen" of Miami Beach. "Nothing annoyed Carl more," wrote Jane. "He hated personal publicity. The only publicity he wanted was for the new city." On January 16, 1924, the *Miami Beach Register* noted that "Some day, if the migration of celebrities continues, it won't be necessary to publish *Who's Who in America*. The Miami Beach city directory will be all that's needed." The promotion of Fisher's tropical paradise sparked a Florida land boom. Six million people poured into Florida in three years. By the end of 1925, Fisher was worth more than $50 million, but his personal life was in shambles. Devastated by the death of his only child in 1921, Fisher became a heavy drinker and womanizer.

Always restless, with boundless energy, Fisher was no sooner established Miami Beach than he started looking for his next great challenge. He found it in Long Island's Montauk, three times the size of Miami Beach, almost entirely undeveloped. It was to be the culmination of his life's work. He bought 10,000 acres in 1925, for the relatively modest sum of $2,500,000. He estimated it would take another $7,000,000 to develop it. "Miami in the Winter, Montauk in the Summer", was Fisher's slogan. He would provide the elite who had flocked to his Miami Beach, with a comparably exclusive summer resort just hours from the social centers of New York City and Newport, Rhode Island.

As a primary lure for the globe-trotting set, Montauk would become a Sportsman's Paradise- a diversion that was much in vogue with the very rich. As embraced by the gentry of the 1920s, a proper summer vacation consisted of vigorous outdoor activities centered around the main pursuits of the not-so-idle rich- yachting, fishing, golfing, shooting, tennis, polo and swimming. Naturally, it would be ideal if the prospective vacationers could pursue all those diverse activities in the exclusive company of their social and economic peers. In short, for Fisher's dream of a "Miami of the North" to succeed, he needed to construct a first-class destination that offered the litany of activities for the Astors, Vanderbilts and Goulds, as well as first-class hotel facilities. Diversity of activities in a socially homogeneous setting was Fisher's aspiration, and Montauk was designed to be that arena.

Montauk's 1932 promotional brochure emphasized the notion of social exclusivity: "Now Montauk Beach, through the vision and resources of a group of distinguished builders, is being transformed into America's finest out-of-door center, where the real aristocrats of modern America may find new health, new relaxation, new ways to play amid luxurious surroundings."

By the time Fisher arrived, Montauk was already well known among connoisseurs, as a first- class fishing and hunting retreat. Ever since the late 1800's, well-heeled hunters and anglers had gone "on Montauk" for extended expeditions. What they found was a beautiful, rustic outpost nearly untouched by the modern era. Teeming with geese, duck, turkey, fox, rabbit, and deer, Montauk was a hunter's heaven. Inshore and offshore, no finer fishing could be found on the east coast. As a first-class resort – or a resort of any kind – it left nearly everything to be desired. Outside of a few private homes and a small inn that stood on the site of today's Montauk Manor. All that existed in the current downtown area was a hangar on the eastern shore of Fort Pond which housed a World War I observation balloon. On the shore on Fort Pond Bay, near the current railroad station, the village of Montauk crowded the water with fishing shacks, warehouses, commercial docks, and piers. In general there was no electricity, no running water, no indoor plumbing, and little in the way of creature comforts anywhere in town.

Fisher was faced with the formidable task of transforming those 10,000 virgin acres into a world- class resort. Within weeks of his purchase, a crew of some 800 men were working around the clock, clearing roads, installing sewers, power lines and laying the infrastructure for a large scale, modern village. On June 1, 1927 the palatial Montauk Manor was opened and its 178 modern guest rooms were immediately filled with summer vacationers.

The Montauk Manor was opened in 1927 with 178 guest rooms. Guests had a wide variety of outdoor activities: oceanfront bathing pavilion with 1600 feet of boardwalk, golf, 12 outdoor clay and 6 indoor tennis courts, polo, horseback riding, fox hunts and deep sea fishing.

The manor's guests could choose from a variety of daily activities. An oceanfront bathing pavilion, complete with outdoor pool and 1,600 feet of boardwalk along the beach, was constructed on the site of the current Surf Club. Eighteen quality holes of golf could be played at what is now Montauk Downs. Tennis players could choose from twelve outdoor clay courts near the Manor, or six indoor courts (located in what is now the sadly-abandoned playhouse near the Manor). For polo enthusiasts, playing fields complete with paddocks, stables, and herds of ponies were maintained at the nearby Deep Hollow Ranch. The horsy set could ride on established trails and the beach, and even run with the hounds in a traditional English-style fox hunt. Add to all that recreation the nearly unlimited fishing and hunting Montauk always provided, and it's easy to see how a visitor's day was filled. Established in his headquarters suite atop his new six-story Montauk Improvement Building – at the time the tallest building on Long Island– Fisher watched his vision and plans become a reality.

Perhaps Fisher's most ambitious piece of engineering was the reconfiguration of present day Lake Montauk. It was, until 1927, a true lake – fresh water, land locked, and as such of no use to Fisher. He needed a yacht club, with deep water berths capable of docking the grand vessels of the Astors, Vanderbilts, and Whitneys. Unfortunately, Montauk's only available anchorage, at Fort Pond Bay, was unsuitable- it was unprotected and subject to devastating storms and high tides. Unperturbed, Fisher imagined the possibilities and came up with a grand solution: he blasted open a channel from Block Island Sound to connect Lake Montauk to the open sea. Once done, he dredged roughly half the lake to a depth of 12 feet and established the Montauk Lake Club, on Star Island. It remains in operation today, and is capable of docking ocean-going vessels up to 150 feet in length.

In the 1920's Montauk was a cosmopolitan resort, a Monte Carlo on the Atlantic that attracted the world's elite. Montauk Manor was the most luxurious hotel on Long Island, a favorite of the New York/Newport crowds. Indeed, at the time the manor's popularity supported direct steamer service to Manhattan. Each night of the summer season lines of fancy touring cars and limos would disgorge scores of blue bloods and society swells who were bound for a champagne dinner and secret midnight rendezvous within the Manor's cavernous rooms. The Star Island Casino, next to the yacht club, was jumping every night, with fine food, excellent wine and the ever-present sound of money hitting the tables. It was there that the then-mayor of New York City, Jimmy Walker, was nearly arrested during an infrequent raid by the local authorities. For the first few years, Fisher's dream city of Montauk was a genuine and profitable reality.

Fisher had planned for everything, everything that is, except weather and the Great Depression. On September 17, 1927, a hurricane hit Miami Beach. Although the actual damage was not as severe as reported in media accounts, the news was sufficient to warn off travelers and the 1927- 28 tourist season was a bust. Then in 1929 the bottom fell out of the stock market and real estate values began a dizzying fall. Since much of Fisher's wealth was based on real estate, his fortune began to

crumble. Within the year his empire had lost a third of its value, and the bankers who held his notes began to become nervous.

As his credit began to thin, Fisher sold his holdings – the Indianapolis Speedway, Miami Beach hotels, homes, yachts, land- that is, nearly everything that could be liquidated. Stretched beyond even his formidable means, his empire collapsed into bankruptcy in 1932. Three years later, Fisher declared personal bankruptcy. When he died in 1939, his personal estate amounted to just $52,198.

Although Montauk itself had a few good years in the 1930's and 40's, Fisher's dream of another Miami Beach was buried along with him. Without his considerable talent and salesmanship, Montauk was left with the imposing infrastructure of a grand resort, but with few of the details completed. Within years of its zenith, much of Fisher's Montauk fell into decay and ultimately abandonment. By the 1950's his office building stood empty, Montauk Manor was a brooding wreck, and his grand boulevards ran off to nowhere. Montauk's caretakers were left with no other choice but to fill in the gaps as best they could, the result being a somewhat uneven resort community.

Montauk today is an amalgam of Fisher's original vision of a getaway for the rich and the reality of an affordable vacation village. Admittedly, Montauk now has over 3,000 quality hotel rooms, some 50 restaurants 1,000 deep-water boat slips, a world-class golf course, and some of the most beautiful ocean and bay beaches in the world. Even some of Fisher's original projects have been resurrected in the past few years. For example, the Montauk Manor and Fisher's six-story headquarters building on the green are now deluxe condominiums. The yacht club is under new management, with restoration of its remaining Fisher sections in full swing. The golf course is better than ever, as is Montauk Downs.

The Indianapolis attorney who often represented Fisher, Walter Myers, remembered the last time he saw his former client. Visiting Miami Beach on business during the Great Depression, Myers spotted Fisher standing with one foot on a park bench. Myers walked up to Fisher, shook his hand, and asked him how he was doing. The answer Myers received from Fisher was not encouraging:

I can tell you in a few words. The bottom dropped out of the sea. New York and Long Island took everything I had. I'm a beggar—dead broke, no family to fall back on. Yes, the bottom dropped out of the sea and I went with it.

You know, I promoted Miami Beach here. The grateful people got up a purse, $500 a month for me. That's what I live on. I used to make dreams come true. Can't do it anymore. I'm only a beggar now. The end can't be far away.

Fisher died from a gastric hemorrhage on July 15, 1939 in Miami Beach. Jane Fisher, who was divorced from Fisher in 1926 and thereafter remarried, never forgot her life with a man some Hoosiers had labeled "crazy." Living with her first husband, said Jane Fisher, was like "living in a circus: there was something going on—something exciting going on—every minute of the day. Sometimes it was very good; sometimes it was very bad. Still, it was living. It was excitement, aliveness, that I never found again."

SOURCE MATERIAL

1. Marvin Dunn, *Black Miami in the Twentieth Century,* University Press of Florida, Gainesville, 1997

2. Jane Fisher, *Fabulous Hoosier: A Story of American Achievement,* Robert M. McBride & Company, New York, 1947

3. Jerry M. Fisher, *The Pacesetter: The Untold Story of Carl G. Fisher,* Lost Coast Press, Fort Bragg, California, 1998

4. Mark S. Foster, *Castles in the Sand: The Life and Times of Carl Graham Fisher,* University Press of Florida, Gainesville, 2000

5. Howard Kleinberg, *Woggles and Cheese Holes: The History of Miami Beach's Hotels,* The Greater Miami & The Beaches Hotel Association, Miami Beach, 2005

6. Marianne Lamonaca and Jonathan Mogul, Editors, *Grand Hotels of the Jazz Age: The Architecture of Schultze & Weaver,* The Wolfsonian-Florida International University, Miami Beach, 2005

7. Dolly Redford, *Billion-Dollar Sandbar: A Biography of Miami Beach,* E. P. Dutton & Co., New York, 1970

Henry Morrison Flagler (1830-1913):
THE ROBBER BARON WHO INVENTED FLORIDA

Several figures stand out in the development of Florida into a world-class tourist destination, including Walt Disney and his predecessors, Addison Mizner, Carl Graham Fisher and Henry Bradley Plant. The earliest and arguably the most influential of Florida's early developers, however, was Henry Morrison Flagler, who invented the concept of the Florida vacation as we know it today.

Henry Morrison Flagler left his home in western New York in 1844 at 14 years of age to join his half-brother, Daniel M. Harkness, in Republic, Ohio. Young Henry, tall and handsome for his age was eager to leave farm life in Medina, New York and to seek his own fortune. His father, Isaac Flagler, was a poor preacher-farmer who had served several Presbyterian congregations in Western New York and northern Ohio. Henry worked on a small boat headed for Buffalo in exchange for his fare. Early on the second day away from home, Henry found another boat headed for Sandusky, Ohio. The trip across Lake Erie was rough and lasted three days and nights. Henry was seasick and unhappy until the boat reached Sandusky. On the very next day, young Henry went to work for L.G. Harkness and Company under the watchful eye of Dan Harkness, whose uncle Lamont Harkness owned a general store business. After five years, 19 year-old Henry Flagler joined the firm of Chapman, Harkness and Company in Bellevue, Ohio where he met and married Mary Harkness on November 9, 1853.

As Chapman, Harkness and Company expanded into the grain distillery and liquor fields, Flagler was able to buy the Chapman interest. One commission merchant in Cleveland, John D. Rockefeller, handled most of their shipments and got to know Flagler fairly well. This association later paid dividends when Flagler relocated some years later to Cleveland. Rockefeller was born in Richford, N.Y. on July 8, 1839 and was nine

years younger than Flagler. His father peddled medicine throughout western New York. John D. Rockefeller graduated from high school in 1855 but did not go to college. During the 1860s oil discoveries in western Pennsylvania led to an oil boom in search for "black gold". Thousands of Civil War veterans joined the oil rush. Among them were horse traders, gamblers, get-rich-quick seekers and dead-beats. All were interested in one purpose: to make a fortune quickly. By 1865, Cleveland was the leading petroleum center with 30 refineries. In 1867, a partnership between Rockefeller and Flagler was formed. The Cleveland Leader commented,

> Our readers will notice by the advertisement in another column, that the old and reliable firm of Rockefeller and Andrew has undergone a change, and now appears under the new title of Rockefeller, Andrews and Flagler..... Among the many oil refining enterprises, this seems to be one of the most successful; its heavy capital and consummate management, having kept it clear of the many shoals upon which oil refining houses have so often been stranded.

While Flagler and Rockefeller were close business associates, they were also friends. Flagler once remarked that it was "friendship founded on business rather than a business founded on friendship." Flagler's life at the time consisted mostly of business and family. He rarely partook of Cleveland's social life, mainly because of his wife's increasingly poor health. From 1864 to 1881 until Mary Flagler's death, it was said that Flagler spent only two evenings away from home.

Flagler probably invented the practice of negotiating special rates and rebates with the railroads which enabled him to outdistance his rival refineries. The formation of the Standard Oil Co. was based on acquisition of and merger with smaller and weaker refineries. When Flagler first proposed such combinations, Rockefeller replied, "Yes, Henry, I'd like to combine some of these refineries with ours. The business would be much more simple. But how are you going to determine the unit of valuation? How are you going to find a yardstick to measure the value? In a few minutes Flagler answered, "John, I'll find a yardstick." And find it he did if only when they had taken over

most of the small refineries in Ohio. In 1869, Flagler and Rockefeller decided to incorporate their holdings into the Standard Oil Company. When asked if this was his idea, Rockefeller said, "No, sir, I wish I'd had the brains to think of it. It was Henry M. Flagler."

Standard Oil continued to expand by merger, acquisition and consolidation. By 1878, Standard Oil controlled most of the pipe lines carrying petroleum from the oil-producing regions. In just four years, Rockefeller and Flagler's Standard Oil Company controlled 95% of the country's petroleum industry.

When Flagler relocated to New York City in 1877, he gradually separated himself from the management of Standard Oil. After Mary Flagler died in 1881, Flagler's influence steadily diminished in Standard Oil but he remained the second largest stockholder after John D. Rockefeller. By the time Standard Oil was dissolved in 1911, Henry Flagler was an extraordinarily wealthy former founder and stockholder. His various interests in Florida had completely replaced his attachments to the Standard Oil Company.

In 1883, Henry Flagler married Ida Alice Shourds at the Madison Avenue Methodist Church in New York City. She was 35 years old and he was 53. Miss Shourds had been an attendant to his first wife before Mary Flagler died. Because Flagler hated cold weather, he planned a belated honeymoon in Florida in December, 1883. Their trip from New York to Jacksonville took 90 hours because of the different gauges of railroad tracks along the way. In 1870, Harper's Weekly reported:

> There are two ways of getting to Jacksonville (from Savannah) and whichever you choose you will be sorry to have not taken the other. There is the night train by railroad, which brings you to Jacksonville in about 16 hours; and there is the steamboat line, which goes inland nearly wall the way, and which may land you in a day, or you may run aground and remain on board for a week.

Florida's population in 1880 was 270,000 people, of whom 40,000 lived in the long-settled northwest coast between Jacksonville and St.

Augustine. Today, instead of rail or packetboats, the chief method of traveling to Florida is, of course, by air or highway. Although airlines are certainly critical to Florida's tourism enterprises, contrary to the popular view, the airlines did not develop the original tourism market for Florida. That distinction should go to Henry M. Flagler, when he took his second wife on a honeymoon to Jacksonville and then farther south to the seaside village of St. Augustine, (the oldest permanent European settlement in the United States). Flagler loved the breathtaking expanse of sea and shore, and enjoyed the clear skies and balmy weather when most of the rest of the country's residents (then concentrated in the northeast) were locked in by ice and snow.

St. Augustine had been used by invalids even before the Civil War but wealthy northerners were just beginning to discover its balmy weather at the end of the nineteenth century. While the Flaglers stayed at the new six-story San Marco Hotel they were surprised at the lack of large hotels and other real estate development. After consultation with the owner James A. McGuire, his hotel manager Osborn D. Seavey, Dr. Andrew Anderson, a St. Augustine resident and Franklin W. Smith, a Bostonian, Flagler decided to build a new hotel. One event that might have heightened his interest was the celebration of the landing of Ponce de Leon in March, 1885. He later recalled the difficulty of deciding on the design of the Hotel Ponce de Leon, "Here was St. Augustine, the oldest city in the United States. How to build a hotel to meet the requirements of nineteenth century America and have it in keeping with the character of the place - that was my hardest problem."

Ponce De Leon, St. Augustine, Florida, completed in 1887, designed by Carrere and Hastings with interior decorations by Louis Tiffany of New York. Built with beautiful courts, plazas, mosaics, fountains, verandas of the Spanish Renaissance period. After eighty seasons, the Hotel closed in 1967 and was converted into Flagler College.

Flagler went to McKim, Mead and White of New York, the leading architectural firm in the United States and hired two young architects: John M. Carrere and Thomas Hastings. The 540-room Ponce de Leon Hotel opened on January 10, 1888 on a five-acre lot with Spanish Renaissance architecture. On opening day, Flagler's invited guests arrived on the first plush vestibule train ever to arrive in St. Augustine. That evening, Mr. and Mrs. Flagler entertained the hotel's architects, builders, artists and railroad executives. The first impression of the Ponce de Leon was of size, since the mammoth structure covered most of its five acre lot. The building was only four stories high but it was large and extensive. Inside the front gate was the beautifully landscaped 10,000 square foot interior court containing a large fountain with a grand entrance to the rotunda. The building's design and ornamentation embodied the style of Spanish Renaissance architecture.

The heartbeat of the hotel was in the spacious rotunda. Its great dome was supported by massive oak columns and its floor was brilliant with inlaid colored mosaics. The architects tried to capture the spirit of Old Spain with allegorical representations of the four elements: fire, water, air, earth and four figures: adventure, discovery, conquest and civilization. Behind the dome of the rotunda was the oval-shaped dining hall seating 700 with stained glass windows, highly polished floors and enormous columns of antique oak. The ceiling art representing the history of St. Augustine was painted by Virgilio Tojetti, one of the foremost artists of the day.

The success of the design of the Ponce de Leon is recorded by the noted Gilded Age author, Henry James in his 1907 book, *The American Scene*. James writes, "The Ponce de Leon, for that matter, comes as close as near producing, all by itself, the illusion of romance as a highly modern, a most cleverly-constructed and smoothly-administered great modern caravansery can come...and is, in all sorts of ways and in the highest sense of the word, the most 'amusing' of hotels."

The hotel had electric lights, steam heat, private parlors, reading and game rooms, exquisite draperies, imported rosewood, walnut and mahogany furniture and Brussels carpet. Since standards of the day deemed public bathrooms sufficient, the hotel originally had only one private bathroom- in Flagler's suite. Almost immediately after opening it became necessary to add private bathrooms to the hotel rooms.

Among the hundreds of first-night guests were Mrs. Ulysses S. Grant, Frederick Vanderbilt and William R. Rockefeller. During its first five years, the Ponce de Leon was the most exclusive winter palace resort in the United States. Its guests included Hamilton Disston, the nation's largest landowner; Vice President Levi P. Morton; Governor Roswell Flower of New York; Chauncey Depew; Charles A. Dana of the New York Sun; and President Grover Cleveland who later visited the hotel in 1889, 1893, 1899, 1903 and 1905. Four other presidents visited the hotel: William McKinley, then governor of Ohio was a guest in 1895; Theodore Roosevelt in 1905; Warren G. Harding in 1921; and years later Vice President Lyndon B. Johnson in March 1963.

The Ponce de Leon was the center of formal entertainment dances. One of these affairs was the Hermitage Ball held in 1892 to raise money for the restoration of Andrew Jackson's Tennessee home. There were swimming exhibitions at the Casino pool, horsemanship tournaments, bicycling and tennis. In 1895, the first golf links were laid on the Fort Marian green and there was great interest among the winter guests in golf equipment and professional instruction. In a manifestation of Jim Crow racism, guests would sometimes attend cake walks sponsored by the Negro bellhops and waiters. The event would begin with a "buck dance", a brisk double-shuffle by one black performer followed by singing and the cake walk itself. Well-dressed white couples would then stroll in time to the music and vie for prizes awarded by a panel of judges of their peers. Later, cake walks were replaced by black-faced white performers in minstrel shows.

In order to attract northern vacationers so soon after the Civil War and Reconstruction, Florida had to remake its image. After all, Florida was the third state, after South Carolina and Mississippi to secede from the Union and join the Confederate States of America. In the years after the Civil War, U.S. federal officers visiting the South observed that the feeling toward northerners in Georgia, South Carolina and Florida was bitter and hostile. Throughout the 1860s, the Ku Klux Klan and other terrorist organizations brutalized black landowners and officeholders with lynchings, murders and arsons. As late as 1873, Harper's Weekly reported that Florida was "suited for cultivation as a resort.... but for its ceaseless political disturbances...." Northern reporters stated that Floridian's intolerance would drive away potential investment and reduce the state to a perpetual wasteland. In St. Augustine, Henry Flagler's choice of Spanish Renaissance Revival design for his hotels was not accidental. It solidified the city's claim to Spanish heritage and helped to stimulate tourism by erasing memories of Florida's participation on the Confederate side of the Civil War conflict. Founded in 1565, St. Augustine had Spanish origins and was known as "the Ancient City". Flagler could, therefore, be a modern-day Ponce de Leon rather than a carpetbagger and promote Florida as a more desirable vacation destination for Northerners.

The George Maynard paintings and murals "Adventure, Discovery, Conquest and Civilization" in the ceiling of the Ponce de Leon's rotunda and dining room reflected the history of Spanish Florida, not the history of slavery or of racist sectional strife. There was no place in this selective history for slaveholders and secessionists but only dashing Spanish explorers. The "Change of Flags" segment of a local festival included Spanish, French, English and American flags but not the Confederate flag.

The management of the Ponce de Leon had to provide housing for the hotel employees. Behind the main dining hall was a large building which contained the kitchen, workshops, living quarters for the hotel's white employees and several employee dining rooms. A quarter of a mile away on Cordova Street, black males were housed in the so-called "colored barracks" while black women lived in the large laundry building near the railroad depot. A variety of other skilled employees worked in the Flagler hotels: plumbers, gardeners, chefs, musicians, engineers and two Pinkerton detectives to protect wealthy guests from "bunko" artists. Most of these employees worked in northern hotels in the summer and in southern resorts in the winter.

In 1899, Flagler built seven studios in the rear of the Ponce de Leon which were occupied by famous New England painters whose landscapes promoted Florida to the rest of the country. The weekly receptions held by the artists were among the social highlights of the winter season.

No sooner did the Ponce de Leon Hotel open than Flagler realized that the market would require a companion hotel catering to a more modest clientele and to accept the overflow from the Ponce de Leon. Flagler hired Carrere and Hastings to design the Hotel Alcazar (an Arabic word meaning "royal castle") and its Casino across the street from the Ponce de Leon. Flagler's army of laborers crossed King Street and began construction of the Alcazar. The site had been cleared by the removal of the Olivet Methodist Church, the demolition of the San Marco roller-skating rink building and the landfill of the creek bed on the site. The Alcazar was smaller than the Ponce de Leon. The structure, 250 feet by 400 feet, was four stories high and was built around a court and arcades with stores, restaurants, shops and salons. The façade was a reproduction of the famous Alcazar in Seville, Spain.

The Alcazar, while not as elaborate as the Ponce de Leon, nevertheless had some unique features such as the Casino and Baths which were opened in early February 1889. In anticipation of the spa development of one hundred years later, Flagler incorporated the following:

- A Turkish bath (the Senate) with dry heat of 160-180 degrees where patrons sat on marble tiers wrapped in togas to endure the heat. Flagler hired a Turkish attendant from Chicago's Palmer House hotel to supervise the baths. Hotel advertising touted the baths as cure-alls for heart disease, as well as for gout, rheumatism, liver and kidney diseases, neurasthenia and obesity. Patrons would enter the baths from the hotel or the Casino and go to one of forty cubicle dressing rooms to disrobe. Then they would follow a regimen prescribed by their physician or by the staff, which might involve being sprayed from a hose and given a shampoo followed by a steam soak in the Russian bath, where a variety of jets of water would be sprayed; then back to the steam room, and finally, a quick cold plunge in the center of the bath area. Afterwards, the guest would probably have a massage and a glass of Clarendon Springs mineral water.

- The baths also contained a small well-furnished gymnasium where guests could exercise amid the Carrere and Hastings version of the modern fitness center. There were dumb-bells, pulleys, weights, Indian clubs, punching bags, parallel and horizontal bars and oriental rugs serving as mats. Women could use the baths and gymnasium at specially scheduled times when female attendants supervised the treatments.

The Casino building was huge structure that contained a swimming pool 120 feet long and 50 feet wide, ranging in depth from 3 feet to more than 12 feet. Light was provided in the daytime from the glassed-over roof above the pool. In the evening, one thousand electric lights illuminated the interior. One floor above, completely encircling the pool area, was the ballroom with its highly polished floor.

The water in the pool came from an artesan well sunk 1,400 feet deep into the Florida aquifer. While the water's natural temperature was above eighty degrees, it was permeated with sulphur which, despite aeration, gave off a "rotten-egg" smell. The eastern end of the pool was for the men while the western end for women was partitioned off so that those too modest to swim in public could take a dip in private.

Flagler was proud of the Alcazar and described it as follows:

> (It) will furnish superior accommodations for those who do not wish to stay at the other hotel. Amusements will be provided and the vicinity of the hotel made as attractive as possible. The Methodist Church, which I am constructing across the avenue on the north, will be the finest church edifice south of the Potomac. The Casa Monica (a hotel designed by Franklin Smith, later purchased by Flagler and renamed the Cordova) is very near and it is a handsome structure. These, with the big hotel (Ponce de Leon) and the Alcazar will make a beautiful group.

Flagler's operational policy was a forerunner of the "loss leader" theory of hotel management. He believed that a fine hotel or restaurant was bound to lose a certain amount of money before it established itself as a place of bona-fide quality. In the 1890's as the Ponce continued to operate at high occupancies, a new hotel manager decided to economize. He wired Flagler for permission to discharge the costly French chef and an equally costly dance band. Flagler wired back, "Hire another cook and two more of the best orchestras."

By the early 1890's, Henry Flagler was St. Augustine's greatest benefactor. He built a modern hospital; contributed money toward the building of a City Hall and an African-American school. He donated money to install electric lights, pave streets, lay sewers, build railroad car shops and homes for his employees. He was 60 years old and apparently was the beneficiary of Ponce de Leon's supposed fountain-of-youth. His greatest accomplishments still lay ahead of him.

For 15 years after the Civil War, there was no new railroad construction in Florida. By 1884, the few railroads along Florida's Atlantic coast each had a different track width. Therefore, none of the early railroads could interchange rolling stock. In order to service his planned resorts, Flagler needed standardized track and dependable railroad service. With characteristically direct action, Flagler purchased the Jacksonville, St. Augustine & Halifax River Railroad and had the track between Jacksonville and St. Augustine widened to standard gauge. Subsequently he acquired the St. Augustine and Palatka Railroad, the St. Johns Railroad and the logging road to Daytona. After standard gauge tracks were laid along these routes, Flagler's entire railroad was as modern as could be found anywhere in the South. Flagler's insatiable business interests continued to lead him to South Florida along the Atlantic coast.

Near Daytona, Flagler bought the Ormond Beach Hotel in 1890. Flagler enlarged the building to 150 rooms, beautified the grounds and constructed a new 18-hole golf course. In 1890, Daytona Beach was the southern terminus of all standard gauge rail on the East coast. At that time it was possible to board a Pullman in New York City and ride all the way to St. Augustine, Ormond Beach and Daytona Beach without changing trains. For the first time, Flagler became a railroad builder, pushing south through the coastline of eastern Florida to New Smyrna to Rockledge to Eau Gallie. By the end of January 1894, new rail had been constructed to Fort Pierce, 242 miles from Jacksonville. In less than two years, Flagler had built 130 miles of standard gauge railroad.

After two years of study, Flagler obtained a charter from the state of Florida in 1892 authorizing him to build a railroad along the Indian River as far south as Miami. Awarded 8000 acres of land for each mile of railroad built south of Daytona Beach, he eventually owned two million acres of Florida land.

Flagler created the Model Land Company which probably did more than to build up Florida's east coast than any of his other undertakings. The Model Land Company, under the direction of Henry Plant's former top executive, James E. Ingraham, hired expert agriculturists, horticulturists and stockmen who were well versed on soils, crops and farm production. Flagler's land policies resulted in the settling of Delray, Deerfield, Dania, Ojus, Peerine, Homestead, Kenansville and Okeechobie as well as Fort Lauderdale, Miami and West Palm Beach.

As the railroad moved south, Flagler did not neglect St. Augustine, buying the Hotel Casa Monica and renaming it the Cordova. Flagler also donated funds to build the Memorial Presbyterian Church, a hospital and to rebuild the Catholic Cathedral when it burned down. He underwrote the construction of the City Hall and a segregated school for colored children, the first installation of electric lights and public water works and the paving of St. Augustine's streets.

In the spring of 1893, Flagler purchased a large tract of land lying between Lake Worth and the Atlantic Ocean. It was located in what is now Palm Beach County. In 1894, Palm Beach was a barrier island separated from the mainland by an arm of the ocean called Lake Worth. It was named after General William J. Worth who had been sent there before the Civil War to settle Indian troubles. The lakes shores were beautiful with overhanging trees, jungle vines and exotic foliage. One of the first settlers in the late 1870's was Robert R. McCormick, founder of the International Harvester Company. He built a home on Lake Worth with a fabulous tropical garden containing a wide variety of Southern Florida's flowers, shrubs, trees and palms. Meanwhile, Flagler acquired about a half mile of frontage for $45,000 on the mainland which ultimately became West Palm Beach. He broke ground on May 1, 1893 for what was to become the South's largest hotel, the Royal Poinciana.

The story of how Palm Beach got its name is worth remembering. In 1878, the Spanish ship Provindencia, sailing from Trinidad to Spain, sank in a storm off the Florida coast. The residents of the Lake Worth community salvaged the cargo of fledging cocoanut palm trees, planted them on the scrubland and adopted the name of Palm Beach. Flagler assembled land which formed the nucleus of the new town of West Palm Beach.

The six-story 439-room Royal Poinciana opened for guests in February 1894 and operated only during the winter season. In order to build the Royal Poinciana and the Florida East Coast Railway extension at the same time, black workers were brought from the Bahamas. They lived in a segregated camp, called "the Styx" without running water and electricity.

The Royal Poinciana was called the "Queen of Winter Resorts" and was considered the largest resort hotel in the world when it was built. In the center of the six-story building was a large rotunda from which ran several miles of corridors. There were lounges, parlors, drawing rooms and a casino. The interiors were designed with the utmost care and taste. The building was enlarged in 1899 and again in 1901. The hotel was the center of social activity for the wealthy and fashionable. Approximately 1400 employees were on duty during the open season, usually from December to April. In addition to the gala annual Washington Birthday Ball, there were cake walks, teas, balls, dances and expensive catered social events. Extensive outdoor activities included two 18-hole golf courses, tennis courts, motor boats, wicker wheel chairs, bicycles and a mule-drawn trolley car to and from the beach. There were two swimming pools, one with "fresh" sulphur water and one with salt water from the ocean.

Unlike his hotels in St. Augustine which were built of stone and coquina, Flagler used wood for the Royal Poinciana. In season, the Royal Poinciana Hotel employed 400 waiters, 287 chambermaids; it had a separate dining room for the lower echelons of hotel staff, another for first officers, a third dining room for the second officers, a fourth for servants of the guests, and a fifth for children. The staff had its own orchestra for their dances and other social functions. The head housekeeper had a three-room suite. Outdoor activities were very popular at the Royal Poinciana including golf, tennis, boating and fishing and more. In an unfortunate manifestation of the racism of the day, African American bicyclists pedaled guests seated in attached wicker chairs called "Afrimobiles".

The hotel contained a spacious dining room, fancy shops and an "Ask Mr. Foster" travel office. Outdoor activities included ocean swimming, boating, tennis, golf and day trips on the hotel's houseboat. The hotel was so popular that it was expanded in 1899, 1901 and 1929 with new guestrooms, dining rooms and a new greenhouse restaurant. Some wealthy guests arrived in their own private Pullman cars which housed their servants during the vacation.

Karl Abbott wrote in *Open For the Season* in 1950,

> When the Royal Poinciana opened in January 1894, additions followed swiftly, until the hotel had a thousand guest rooms. It was the largest frame strictly resort hotel in the world, and so far as I know there was never been another so large. The hotel accommodated seventeen hundred and fifty guests and required a staff of about twelve hundred employees, all of whom were housed and fed in a dormitory which was a great hotel in itself. There were approximately three hundred colored waiters, and as they left their dormitory on a sunny day, dressed in their uniforms with snowy white shirt bosoms, they looked like a miniature army advancing upon the hotel. The dining room accommodated two thousand guests at a single sitting, and to quote Ring Lardner: "From one end of the room to the other was a toll call."
>
> Business tycoons, the Newport set, theatrical stars, politicians of the day made the Poinciana a mecca for their winter vacations, and the winter colony round about grew apace; Colonel Bradley built this wonderful gambling Casino; Flagler, his beautiful residence, Whitehall, and the magnificent Hotel Breakers on the beach.

Colonial Bradley's Beach Club and Casino was a notorious private club and restaurant with an octagonal gaming room where guards carried machine guns. Flagler disapproved of the gambling but did not shut Bradley down because hotel guests enjoyed the club.

The hotel had the back-of-the-house boiler rooms, generators, kitchens, laundry and staff housing in separate buildings. An 1894 souvenir brochure showed the layout of the laundry and praised its up-to-date technology. Advanced techniques were also evident in the unique fire escape equipment. Each guestroom was equipped with a rope ladder that allowed guests to be lowered mechanically to the ground level. These ladders had seats and galvanized fixtures with ladder hooks.

After Flagler built the Royal Poinciana; he became a major benefactor of the area. He built houses for his employees, contributed to public funds for the contribution of West Palm Beach's prominent buildings. He gave a plot of land for a municipal cemetery. He also built a Catholic Church in the city because a large number of his employees were Catholics.

Flagler's second hotel in Palm Beach was the unpretentious Palm Beach Inn, about a quarter mile east of the Poinciana on the Atlantic Ocean which was built as an annex for bathers and swimmers. It became as popular as the Poinciana with its name changed to the Breakers Hotel. It was destroyed by fire in 1903, rebuilt in 1906 and destroyed again by fire in 1925.

The heirs of Henry Morrison Flagler vowed that this disaster would never happen again. They engaged the architectural firm of Schultze and Weaver (who later designed the Waldorf-Astoria, the Pierre and the Sherry-Netherland in New York City) to build a concrete structure reinforced with eleven hundred tons of steel. The owners, determined not to miss the upcoming December-to-May social season, employed some twelve hundred construction workers, who completed the hotel in less than a year. Seventy-two Italian artisans were imported to execute the paintings on the ceilings of the lobby and other first-floor public rooms. From its opening day, December 29, 1926, the Breakers was the resort hotel of choice for the American social set, who arrived in private railroad cars, like a flock of exotic birds on their annual migration some for three-to-four month stays. These wealthy guests were accompanied by dozens of steamer trunks, gold-encrusted jewelry cases, lizard-encased golf clubs and a retinue of servants who resided in tiny cubicles equipped with call bells to provide their employers with twenty-four-hour access to their services.

Between the two hotels Flagler developed a vast park with spectacular landscaping and a miniature railway with cars pulled by donkeys. Serpentine walkways crossed acres of lawn and intersected with hundred of flower beds and rows of palm trees and Australian pines. In the Roaring Twenties gentlemen drank bootleg gin and smoked cigars in a gallery overlooking the Circle Dining Room. Guests danced the Charleston till dawn. For a time a three-to-seven A.M. "nightcap breakfast" was served. But with the stock market crash of 1929, the Breakers' popularity began to wane. During World War II the hotel was converted to a U.S. Army hospital. The Royal Poinciana was demolished by the Flagler System in 1935.

Following the end of World War II, the Breakers struggled to regain its former opulence. Every spring it closed its doors, the windows were rubbed with soap to keep out the sun, and the furniture was covered with sheets. During the winter season, the room-sized safe, lined with boxes that once held an emperor's treasure of emeralds, rubies and diamonds, stood empty. In the abandoned gallery, the paintings of nymphs on the ceiling were peeling; the cracked walls still reeked of stale cigar smoke. By 1970, in an effort to enter the modern world, the hotel had added air-conditioning and convention facilities, but it never regained its former glory until the 1990 renovations. The Breakers has long been controlled by the Kenan family, relatives of Mary Lily Kenan, the third wife of Henry Morrison Flagler, and in 1990 they finally committed $75 million to a complete renovation. Among the more recent additions are the Flagler Club, twenty-eight deluxe rooms with special services, including those of a dedicated concierge. There are fourteen tennis courts and two 18-hole golf courses. (The first, completed in 1896, is the oldest in Florida). The beach club has a massive pool, a kiddie pool, beach cabanas and an outdoor and an indoor restaurant. Personal trainers, fitness classes and massage are available.

At the age of 70, Flagler built a fabulous Palm Beach mansion, called Whitehall, which was reputed to cost $2.5 million. A reporter for the New York Herald, writing in March 1902, described the mansion as "more wonderful than any palace in Europe, grander and more magnificent than any other private dwelling in the world..... the Taj Mahal of North America." Whitehall was a wedding present for his new bride, Mary Lily Kenan.

Then, as now, northern Florida was subject to periods of wintry cold. After an intense cold snap in 1894, Flagler turned his attention farther south. Fort Dallas, an outpost located at the mouth of the Miami River, was built after the outbreak of the Seminole War in 1836. Julia Tuttle, a friend of John D. Rockefeller, lived there and owned 640 acres of woodlands and marshland bordering the Miami River and Biscayne

Bay. Tuttle promised to share half her land with Flagler if he would extend the Florida East Coast Railway to Miami. Flagler agreed and Tuttle then divided her land into small plots, giving every other plot to Flagler, which caused him to purchase her remaining plots in order to secure a contiguous 640 acres of land. Acquiring more land on Biscayne Bay, Flagler extended his railroad in April 1896 to Miami where he built a railway terminal, streets, and a municipal water system. Soon thereafter, Flagler built a new inn, the five-story Royal Palm. Upon the incorporation of the new city, the residents wanted to name the new city "Flagler" in appreciation. Instead, Flagler urged that it be called "Miami", the Indian name for the river that ran through the city.

With an eye toward expansion in the Caribbean, Flagler acquired a hotel in Nassau, the Royal Victoria and started steamship service between Palm Beach and Nassau. In order to qualify for a subsidy of 8500 English pounds for ten years, Flagler contracted to build a new hotel, the Colonial, with 340 rooms. The new Colonial far surpassed the Royal Victoria which closed after the 1901 season.

Most of the laborers in Flagler's workforce were blacks from southern states, from the Bahamas and other Caribbean islands. The center of the South Florida black community was Colored Town which was created in 1896 in northwest Miami. Blacks were denied equal housing, business opportunities, voting rights and the use of the beaches. But one black construction laborer who worked as a carpenter for Florida's East Coast Railroad recognized the need to provide housing for black workers. Dana Albert Dorsey was the son of former slaves whose formal education stopped at fourth grade at a school run by the Freedmen's Bureau in Quitman, Georgia. After moving to Miami in 1897, Dorsey engaged in truck farming but soon began to invest in real estate. He purchased lots for $25 each in Colored Town and constructed one rental house per parcel. He built many of the so-called shotgun houses and rented them out, but never sold any.

According to his daughter Dana Dorsey Chapman, in a 1990 interview, her father's excellent penmanship was the product of his early formal education at the Freedmen's Bureau during Reconstruction. Dorsey's business expanded as far north as Fort Lauderdale. He donated land to the Dade County Public Schools on which the Dorsey High School was built in 1936 in Liberty City. In 1970, its purpose was changed to meet the needs of the adults in the community by becoming the D.A. Dorsey Educational Center. In Overtown (formerly Colored Town), the Dorsey Memorial Library which opened on August 13, 1941, was built on land he donated shortly before his death in 1940. That building is now being renovated and restored under the direction of my brother, Leonard Turkel, a Miami philanthropist and businessman. The first black-owned hotel in Florida was the Dorsey Hotel in Overtown. The hotel placed advertisements in black and white newspapers and was constantly upgraded by Dorsey, including adding hot and cold running water. Marvin Dunn in his fascinating book, *Black Miami in the Twentieth Century* reports that,

> The Dorsey house was always filled with important dinner guests. Some of the white millionaires who visited were awed by Dorsey's accomplishments, achieved under difficult circumstances. Some even went to him for financial help. According to his daughter, during the Depression, Dorsey lent money to William M. Burdine to keep his store open. When Dorsey died in 1940 flags were lowered to half-staff all over Miami.

In 1918, Dorsey purchased a 216 acre island sliced from the tip of Miami in 1905 when the government dredged out a sea-lane from Biscayne Bay. His intention was to create a beach resort for blacks because they were forbidden to use all other public beaches. When his efforts were rebuffed by the blatant racism of the time, he sold the island in 1919 to the Alton Beach Realty Company owned by Carl Graham Fisher who named it Fisher Island. It is now one of the wealthiest enclaves in South Florida.

At age 75, Flagler still had ambitions. This time he turned his attention to the string of coral islands that extended in a graceful, 150- mile westward arc from Biscayne Bay to Key West. He determined to connect Key West to mainland Florida with a rail line. This vast construction project, called the Overseas Railroad, required the construction of causeways, bridges, roads, and trestles across the open sea from island to island. Flagler became especially interested in this Key West Extension when the United States announced the construction of the Panama

Canal. Flagler thought that Key West, the closest deep water port to the Canal (300 miles closer than any other Gulf port), would stimulate Central and South American trade with the United States. After the Spanish-American war of 1898, Flagler anticipated increased trade with Cuba bringing oranges, pineapples and sugar by ferry to Key West and then by rail to New York. The physical obstacles facing the Key West extension were very difficult and seemingly insurmountable.

In 1904, Henry Morrison Flagler made the fateful decision to build the Overseas Railroad, some 156 miles from Miami to Key West. His agents made surveys and estimated costs for several years and then got the go-ahead signal from Flagler, "Very well, then. Go to Key West." The construction required many engineering innovations, vast amounts of material, labor and money. All building materials, food, fresh water and medical supplies for a 3000 to 5000 workforce had to be brought in by barges.

For construction, there were cargo ships carrying crushed rock, cement and coal. There were tugs, houseboats, work boats, dynamos, floating pile drivers, hundreds of barges with derricks and concrete mixers, eight stern-wheel Mississippi River steamboats and power excavators. For nearly 75 miles, the railroad was raised over water or wetlands on steel and concrete bridges. Over the seven years of construction, five hurricanes caused extensive damage, delays and deaths. It is estimated that the project cost more than $49 million and several hundred lives. The first official train to travel the newly built extension arrived at Key West on January 22, 1912 at 10:43 A.M. with the 80-year old Henry Morrison Flagler on board. The Key West Extension was variously called "Flagler's Folly", "The Overseas Railroad" and "The Eighth Wonder of the World."

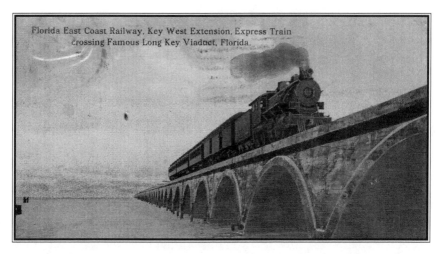

Florida East Coast Railway, Key West Extension, Express Train crossing Famous Long Key Viaduct, Florida.

The Florida East Coast Railroad's Key West Extension was called "Flagler's Folly" or "The Eighth Wonder of the World." Until its destruction by hurricane on September 2, 1935, it had carried some half-million passengers from Miami to Key West on the 156-mile Overseas Railroad. After the state of Florida acquired the right-of-way from the Flagler family, they converted the railroad to the spectacular Overseas Highway still in operation.

The route of the Overseas Railroad between Miami and Key West was:

	Miles
Miami to Homestead	28.00
Homestead to Jewfish Creek	21.39
Jewfish Creek	.02
Key Largo	16.64
Tavernier Creek	.06
Long Island	4.88
Windley's Island Creek	2.01
Matecumbe Key	14.05
Long Key	4.05
Long Key Viaduct	2.68

Grassy Key	15.57
Knights Key to Little Duck Viaduct	8.95
Bahia Honda Key	2.22
Bahia Honda Viaduct	1.04
Big Pine Key	28.41
Boca Chica Viaduct	1.68
Key West	4.19
Total	155.84 miles

The Overseas Railroad operated for 22 years, until Labor Day 1935, when the line was irreparably damaged by a severe hurricane that toppled bridges, twisted rails, overturned causeways, and smashed trestles. Over that time, it carried some half million passengers over the twenty-nine islands from Miami to Key West. When the railroad's directors refused to rebuild the ruined rail line (owing to the Depression), the state of Florida acquired the rail right of way and reengineered and rebuilt it to open in 1938 as the spectacular automobile highway to Key West that is still in use today.

Only three hotels were purchased by Flagler: the Casa Monica (1889) in St. Augustine, the Hotel Ormond (1887) in Ormond-on-the Halifax; and the Royal Victoria Hotel (1861) in Nassau. The Flagler system leased two hotels: the Hotel Key West (originally the Russell House, 1887) and the Hotel Biscayne (1896) in Miami. After Flagler's death, the Flagler Company built two hotels: the Casa Marina (1921) in Key West and a new Breakers Hotel (1926) in Palm Beach. Flagler was unique in many ways, not the least of which were his hands-on business practices. He personally selected his architects, builders and managers. He monitored the construction contracts, staffing and payrolls and the cost of building materials.

The death of Henry Flagler in 1913 marked the end of an age. During the last few years of his life he returned often to St. Augustine. But the last decade of his life was filled with personal tragedy. He was estranged from his only son, Harry. His daughter Jennie Louise Benedict died in 1889, a few weeks after giving birth to a baby girl who lived only a few hours. His wife Ida Alice became erratic in behavior and delusional.

Flagler had her committed to a mental institution in 1895 and some years later divorced her. However, he established a trust fund to provide for her care until her death in 1930. After his death in Palm Beach, Flagler's body was buried with those of his first wife and daughter in St. Augustine. His body was rested in state in the rotunda of the Ponce de Leon Hotel in St. Augustine.

What was Flagler's legacy? In addition to the magnificent Overseas Highway and the right-of-way to Key West, some of Flagler's other developments also remain. In St. Augustine, the Alcazar and Cordova hotels became city and county office buildings. The Ponce de Leon now bears the name of Flagler College. (Flagler's name is also on a county and graces the village of Flagler Beach, south of St. Augustine.) The Ormond Beach Hotel became a retirement home. The Whitehall in Palm Beach was converted to a hotel in 1925 with the addition of a 300-room tower. The hotel tower was removed in 1959, and the restored mansion was dedicated as the Henry Morrison Flagler Museum.

Flagler's East Coast Railroad gave strong impetus for new communities to be developed along the railroad right-of-way. The railroad also attracted tourists to vacation in Florida and to use Flagler's grand hotels. The isolated Flagler Memorial on Monument Island has a battered concrete obelisk dedicated to Henry Flagler, which sits on a tiny man-made island in Biscayne Bay, reachable only by boat or, more typically, Jet Ski.

Other landmarks are gone. The Royal Poinciana in Palm Beach and the Royal Palm in Miami were demolished to make room for other developments. The magnificent Breakers Hotel continues operation today more than a century after it opened, and with the nearby Flagler Museum are fitting tributes to Henry Morrison Flagler, the robber baron who invented Florida.

SOURCE MATERIALS

1. Edward N. Akin, *Flagler: Rockefeller Partner and Florida Baron*, Kent State University Press, Kent, 1988.

2. Susan R. Braden, *The Architecture of Leisure: The Florida Resort Hotels of Henry Flagler and Henry Plant*, University Press of Florida, Gainesville, 2002.

3. David Leon Chandler, *Henry Flagler*, Macmillan Publishing Company, New York, 1986.

4. Marvin Dunn, *Black Miami in the Twentieth Century*, University Press of Florida, Gainesville, 1997.

5. Flagler Museum, *An Illustrated Guide, Palm Beach, Florida* 1998.

6. Gerald W. Glover, Scott R. Morrison, Jr., and Alfred C. Briggs, Jr., *"Making Quality Count: Boca Raton's Approach to Quality Assurance."* Cornell Hotel and Restaurant Administration Quarterly, Vol. 25, No. 1 (May 1984).

7. Thomas Graham, *Flagler's Grand Hotel Alcazar*, St. Augustine Historical Society, 1989.

8. Thomas Graham, *Flagler's Magnificent Hotel, Ponce De Leon*, Reprint, St. Augustine Historical Society, 1990.

9. Reiko Hillyer, *The New South in the Ancient City: Flagler's St. Augustine Hotels and Sectional Reconciliation*, The American Hotel Journal of Decorative and Propaganda Arts, The Wolfsonian-Florida International University, Miami Beach, 2005.

10. Marianne Lamonaca and Jonathan Mogul, Editors, *Grand Hotels of the Jazz Age: The Architecture of Schultze & Weaver*, The Wolfsonian-Florida International University, Princeton Architectural Press, New York, 2005.

11. Sidney Walter Martin, *Florida's Flagler*, The University of Georgia Press (Athens 1949).

12. Brian McGinty, *The Palace Inns*, Stackpole Books, Harrisburg, 1978.

13. Edward A. Mueller, *Steamships of the Two Henrys: Being an Account of the Maritime Activities of Henry Morrison Flagler and Henry Bradley Plant*, E.O. Painter Printing Co., DeLeon Springs, Florida 1996.

14. Pat Parks, *The Railroad That Died At Sea*, The Stephen Greene Press, Brattleboro, Vt., 1968.

15. Polly Redford, *Billion-Dollar Sandbar*, E.P. Dutton & Co. Inc., New York, 1970.

16. Charles A. Reynolds, *Tribute: The Architecture of the Hotel Ponce de Leon in Its Relation to the History of St. Augustine*, Brochure 1890.

    The Ponce de Leon set a new standard in American architecture and propelled its architects Carrere and Hastings to the forefront of their profession. Among their subsequent commissions were the interior of the original Metropolitan Opera House, the New York Public Library, the Senate and House Office buildings in Washington, D.C., the Carnegie Institution of Washington, D.C. and the Memorial Amphitheater of Arlington, Va.

17. Ida M. Tarbell, *The History of the Standard Oil Company*, 2 Vols. Macmillan, New York, 1925.

18. J. W. Travers, *History of Beautiful Palm Beach*, Palm Beach Press, West Palm Beach, 1931.

John Q. Hammons (1919-   ):
MASTER HOTEL DEVELOPER, BUILDER, OWNER AND MANAGER

Have you taken notice of the living hotel legend called "John Q". He's been on a unique and singular track for 90 years and, if you don't know who he is, you're missing one of the great hotelier/developers of our time.

Of course, I'm referring to John Q. Hammons who received the prestigious 2007 ALIS Lifetime Achievement Award. Over his 49-year career he has developed 185 hotel properties in 40 states. But the statistics hide the essence of Mr. Hammons special development techniques. Hammons disdains the standard feasibility studies when assessing potential sites for hotel development. Instead, he relies on his own experience, knowledge and intuition.

From a modest beginning in Fairview, Missouri, John Q. Hammons has become one of the country's leading hotel and commercial developers. He develops, builds and operates upscale, full-service hotels in secondary and tertiary locations in 22 states.

Among many success stories, here's a recent one that defines his techniques:

- In Charlotte- Concord, NC, Hammons is building a 308 suite Embassy Suites Hotel Resort and Spa with 55,000 square feet of meeting space adjacent to the Concord Convention Center. He will manage the convention center and the adjacent 18-hole Rocky River Golf Club. Hammons has an exclusive marketing partnership with the Lowe's Motor Speedway located a half-mile from the hotel. The Speedway hosts six NASCAR events a year and receives 1.7 million visitors annually in its 165,000 seat stadium.

Here are some reflections by John Q. Hammons on being an exceptional hotelier:

- Be in Tune With Change: Have a Plan of Action. "People do not stop to think what change means. That's the thing about success. You have to watch change in people, change in habits, change in style, change in desire, change in everything. It's happening every day, and nobody thinks about it. I do."

- Live by the Bedrock Rule. "They're not making any more land, so if you hang onto it long enough, you're bound to make a profit, either by selling it or by developing it."

- Commit to Quality and Location. "During the late '80's and early '90s when the banks closed, I told our regional managers, we are going to stay in the quality business. I said I've made up my mind that the day is coming that there will be so many budgets built that you won't believe it. The price of entry is low, and you don't have to be very smart to do 50 or 100 rooms. We're not going to travel there. We're going to get with the colleges, universities and state capitals. We're going to get into solid markets, and we're going to build quality hotels."

- Keep Your Word. "My reputation allows me to make deals no one else could make, certainly not on a handshake. I always live up to what I say I'll do... and more. If you don't do what you say, word of that will travel the country. I've never had that kind of reputation, and I never will."

- Give Back. "If you're able to succeed monetarily in life, you should share, and that's what I've done."

- Forge Ahead in Good Times or Bad. "No matter what the economy does, no matter the circumstances, forge ahead. I've weathered a lot of storms, but I stay positive. Experience has taught me that I will prevail, no matter what fate throws at me."

As a long-time hotel consultant, I stand in awe of the Hammons organization which now operates 73 hotels located in secondary and tertiary markets and has several others under development. These were developed near demand generators, such as state capitals, airports, interstate highways, universities, golf-courses, corporate headquarters, state parks, and even on the top of a mountain on Table Rock Lake in Branson, Missouri in the Ozark Mountains.

Taking a drive through Springfield, Mo. reveals the Hammons impact: there's John Q. Hammons Parkway and Hammons Field, home of the Springfield Cardinals, a Double A affiliate of the St. Louis Cardinals. In 2005, the 8000-seat Hammons Field was honored by Baseball Parks. com as the best park in professional baseball. In the mid 1980's, John Q saw that the downtown of Springfield was crumbling. "It looked like East Berlin around here", he said. Hammons developed his University Plaza Hotel and Convention Center and the 22-story Hammons Tower, Springfield's tallest building. On the campus of Southwest Missouri State University, John Q's name, or his wife Juanita's, will be on four buildings and a fountain near a new Hammons Sports arena. It's already on the Hammons House Dormitories, the Juanita K. Hammons Hall for the Performing Arts and the Hammons Enterprise Center.

Then there is the Hammons School of Architecture at Drury University, the Hammons Fountains at the Ozarks Technical Community College and the John Q. Hammons Library at the Missouri Sports Hall of Fame.

John Quentin Hammons was born on February 24, 1919 in Fairview, Missouri to James O. and Hortense Bass Hammons who operated a dairy farm. John Q. remembers that at 12 years of age he would set 20 or so rabbit traps. "I would make the traps out of old wood because if you made them out of new wood, the rabbits wouldn't go in. I'd bait it with an apple or turnip," he says. "I was averaging five to six pelts a day and I sold them for five cents apiece. So I was getting rich." One day, however, when he arrived at his customary 6AM to collect his rabbits, there were none. The next day none and three days in a row. Finally, a neighbor told Hammons' father that a boy who lived nearby was arriving before John and stealing his catch. "It was a 16-year-old, bully-type kid, "says Hammons. "That kid was a thief." John's method of solving the problem was to get up at 4AM. "I had four rabbits the first morning so I beat the thief. That's a true story." If you visit the John Q. Hammons Library, you will see a replica of a rough-hewn rabbit trap given to him by his friend, Dr. Marshall Gordon.

During the Great Depression, Hammons' parents lost their farm and his ailing mother had to go to work in a tomato factory while his father became an insurance salesman. In 1937, John graduated from Fairview High School where he played varsity basketball. He went on to Monett Junior College (now University). After receiving his teaching certificate in 1939, he taught history, science and physical education at Cassville Junior High School, where he coached the basketball team. Hammons remembers that "I took a little junior high team and they had never played a basketball game in their life as a group. I taught them passes, put them in nice clean uniforms. Got a schedule. We lost one game the first year and then went undefeated the second year." During those years, Hammons also volunteered as a Cub Scout Cubmaster.

After December 7, 1941 (Pearl Harbor Day), Hammons went to work as a cost accountant for the Lytle-Green Construction Co. of Des Moines, Iowa on the Alaskan- Canadian (Alcan) Highway. Stretching 1,522 miles from Dawson Creek, British Columbia to Fairbanks, Alaska, the road served as an inland route to Alaska. During the building of the highway, Alaska hit a record of 72° F below zero. When the highway was completed in 1943, Hammons joined the Merchant Marines and served in both the Atlantic and Pacific Oceans as a Lieutenant Junior Grade.

After discharge, Hammons met Juanita K. Baxter who was raised on a farm in Marionville, Missouri and came to Springfield to attend Southwest Missouri State Teacher's College. They were married on September 2, 1949 at the Westminster Presbyterian Church in Springfield.

Hammons began his development career by building housing for World War II veterans in Springfield. When the city planning commission refused to approve a high-end shopping center, Hammons traveled to California where he saw Del Webb's Highway Houses: a pioneering motor hotel concept that followed Route 66. When Hammons returned home, he contacted a Memphis, Tenn. builder named Kemmons Wilson who was undertaking a similar concept named Holiday Inns. Hammons formed a partnership with a plumbing contractor named Roy E. Winegardner and in 1958 became one of Holiday Inn's first franchisees. During their partnership, they developed 67 Holiday Inns, about 10% of the system. This development coincided with the creation of the Interstate Highway System when President Dwight D. Eisenhower signed the Federal-Aid Highway Act of 1956: a 13 year plan that would cost $25 billion, funded 90 percent by the federal government.

Winegardner and Hammons were building Holiday Inns so fast that they sometimes bypassed the customary approval process. David Sullivan, a 40-year hotel veteran and a member of Hammons board of directors, was a Holiday Inn executive in charge of franchise administration for Holiday Inns. He recalls the Hammons technique: "We had a long process where a potential owner would make an application, and then we'd study it, and take it to a committee for approval, and make sure that the person who was building it was the right person, and we believed in the study and in the product he was going to do. It was a long, tedious process. Well, we'd get these applications in the mail from John Q and we'd start the process, and when we called John he'd say 'Don't worry about it; the hotel's already been built. In fact, it's opening next week.'"

While Hammons and Winegardner were successful partners, they didn't always see eye to eye on strategies or locations. They agreed to maintain the partnership but to also go their separate ways. In 1970, they sold 23 hotels for $60 million to Holiday Inns in exchange for Holiday Inn stock and that made John Q and Roy among the largest stockholders of the Holiday Inn Corporation.

Hammons describes in his own words, two defining moments of his life:

> **Defining Moment:** "In 1969, my entrepreneurial spirit eventually led me to start my own company, John Q. Hammons Hotels. Even though Holiday Inn helped me become a great success, I switched gears after seeing economy hotels popping up next to each other. We had to specialize, so we focused on the upscale market, primarily building Embassy Suites and Marriott hotels with convention centers. We decided to build quality hotels that exceeded customer's expectations. None of our hotels are alike and we use atriums, water features

and local art to create individuality. We also strive to surpass the brand standards in each hotel, such as widening the hallways to seven feet and implementing pod check-in systems. If you build it right, locate it correctly and give the customers what they want, they will buy. The best way to sell is to let the other person buy."

Defining Moment: "After 9/11 hotel development came to an abrupt halt. Companies were too fearful to move forward. While everyone was stagnant, we forged ahead. The advantage of continuing to build hotels was the availability of materials and labor. We knew the economy would rebound and people would begin traveling more. Our hotels needed to be ready to welcome them. We have built and opened 16 hotels since 9/11, and that decision was well worth it. Recently the cost of cements and steel ignited, increasing 25%. By developing hotels during an uncertain time, our company has saved US$80 million. No matter what the economy does, no matter the circumstances, forge ahead.

I have made it my life-long business to find markets and develop quality hotels. Since 1958, we have built 185 hotels from the ground up. Along the way, we have never forgotten to give back to the cities that help us succeed. We also have learned that you have to be fearless to succeed.

I am humble, appreciative and thankful for one opportunity I have to live each day doing what I enjoy most. This is what I consider to be the defining moment of a lifetime."

Hammons' number one piece of advice is "you never build without the market…. Everyone says 'location, location, location'. But it's not true. It's market, market, market. What I do is go throughout (the country) and look for those nooks and crannies where industry has grabbed a spot and gone to work." Hammons never builds in primary locations. He selects secondary and tertiary markets where large corporations have regional offices or factories as well as university towns and state capitals. When Hammons and his senior vice president Scott Tarwater board Hammons' private jet, they are looking for the confluence of interstate highways, transportation centers, universities and state capitals. They do not need to be right in the middle of the existing action; in fact, they prefer to be in a stable and underutilized location. Listen to the Hammons strategy: "After going through (numerous) recessions, I decided I'm going to universities and state capitals, and if I could find both, (for instance) Madison, Wisconsin or Lincoln, Nebraska, you've got a homerun. Because when recessions come on, people still go to school and government employees still get paid. After 9/11 all the big players who have big hotels at big airports and city centers took a huge blow. They were helpless. (Whereas) we were out here in universities and capital cities and strong farming/agriculture communities."

Hammons does not believe in formal, third-party feasibility studies. When he started his development work, Hammons would go into towns to do his own type of feasibility study. That meant talking to bellman, taxi drivers, all the regular people. He relies on his own judgment and the opinions of his top executives. Of course, his balance sheet is so strong that he often does not need mortgage financing and therefore does not have to please the bankers. For example, when Hammons built the five-star Chateau on the Lake in Branson, Missouri, "the banks thought I was over the edge and gone. Put a hotel like that in Branson territory? You're out of your mind. So when we finished we had $60 million in cash in it and I couldn't get a loan. So I went ahead and opened. Four months later, I got a loan for $35 million. Just like that."

In "*They Call Him John Q*," Susan M. Drake wrote:

> In 1974, John Q. Hammons paid a Jeep driver $25 to take him to the top of the mountain on Table Rock in the Ozarks. Atop that mountain, Hammons was convinced, he would build a hotel one day. No matter that he would have to blast 50 feet off the mountain to flatten it enough to build the hotel. No matter that it

was far from any major highway, without much chance of drop-in traffic. No matter that the closest civilization, Branson, Missouri, was just a two-lane town with a few entertainers. No matter that it would cost $60 million and take almost two years to build the hotel. When John Q has a vision, nothing stands in his way. He bought the property, held it for 26 years and when he believed the time was right, he made his move.

Hammons provides the following analogy: "Mackinac Island has The Grand. Colorado Springs has the Broadmoor. I knew that that lake country would become something."

Was Hammons right? Just consider the following:

- 7 million people drive into Branson each year to attend the 50 theatres and live shows in town

- Forget Las Vegas and New York's theater district. Acre for acre, Branson is the live-entertainment center of the nation.

- Branson is a $1.7 billion tourist mecca, the number one motor coach destination of the decade.

- Located in the heart of the Ozark Mountains on the shores of Lake Taneycomo, Branson is a popular tourist destination, famous for its many live music theaters, clubs and other entertainment venues, as well as its historic downtown and surrounding natural beauty.

The Chateau on the Lake, a 5-star, 301 room hotel with a 46 foot, $85,000 tree in its atrium, is the best hotel in Branson, by far. Its function space includes a 32,000 square foot Great Hall, eight hi-tech breakout rooms, two corporate boardrooms and a 54-seat theater. The Chateau has a full-service marina with everything from jet skis to ski boats, scuba diving, fishing and other water sports. A luxurious $6 million, 14,000 square foot Spa Chateau just opened in 2006.

John Q loves to tell the story of when Walter Cronkite visited the hotel. He asked Cronkite what he thought of the property. "He told me 'I can't believe this hotel; I've been all over the world and it ranks at the top.'"

After the Chateau on the Lake opened, the Hammons management team was split about whether they should operate year-round. The major issue was the drop in business during the winter's inclement weather which sometimes made the Branson roads impossible. Hammons made the decision in the following note to his staff:

> For your ready reference, I thought you should know that I have just completed contract negotiations with a music composer, Sir Lancelot Bourguine. When he is in Europe, he has an office in Paris; he is very famous. The contract calls for him to write the lyrics to "How to Get to Branson in the Wintertime" and also another composition, "Upon Arrival, How Do I Stay Warm Enough to Sing Old Lonesome Me."

By 1987 Hammons was on the *Forbes* magazine list of the 400 richest people in the country. In 1986, he was number 383 and in 1987, he jumped to 286 with a net worth estimated at $300 million. In 1994, John Q. Hammons took his company public in order to raise the capital he needed to continue to develop hotels. The company sold six million shares for more than $100 million. Over his business career, Hammons has invested in other ventures: casino in Reno, restaurants and IMAX franchises. But, while he may be attracted to other businesses, he is first, last and always a hotel developer. Everything else is a sideline.

In hotel development, Hammons has followed his own techniques for selection and development. It is a unique formula which requires both capital and patience. Hammons develops hotels by at least six major rules:

Rule No. 1: Pick the Right Location- Hammons doesn't develop in New York, Chicago or Los Angeles. He concentrates on secondary and tertiary markets like Charlotte- Concord, NC; Joplin, Mo; Huntsville, Ala; Bricktown, Oklahoma City, Okla; International Airport, Kansas

City, Mo; Ft. Smith, Ark; Phoenix- West, Ariz; Rogers, Ark; Omaha, Neb; Greensboro, NC; Hot Springs, Ark; Des Moines, Iowa; Tampa, Fl; Tulsa, Okla; Grapevine, Texas; Frisco, Texas; Little Rock, Ark; North Charleston, S.C., among others.

He picks locations where he can be the dominant player and then builds a more elaborate hotel than the community expects. He always locates where some of the following facilities are present: State capitals, universities, interstate highways and sometimes convention centers (yet to be built). He does his feasibility study and market research from an airplane or helicopter. He spots where the rivers flow, where the valleys connect and what direction the interstates are likely to go.

Rule No. 2: Know the Market- "When I first started in business, I was trying to sell a big shopping center in the middle of a cornfield. An old-timer said to me, 'Son, you haven't run the BB test! I asked what that was, and he said, 'Son, that's when you have to count the bellies on the block. There has to be a market for something, people to buy your product." Since then, Hammons makes it his business to count the bellies on the block.

"I study the market conditions of one community and if I see something that works, I always wonder why wouldn't it work in another similar area. It usually does."

Veanne Stocking, regional vice president, John Q. Hammons Hotels & Resorts, says that when she travels with him, he arrives in the airport and speaks to the people who work there like the person at the shoeshine stand and the car rental agents. "Within minutes, he's surrounded by 20 people and he's listening to their stories, asking them about how business is, what the area is like and what their own experiences are." John Q absorbs all these opinions and builds an internal stockpile of information about the local marketplace. A favorite technique of his is to ask "Where are you from?" And then to inquire about some special feature of their hometown. That's how his good memory enables him to establish an immediate rapport with strangers and get useful market information.

Rule No. 3: Use the following five-point approach to evaluate potential locations:

- Evaluate economic conditions and the flow of money in the community

- Look at the history of the banks. Have they grown over time? What has the story been for the last 10 or 20 years.

- Consider if the people in the city are conservative or aggressive in their saving habits.

- Find out if the city's administration is progressive and favorable to business. Attitude is the most important factor in every city's potential.

- Determine the quality of the schools in the community. As training grounds for the city, they shape the people who work in and influence the community.

Hammons' years of experience are worth more than any feasibility study. "I get the ingredients. I look at their economy, and whether they're growing or not, how many projects they've completed successfully and how many are on the drawing board. I'll go in and ask a lot of questions of the city and they don't know why the hell I'm asking, but I do. The first thing I want to know is what their operating budget is. What's their budget 10 years from now, and so forth. I just want to know how they're planning to do it. I can ask questions like that, and that plays into my reasons for why I want to build there."

Rule No. 4: Build the best hotels- J.W. Marriott, Jr. puts it this way, "He (Hammons) has a real sense of obligation about the business. He's on a mission to provide quality lodging in all locations, whether they are smaller towns or bigger towns. His idea of quality lodging experience is a full-service hotel that's secure, where he can keep his guests safe and they have a great service experience. He's one of these guys who doesn't come in and out with fads. He believes what he believes, and he keeps moving ahead. Sometimes he falls out of fashion, but he always comes back because he just keeps doing what he's doing. He's been successful for 40-some years. There's no doubt that he'll just keep going and being successful as long as he lives."

Hammons project manager Marty McGahan says, "Mr. Hammons looks for the details. He wants us to watch our costs; he want to create projects that are a notch above our competition. Our guest rooms are often larger than the franchise brand requires, and we often install higher levels of finishes throughout the project, too. An eye for the details is one of the ways Mr. Hammons stays ahead of his competition. He's become a great admirer of European-style hotel architecture and wants to incorporate this look into his newer hotel projects. Our challenge is to re-create this look on his tight project budget. European-style hotel architectural looks are a very expensive look to construct."

Hammons inevitably builds a better and bigger hotel than the community expects and than the franchise company requires. He says, "I've always survived because I believe in quality. At that manager's conference where I told our people I intended to stay in the upscale, quality business, I told them I was going to put meeting space in our hotels. And that the meeting space will be big, like 10, 15 or even 40,000 square feet, because that's our insurance policy. I knew that the trends for big conventions like in Chicago, New York, Miami, San Francisco and Los Angeles, Seattle, etc., were going to be a thing of the past because you can't afford to get there. I knew. I could see that coming. That's why I wanted to go into a region where I could be in the dominant position. ….Keep your properties up and go upscale. Put that convention center there and you can still be in business having your meetings and things like that."

Although Hammons got his start building Holiday Inns, he subsequently developed more upscale properties such as Marriott, Hilton, Embassy Suites, Renaissance. Hammons says,

> I've always survived because I believe in quality. At that manager's conference where I told our people I intended to stay in the upscale, quality business, I told them I was going to put meeting space in our hotels…. I saved many hotels by doing that, because when the down times come, if you just have a hotel, you may have

a pretty good piece of real estate but your budgets in the discount bin, and you don't have anything to offer. I've got something to offer. Keep your properties up and go upscale. Put that convention center there and you can still be in business having your meetings and things like that.

Rule No. 5: Hire Great People- Hammons hires great people to operate his hotels. He knows that just building a monument is not enough. He attracts and keeps the best managers he can find.

Rule No. 6: Control Costs- Hammons was raised during the Great Depression and its effect is continuous and lifelong. He is a product of his upbringing in a family that suffered financial setbacks. The same man who financed the building of the $60 million Chateau on the Lake sees no reason to waste paper clips. Board member Daniel Sullivan says, "We have a board dinner and it just kills him if they serve steak, I'm not kidding you. He'll say, 'We can't afford this. Next time we're having hamburgers'".

Hammons serves as his own oversight manager, often calling a general manager when occupancy dips or profits drop. He believes that "Revenue hides a lot of things. When things get tough, you'll find out which managers are swimming naked." Here's a memo he sent to GM's in 2000:

> To: All General Managers
> From: John Q. Hammons
>
> This subject is IMPORTANT! What happened to our business during the month of July? Many of our hotels were caught sleeping at the wheel by the 4th of July holiday, and this was very disappointing!
>
> Since ringing in the New Year, everyone has had access to a July calendar for business planning purposes. It's a well-known fact that whenever a holiday falls in the middle of the week, serious trouble lies ahead. While the holidays may be great fun for the masses, they affect many business livelihood- and particular hotels!

I've been in the hotel business for over 40 years, and many of you have also been around for a number of years. We will always experience the same 'holiday cycles' year after year, so why weren't you alert to the business downturn, which historically takes place during these times?

The first six months we sailed along with well over $1.4 million at the NOI level, and then July comes along and we're back to square one. We continue to approve recommendations for salary increases, bonuses and advancements when requested. And then a month like July comes around, and we question not only your attention to detail but also the wisdom of our decision to reward poor management judgment.

Everyone knows how hard we have all worked to make our company successful. It is your company, and we depend on your performance. We can't continue to accept lack of planning and preparation any more. If you had anticipated the 4th of July holiday weeks in advance, a lot of expense could have been avoided.

Will you please help us? We need your teamwork. We need the experience of your many years in the hotel business.

Leave the sleeping to our guests!

Hammons deal making ability is legendary. Here's a typical scenario in a city where he intends to build a hotel:

Listen, here's what I'll do: I'll take this city block that you have down here, and you're going to lease it to me for a $1 a year or sell it to me for a $1. I'll build you a 250-room, nine-story atrium hotel with glass elevators, waterfalls, two restaurants, two lounges, and 15,000 square feet of meeting space. You're going to build a parking deck behind it for me and lease that to me for so much. Now if you all don't want to do this, I understand. It's your property, and it's your city. But I'm going from here to Lincoln, Nebraska. I can do four projects this year at $25 million a project, and it really makes no difference to me whether I do it here or in Lincoln. They're both state capitals, they both have interstates, both have airports and I'm prepared to go to the next place over here. You just let me know what you want to do.

According to people who have been there, that's when the city council or the mayor would flinch from what they could tell is a man telling the truth. Whereas some developers would come hand in hand to beg for permission to do a deal, John Q merely puts his offer out there and says take it or leave it. It's not unusual that within a day or so, a mayor will call and say "Mr. Hammons, I think we're going to be able to deliver that land to you up there for a dollar after all."

Hammons "Aw shucks, country-boy-from Missouri" demeanor is often off-putting to the people with whom is negotiating. It is said that his computer-like mind has a photographic memory and almost total recall, especially for land prices and hotel development costs. Senior Vice President- Development Scott Tarwater says that John Q would rather read a profit and loss statement than a good novel.

It seems that Hammons can draw the entire Interstate Highway system to dramatize where he has built hotels and, more importantly, where he is going to build them. Terry Bichsel, former Senior Vice President of Operations says, "He knows absolutely every highway, every intersection, every good piece of real estate in the country." This is the same John Q Hammons who has a collection of 300 colorful neckties, a penchant for V8 juice and a loving way of referring to his wife, Juanita, as "Mrs. Hammons". He says about her, "you'll never find anybody that says anything negative about Mrs. Hammons. Never. "As to why he grew his business in Springfield, Mo., "Well, Mrs. Hammons was teaching over here at McDaniel school. I had to have her support me, you know, on that little salary she had".

As of this writing, the backlog of planned Hammons hotel developments and recent openings totals 16 hotels and select convention centers in more than 11 states:

1. Boise, Idaho- a 10-story, 250-room Marriott Hotel in Boise's downtown core that will connect to the city's planned new exhibition facility and also be walking distance from the existing Boise Centre on the Grove convention facility.

2. Concord, N.C.- the 308-room Embassy Suites Hotel Resort and Spa with 55,000 square feet of meeting space and an adjoining 80,000 square-foot convention center opened in January 2007.

3. Fairview, Texas- the 10-story, 280-suite Embassy Suites Hotel and adjoining 80,000- gross-square-foot convention center will join The Village at Fairview, an upcoming 400-acre, mixed-use lifestyle center.

4. Fort Smith, Ark.- the $25 million, 138-room new Courtyard by Marriott opened February 2007, one block from the city's convention center.

5. Glendale, Ariz.- the 12-story, 320-room Renaissance Hotel will be located in the city's West Valley area.

6. Huntsville, Ala.- a new Embassy Suites opened in October, 2006.

7. Joplin, Mo.- 114-suite Residence Inn is adjacent to Hammons Holiday Inn.

8. Kansas City, Mo.- the new Residence Inn near a Hammons Embassy Suites and Homewood Suites at the Kansas City International Airport.

9. Murfreesboro, Tenn.- a 10-story-, 283-room Embassy Suites Hotel and adjoining 80,000 square-foot conference center.

10. Normal, Ill.- a nine story, 229- room Marriott Hotel and 45,000 square-foot convention center located near Illinois State University.

11. Norman, Okla.- a 240-room hotel and a 65,000- square-foot conference center, estimated to cost a total of $50 million, will be part of the university North Park mixed-use project.

12. Oklahoma City, Okla.- the 150-suite Residence Inn located in downtown Bricktown opened in March 2007 and is located near a Hammons Courtyard by Marriott.

13. Osage Beach, Mo.- the 15-story, 320-rooms and suites to be called Chateau on Lake of the Ozarks and to feature 100,000 gross square feet of meeting space, a 40,000 square-foot grand ballroom, and 22 smaller meeting rooms, and a full-service spa.

14. Peoria, Ill.- an eight-story, 266-suite Embassy Suites Hotel and Riverfront Conference Center will be located in East Peoria.

15. Pleasant Grove, Utah- a convention center with an adjoining 10-story, 300- room Embassy Suites Hotel and a 220-room Courtyard by Marriott will be located near Brigham Young University and Utah Valley State College.

16. San Marcos, Texas- the $50 million Embassy Suites Hotel will be adjoined by a $21 million city-owned conference center.

Mr. John Q. Hammons Awards

Throughout his many years in the hotel industry, John Q. Hammons has been honored with countless awards for his achievements as not only a hotelier, but also as a philanthropist:

In January, 2007 John Q. Hammons received the prestigious ALIS Lifetime Achievement Award at the 6th Annual Americas Lodging Investment Summit (ALIS). Hammons was recognized for his commendable accomplishments in the lodging industry as well as his outstanding commitment, leadership and service to the community.

His lifetime achievements were also recognized in October 2006 by IAHI, the Intercontinental Hotels Group owner's association. IAHI honored Mr. Hammons with the prestigious Kemmons Wilson Service Award for his leadership, service to the community and embodying standards and beliefs set forward by Mr. Wilson, the hospitality industry pioneer who created the Holiday Inn brand in 1952 and launched the IAHI to represent his franchisees in 1955.

The November 2003 issue of *HOTELS* magazine featured Hammons as "Corporate Hotelier of the World," an annual award that recognizes excellence in establishment and maintenance of high-quality service and standards, demonstration of management skills, volunteer efforts to support industry committees and local charities, as well as support of educational endeavors.

Additionally, in March 2002, the Hilton Hotels Corporation presented Hammons with the Connie Award (named after founder Conrad N. Hilton), which is usually bestowed internally within the Hilton organization. Recognizing him as one of the most committed developers of the Embassy Suites Hotel brand, Hilton Hotels selected Hammons for his dedication and loyalty to the Hilton organization, as well as his impressive philanthropic efforts in Springfield.

Hilton Hotels also recognized Hammons as the 2003 Embassy Suites Hotel Developer of the Year for developing properties that enhance the brand's image. To be considered, all hotels in Hammons' Hilton Family portfolio had to be rated high quality and in good status.

Hammons and former business partner, Roy E. Winegardner, were presented with a Lifetime Achievement Award during ceremonies at the 15th Annual Hospitality Industry Investment Conference at the Century Plaza Hotel and Tower in Los Angeles the fall of 2000. The award was sponsored by the University of California in Los Angeles Extension.

In October 2003, *USA TODAY's* Newspapers in Education Program honored Hammons with an appreciation award for his ongoing commitment to Springfield-area school students. Since 1993, he has dedicated a portion of funds to provide more than 706,600 copies of USA TODAY to more than 5,464 schools and 682 teachers, to inspire student education of current events.

When Mr. Hammons was recently asked about his awards, he replied, "My legacy is not yet finished. I have exciting plans to still accomplish in the hospitality industry and in my philanthropic endeavors."

SOURCE MATERIAL

1. Susan M. Drake, *They Call Him John Q: A Hotel Legend*, Black Parts Publishing, LLC, Memphis, 2002

2. *"A Passionate Commitment To His Work,"* Celebrity Magazine, July 2006

3. *"The Complete John Q.: The Man, His Gifts, His Legacy,"* Signature Magazine, Spring 2006

4. Author's visit from July 11-13, 2006 to Springfield, Mo. and Branson, Mo. to interview

John Q. Hammons and the following executives:

- Scott Tarwater, Senior Vice President- Development

- Joe Morrissey, Senior Vice President- Hotel Operations

- Steve Minton, Senior Vice President- Architecture

- Cheryl McGee, Corporate Director of Marketing

- John Fulton, Vice President- Design

- Stephen Marshall, Vice President & General Manager, Chateau on the Lake Resort, Branson, Missouri

Frederick Henry Harvey (1835-1901):
CIVILIZER OF THE WILD WEST

Just one hundred years ago, two architectural jewels opened at the Grand Canyon. They are the 95-room El Tovar Hotel and the Hopi House gift shop. Both reflect the foresight and entrepreneurship of Fred Harvey. An immigrant from England, Fred Harvey's business ventures eventually included restaurants, hotels, gift shops, newsstands and dining cars on the Sante Fe Railroad. The partnership with the Atchison, Topeka and Sante Fe introduced many new tourists to the American Southwest by making rail travel comfortable and adventurous. Employing many Native-American artists, the Fred Harvey Company also collected indigenous examples of basketry, beadwork, Kachina dolls, pottery and textiles.

Fred Harvey arrived in the United States in 1850 at 15 years of age from Great Britain. His first job was a "pot walloper", a dishwasher in New York City at the Smith and McNeill Café. In 1859, he married 17 year-old Barbara Sarah Mottas. While the Civil War was bad for restaurants (and the Confederates), it was good for the railroad business. Harvey made a career change and worked for railroads with travel opportunities for twenty years all over the United States. He knew what travelers into the West had to put up with, for he traveled on several railroads, including the Hannibal & St. Joseph, popularly known as the "Horrible & Slow Jolting." He clerked on the first mail train and was traveling freight agent for the Burlington Railroad. His fastidious English tastes were revolted by the unpalatable dry biscuits, the greasy ham and the weak old coffee. The dirty, fly-ridden quarters and the all-too-prevalent custom of fleecing travelers "who wouldn't be back anyway," made Harvey angry enough to change things. He was determined to bring good food, civilized service, and attractive, honestly run eating houses and hotels to travelers in the West. If he could get the cooperation of the railroads, he knew he would succeed. After rejection by the Burlington Railroad, Harvey struck a deal with Charles F. Morse, the superintendent of the Santa Fe Railway and Thomas Nickerson, its president. With only a handshake to seal their agreement, the two companies began a long and fruitful partnership.

The travelers of that era moved through Chicago on a slow journey westward on hard board seats in overcrowded crude coaches. Before Harvey, the stories of vile food and sloppy service were well-known. Dee Brown wrote in *Hear That Lonesome Whistle Blow* that one report said that "the chops were generally as tough as hanks of whipcord and the knives as blunt as a bricklayer's trowel" and "chicken stew was really prairie dog." The lunchrooms were noisy and dirty, tables covered with stained cloths and served cracked dishes and bent flatware. Harvey's timing could not have been better when he started provide appetizing and affordable meals in comfortable dining quarters.

In 1876, Fred Harvey opened his first railroad restaurant in Topeka, Kansas on the second floor of the little red Santa Fe depot. Good food, good cooking, spotless dining rooms, and courteous service, introduced by Fred Harvey in his first Harvey House, brought a booming business that pleased Santa Fe passengers and amazed Topeka residents.

The Santa Fe Railway provided the buildings for the Harvey restaurants where the passenger trains would stop twice daily for meals. The railroad carried all the produce and supplies needed by the Harvey restaurants including transporting the dirty laundry. Fred Harvey hired, trained and supervised all personnel and provided for food and service. Harvey's policy was "maintenance of standards, regardless of cost." He believed that profits would grow if the food and service were excellent. "Meals by Fred Harvey" became the slogan of the Sante Fe Railway. Western hotels, before Harvey, were just shacks with cots. For guest who came from the East, those facilities were intolerable.

From that modest beginning, the Harvey organization grew into a far-flung resort, restaurant, hotel and retail organization, with operations extending from Cleveland to the West Coast. During the 1880s and 1890s, Fred Harvey's unique restaurants and Harvey Houses opened, one after another, approximately every 100 miles along the Santa Fe through Kansas, Colorado, Texas, Oklahoma, New Mexico, Arizona and California. This was necessary, it was said, "To keep western traffic from settling in any one place where Fred Harvey served his incomparable meals."

In a formal contract with the railroad, signed in 1889, Harvey secured the right to operate all restaurants on the Sante Fe line west of the Missouri River. A subsequent 1893 contract gave him the rights to its dining-car service. He supplied the equipment, food, supplies and management and the railroad hauled them and the Harvey's employees for free. The profits were his to keep.

Harvey's food was the best quality, much of it supplied by local farmers. Just imagine the extraordinary planning and organizational efforts required to bring fruits and vegetables from California, beef from Texas, shellfish from the east coast and fresh water fish from the Great Lakes packed in ice to keep it fresh. Harvey owned and operated his own dairies to guarantee fresh milk and cheese. He brought in his own spring water so that Harvey-blended coffee would not be ruined by brackish local water. In the 1880s, Harvey customers were served full meals from oysters on the half shell to homemade pie, ice cream and coffee all along the Santa Fe route. Railroad buff and historian Lucius Beebe wrote in the American Heritage magazine in February 1967, "Harvey imposed a rule of culinary benevolence over a region larger than any Roman province and richer than any single British dominion save India."

A major element in Harvey's success was the excellent corps of waitresses he started to hire in 1883 who became known as the Harvey Girls. The idea began at the Harvey House in Raton, New Mexico where Harvey fired the manager and an all-male staff after some had gotten into a fight. It didn't take long for Harvey to realize that replacing all the waiters with waitresses was a brilliant move. The Harvey Girls matured into an emblem of Fred Harvey's devotion to first-class service.

To maintain this excellence, he hired and trained young women of fine character as waitresses, the famous "Harvey Girls". Harvey placed ads in Eastern and Midwestern newspapers that read: "Wanted, young women of good character, attractive and intelligent, 18 to 30 years of age as waitresses for Harvey Eating Houses in the West. Good wages with room and meals furnished." Harvey Girls were trained to high standards of prompt and courteous service. They were the key to serving hundreds of passengers in about 20 minutes...the average length of time a train would need for servicing every four hours. Their story is unique in American history. Only white women who were hired as Harvey Girls. There were no black women and only a few Hispanic and Indian women who ever served as waitresses. European immigrant women were apparently acceptable. Minority workers, male and female, worked in the Harvey kitchens and hotels where they served as maids, dishwashers and pantry girls. Harvey had no shortage of applicants. It is estimated that a hundred thousand women applied from 1883 until the 1960's. To the frontier outposts of the West where train robberies, horse thieving, and stampeding buffalo herds were commonplace, Harvey girls brought refinement, culture and, often, romance.

Harvey Girls all wore the same uniform, outfits befitting a nun: a long-sleeved black dress with a stiff "Elsie" collar, black shoes, black stockings and hairnets. The company furnished a full white wrap-around apron so stiffly starched that it had to be pinned to a corset. Harvey Girls wore no jewelry, no makeup and chewed no gum. They lived in dormitories where they were closely supervised by their manager (or manager's wife), and curfews were strictly enforced in the early years. They were looked after as carefully as boarding school students in female seminaries in the East. They worked very hard and their eight-hour-a-day shifts were often split to conform to train schedules. They were told what to wear, where to live, whom to date and what time to go to bed. When the Harvey Girls were recruited in the early years, they were asked not to marry for at least a year.

Gentlemen callers were permitted at certain hours in the well-chaperoned parlor; that is, if they left their six-shooters at the door. But it wasn't long before the cowboys and cattlemen who tried to ride their broncos right into Harvey Houses were persuaded to change their manners and took more kindly to the alpaca jackets Fred Harvey kept on hand and demanded his coatless gentlemen diners wear. Before long, the cowboys were seen accompanying the Harvey Girls to church on Sundays. When that happened, everyone took it for granted that marriage was the next step and that the roaming, devil-may-care Westerner was about to become respectable.

It was estimated that at least 20,000 Harvey Girls became the brides of ranchers, railroad men and cowboys, founding many of the first families of the West. And many of the male offspring of those families were named "Fred" or "Harvey" in deference to the man who had the vision to civilize the region. The combination of good food served in a fine dining atmosphere with imported linen, china and silver created a distinctive contrast to the typical eating establishments in turn-of-the century small towns. The hope of catching the eye of one of the Harvey Girls no doubt kept many a farmer, rancher, and railroader coming back to dine again and again.

In the early days before Harvey Houses were established, diners paid in advance, and when they had barely started to eat, train crews were known to conspire with lunchroom owners to shout "all aboard" and passengers had to rush out without finishing their meal or be left behind. In this way, the same food provided many half-eaten meals and the train crew got a cut of ten cents per passenger. In contrast, Harvey Houses followed a foolproof system to assure the comfort and satisfaction of travelers. Trainmen canvassed the passengers on the train, noting the number who wished dining room and lunch counter service and telegraphed the orders ahead to the next Harvey House restaurant. When the train pulled into the station and the passengers began to get off the train, a white-coated Harvey House porter would hit a big brass gong which stood outside the entrance to the restaurant. This let passengers know instantly where to go, and the Harvey Girls were ready to serve them.

The waitresses, taking orders for coffee, tea or milk, arranged cups according to a code and the "drink girl" immediately followed serving accordingly. Then came the grand entrance of the manager himself, bearing aloft great platters of steak, chops or seafood that he served with a flourish. Passengers were assured ample notice would be given before the trains departed and were encouraged to take their time and enjoy their meals. Plenty of coffee was served. Desserts came in time, and five minutes before train time a signal was given for those lingering over a last bite. Then came the "all aboard." Harvey meals included as many as seven entrees- with seconds- for 75 cents. Prices were apologetically raised to one dollar in 1920 and remained at about a dollar until 1927. Menus at Harvey Houses were coordinated to avoid duplication on a trip. If you had prime rib at Needles, you had chicken at Barstow. One of the reasons for the Harvey Houses' success was their ability to serve fresh, high quality meat, seafood, and produce at remote locations across the Southwest. Trains would deliver beef from Kansas City, seafood and produce from southern California year-round.

When Fred Harvey died in 1901, his company had grown to 15 hotels, 47 restaurants, and 30 dining car operations along the Santa Fe line. By 1912, under the leadership of Fred Harvey's sons Byron and Ford, there were more than sixty-five eating houses on the Sante Fe and Frisco railroad lines, a dozen large hotels and sixty dining cars in the Harvey system. They employed about five thousand people, half of whom were women. The company continued in existence until 1968 when Harvey's grandsons sold out to Amfac Parks & Resorts.

Harvey operations at Union Stations in Cleveland, Kansas City, St. Louis, Chicago and Los Angeles included newsstands, gift shops featuring Indian jewelry and weavings, barber shops, liquor stores, private dining rooms, restaurants, coffee shops, cafeteria, haberdashery, candy and fruit stands, miniature department store, cocktail lounges and soda fountains. Harvey was among the first to market its own name–brand "designer" goods: Fred Harvey hats, shirts, shaving cream, candy, playing cards, even Harvey Special Blend whiskey. Except for the prohibition years, Harvey sold exclusively a Scotch distilled by Ainslie & Heilbron in Glasgow. As a forerunner to Starbucks, Harvey packaged its own select coffee for public sale in 1948. The blend was already famous among Sante Fe travelers and Harvey sold 7,000 pounds in the first two weeks. The press dubbed him "Civilizer of the West" and one article from the 1880's said "he made the desert blossom with beefsteak and pretty girls."

The Harvey company built luxurious resort hotels within sightseeing distance of major western attractions in national parks like the Grand Canyon and the Petrified Forest. Mary Elizabeth Jane Colter (1869-1958) was an architect and interior designer who worked almost exclusively for Fred Harvey and the Santa Fe Railway. She was a pioneer who designed hotels, train stations, restaurants and gift shops with a brilliant use of Native American and Hispanic art and artifacts. The famous Western writer Frank Walters wrote, "For years, an incomprehensible woman in pants, she rode horseback through the Four Corners making sketches of prehistoric ruins, studying details of construction, the composition of globes and washes. She could teach masons how to lay adobe bricks, plasterers how to mix washes, carpenters how to fit viga joints."

Colter grew up in St. Paul, Mn. and studied art and architecture at the California School of Design in San Francisco. Her aesthetic tastes were shaped by the Arts and Crafts movement which by the end of the nineteenth century greatly influenced American architecture and design. Colter's first paid commission for the Harvey Company was design of the museum and sales outlet in 1902 for the Indian Building at the Alvarado Hotel in Albuquerque. Her last assignment in 1949 was a Mexican-themed cocktail lounge for the La Fonda Hotel in Sante Fe.

The Alvarado Hotel was designed by architect Charles Whittlesey who was trained in the Chicago office of Louis Sullivan and opened in 1902 with eighty-eight guest rooms, parlors, barbershop, club, reading room and a restaurant. It was a frame stucco building with great lawns surrounding its long brick walkways, private courtyards and a long arcade to the Sante Fe Railway depot. "It opened" reported the Albuquerque Journal Democrat on May 11, 1902, "in a burst of rhetoric, a flow of red carpet and the glow of myriad brilliant electric lights" (electricity was still a novelty) with hopes that it 'would attract the wealthier classes to stop in Albuquerque on their travels to the west." The Alvarado was demolished in 1970 despite the efforts of Albuquerque citizens to save it as a landmark. Mary Colter's adjacent Indian Building launched the Harvey Company's long-time sponsorship of Indian arts and crafts. There were work and exhibit rooms with Indian basketmakers, silversmiths, potters and weavers at work. William Allen White wrote in the Kansas Emporia Gazette about the fine food and music in the dining room, "The Alvarado Hotel at Albuquerque is a Fred Harvey place and is undoubtedly the best railroad hotel in the world. The New Yorkers who have been to Europe say so, and they ought to know." Mary Colter designed a new cocktail lounge in 1940 in the Alvarado and called it La Cocina Cantina to capture the design of an early Spanish kitchen.

Before Harvey, there were few clean hotels out west, only saloons or public rooms with cots. In 1878, Harvey built the Clifton Hotel in Florence, Kansas. The Clifton resembled a fine English home with fountains and candelabra in the surrounding garden and luxurious guest accommodations inside including an elegant dining room. The chef, who was hired from Chicago's Palmer House, received the fabulous salary of $5,000 a year. Linens were imported from Belfast, Ireland; silver from Sheffield, England; china from France. Society balls were held at the hotel and the menus were a gourmet's delight. Harvey's hotel was a civilizing influence in other ways, too. The following notice appeared in a June 1879 Florence newspaper: "Every Tuesday and Friday the ladies of Florence can have the use of the bathrooms in the Fred Harvey hotel. This will be a luxury which will be duly appreciated. All other days the bathrooms will be open to gentlemen." At the turn of the century, another Harvey House of equal beauty was the Bisonte Hotel in Hutchinson, Kansas followed by the Sequoyah in Syracuse and El Vaquero in Dodge City, all built in Spanish Mission style. The first Harvey House hotel in Emporia, Kansas served such celebrities as Shirley Temple, Will Rogers, Jackie Cooper and Gloria Swanson.

The chaotic Kansas frontier included a transient cowtown population of cowboys and herd bosses, cattle-selling Texans, prostitutes and saloon-buffs. Harvey even built the Arcade Hotel in "bloody Newton, the wickedest town in the West", after the cattle industry moved to Dodge City. Later, Harvey moved his district headquarters to Newton from Kansas City including construction of a major dairy, an ice plant, meat locker-rooms, a creamery, a poultry feeding station and produce plant, a carbonating plant for bottling soda pop and a modern steam laundry. By 1921, Newton's central laundry cleaned four million pieces a year.

As the Santa Fe Railway moved across Kansas to Colorado and to New Mexico, Oklahoma and Texas, Harvey Houses opened every hundred miles or so. New Mexico was the home of sixteen, five of which were among the most beautiful in the system: the Montezuma and Castaneda in Las Vegas (NM), La Fonda in Sante Fe, the Alvarado in Albuquerque, El Navajo in Gallup and El Ortiz in Lamy.

"Harvey House" was a generic term. Each individual Harvey House had its own name. The Harvey House in Barstow was named Casa del Desierto and is the finest remaining depot hotel in California, but it almost perished. After World War II, with the decline of rail travel, the Casa del Desierto fell into disuse and was eventually abandoned. The 1992 Landers earthquake destroyed the building's unreinforced brick towers, interior gypsum block walls, and most of the cast stone anchorage. Large sections of the second floor exterior walls collapsed. In the early 1990s, the City of Barstow began to work on restoring the building to its original splendor. The building now houses two museums and serves as a depot for Amtrak.

Each of these hotels was unique but perhaps none more so than the long-forgotten Montezuma Hot Springs Hotel in Las Vegas, New Mexico. An enormous castle-like structure, built adjacent to hot mineral springs, it was the largest wood frame building in the country with 270 rooms and an eight-story tower. Its connected spa-bathhouses served five hundred people a day and competed with the finest health resorts in the United States and Europe. After it burned to the ground in 1884, Harvey and the Santa Fe immediately rebuilt the million dollar hotel. This second structure also suffered a serious fire and was again replaced in 1899. After Harvey's El Tovar opened at the Grand Canyon, the Montezuma closed in 1903.

The Santa Fe Railroad itself went into receivership in 1893 until 1895. The newer hotels and Harvey Houses reflected the Sante Fe's interest in Spanish colonial and Native American history. With the Harvey company's active partnership, they published many books, pamphlets and guidebooks on the Southwest. These publications spurred a boom in Native American arts and crafts. The resident genius at the Harvey Company was Herman Schweizer, a German Jewish immigrant who worked as a newsboy on the Santa Fe until he was hired by Harvey and sent to the Harvey House in Coolidge, Kansas as a restaurant manager. Schweizer soon began to buy Navajo blankets, to commission native silversmiths and to supply turquoise and silver. Erna Fergusson wrote (in *Our Southwest* in 1940) that Schweizer "had the gift of the gods, a sure taste for the authentic and beautiful." Schweizer's talents came to the attention of Fred Harvey's daughter Minnie, wife of Harvey executive John F. Huckel who was an impassioned supporter of Indian arts. It was Minne's idea to create the Harvey Indian department. From 1901 to 1943, Schweizer served as its manager.

Considered the "architectural crown jewel" of Grand Canyon National Park, El Tovar reopened on April 13, 2005 for a centennial celebration of a $4.6 million renovation. Fred Harvey's foresight was becoming apparent again even though he died before actually seeing the completion of two of the best-known structures in the national park systems: the El Tovar Hotel and the Hopi House.

The El Tovar Harvey Hotel, Grand Canyon, Arizona was designed by architect Charles Whittlesey and opened in 1905 with 100 guestrooms and the proportions of a Swiss chalet and Norway villa. El Tovar had the traditional Harvey kitchen, bakery and butcher shop offering the finest meats, fish, fruits, cheeses and raw milk from the Fred Harvey dairy at Del Rio. El Tovar was renovated and reopened with a gala ceremony on its 100th birthday in 2005.

Opening January 1, 1905, the Hopi House was designed by Mary Colter. Colter had already established a reputation as a gifted architect and had designed several of the Fred Harvey Company's gift shops adjacent to its hotels at railroad stops along the route of the Atchison, Topeka and Santa Fe Railway to organize the sale of items created by native craftspeople. The Hopi House was built to resemble a Hopi pueblo which housed

Indian artisans who produced Navajo blankets, pottery, jewelry and other artworks for sale. The consecutive openings of these Grand Canyon architectural jewels was remarkable because they reflected the entrepreneurial commitment, precision and perfectionism of a man who prided himself on the highest standards of performance.

At the turn of the 20th century, a visit to the Grand Canyon was not a simple journey. A stagecoach ride from Flagstaff was a 20-hour teeth-rattling affair and upon arrival at the Grand Canyon, accommodations were rustic, at best. In 1901, the Atchison, Topeka and Santa Fe Railway laid an 80-mile railroad spur from Williams, Arizona to Grand Canyon Village on the South Rim. Like other railroads, such as the Northern Pacific and Union Pacific, the company sought to increase its customer base and began making plans for the construction of a luxury hotel close to its terminal at the South Rim.

Charles Whittlesey who designed the Alvarado Hotel in 1902, was assigned the job. While hotel architecture at the time tended toward Victorian with wooden frame construction, the designers of national park and other lodges along and near the railroad lines were attempting to define new styles using natural and local materials.

"El Tovar is probably the most expensively constructed and appointed log house in America" reported The Hotel Monthly in June 1908. Architect Whittlesey melded the best features of a Swiss chalet and the informality of a hunting lodge. It was a four-story, log and boulder structure located near the Grand Canyon rim. Most of the logs were Oregon Douglas firs. El Tovar opened in 1905 with one hundred guestrooms, hot and cold running water, steam heat, telephones, electric lights and only one bathroom for each of the four floors. The Sante Fe Magazine published "Fred Harvey's Facilities and Service at the Grand Canyon" in 1928 by John Willy who reported,

> El Tovar had the traditional Harvey kitchen, bakery and butler shop offering the finest meat and baked goods found anywhere in the United States. Bulk storage refrigerators held fresh salmon from San Francisco and celery from Michigan, honeydew and Persian melons weighing from twenty-two pounds each, apple, pears

and oranges from California and French and Portuguese sardines, Kansas beef, Camembert cheeses and raw milk from the Fred Harvey dairy at Del Rio.

The front door to El Tovar is a mere 30 yards from the edge of the South Rim of the Grand Canyon. Visitors entering through this door pass through the lobby known historically as the Rendezvous Room. The interior features dark log/slab paneling and exposed log rafters. The Rendezvous Room, registration area, two gift shops, lunge, dining room and a small number of guest rooms are located on the first floor. The Terrace Level as well as the second and third floors contain the remaining guest rooms, including 12 suites. The hotel originally had separate men's and women's sitting rooms, a men's grotto, a photography studio with darkroom, a rooftop garden, wine room and billiards parlor. The dining room became renowned for the high quality of its meals probably because the hotel had its own herd of Jersey cows, a milking barn, poultry barn, butcher shop, bakery and cold storage.

The opening of El Tovar preceded Arizona's statehood by seven years and the Grand Canyon's designation as a national monument in 1908 and a national park in 1919. The hotel's presence was credited with helping to increase visitation and international awareness of the remote Grand Canyon region.

U.S. Presidents who have stayed at El Tovar include Theodore Roosevelt, William Howard Taft, Herbert Hoover, Calvin Coolidge, Dwight Eisenhower Gerald Ford, George H. W. Bush, and Bill Clinton. Among the celebrity guests were Albert Einstein, Elizabeth Taylor, Douglas Fairbanks and Mary Pickford.

The Hopi House continues to be a popular attraction where high-quality, authentic Native American art is sold. The gallery features traditional and contemporary Southwest Native American arts and crafts, many of which are of interest to collectors of Native American art.

Hopi House's success led to the commissioning of a series of unique projects by Mary Colter for the Fred Harvey Company:

- 1914- the Hermits Rest along the Sante Fe Railway's right of way into the Grand Canyon.

- 1914- the Lookout Studio built as a lookout area west of El Tovar

- 1922- Phantom Ranch, eight miles into the canyon

- 1932- the Watchtower, designed after ancient Indian towers and kivas, decorated with wall and cave drawings

- 1935- Bright Angel Lodge, a budget-priced lodge with cabins

- 1936- Men's Dormitory

- 1937- Women's Dormitory

In a thirty-four page brochure published at El Tovar's inaugural on January 12, 1905, William Haskell Simpson wrote:

> Here are expressed a quiet dignity, an unassuming luxury, and an appreciation of ongoing needs. Not a Waldorf-Astoria – admirable as that type is for the city – but a big country clubhouse, where the traveler seeking high-class accommodations also finds freedom from ultra- fashionable restrictions. You may wear a dress suit at dinner or not. You may mix with the jolly crowd or sit alone in a quiet nook. You may lunch at almost any hour of the day or night. You may dine with other guests or enjoy the seclusion of a private dining room.

Simpson continued with a graphic description of the Hopi House:

> A short distance east of El Tovar and a stone's throw from the sheer canyon wall is the Hopi House, an irregular stone structure, plastered with adobe... (that) looks like an Indian pueblo; and so it is, in miniature... Here are Hopi men, women and children- some decorating and burning exquisite pottery; others spinning yarn and weaving squaw dresses, scarfs, and blankets. Go inside and see how these gentle folks live... The floors and walls are as clean as a Dutch kitchen. The Hopis are making "piki", twining the raven hair of the "manas"

in big side whorls, smoking corn-cob pipes, building sacred altars, mending moccasins- doing a hundred un-American things…. It is almost as good as a trip to the province of Tusayan, minus the desert.

Colter's years of successful design solidified her position as one of the most important members of the important members of the Harvey organization. Her knowledge, skill and good taste enabled her to create pleasing aesthetic design in a successful commercial setting.

In 1930, Colter designed the seventy- four room La Posada Hotel in Winslow, Arizona. It was constructed of reinforced concrete with a red tile roof and was 350 feet long. Each of the guestrooms was decorated in a different bright color combination. La Posada had a large restaurant, lunchroom and a railroad depot. All the woodwork in the public areas was sandblasted to create an aging effect. Elizabeth W. De Huff described La Posada in a bulletin for a courier company dated April 1, 1930:

> The new hotel at Winslow is built in the low, rambling style introduced into Old Mexico and our own far Southwest by the early Spanish emigrants- the early emigrants who turned their leisurely attention to the cultivation of the broad vegas and the raising of cattle. With all the effort to recreate the atmosphere of the past, nowhere in the hotel have modern improvements been overlooked and the guest will find himself surrounded at every turn with the creature comforts of hotel service of 1930.

Colter's last major effort was as architect for the Bright Angel Lodge and Cabins at the Grand Canyon. In 1917, the Grand Canyon Working Plan stated:

> The Hotel Management….. decided that even the cheaper rates at the Bright Angel Hotel do not meet the requirement for what is considered to be the most desirable class of tourists and visitors. Educators, scientists and artists as a rule cannot afford to stop at El

Tovar, and pride makes Bright Angel accommodations not quite satisfactory. It is for those that they now propose to undertake an entirely new development; namely the construction of a group of artistic and plain, but clean and light housekeeping cottages.

Although the Bright Angel was moderately priced, Colter did not skimp on the interiors. The Bright Angel lounge has a ten-foot high fireplace that used stone from each major stratum of the canyon. Colter's concern for the authenticity of her design is expressed in the letter she sent to Eddie McKie, chief ranger naturalist at Grand Canyon:

> Won't you please, in the meantime, check the rock Ed Cummings has collected and see if there are any important omissions... I know the design I want but I depend entirely on you for the geology. You know I am not trying to show every strata and variate in every part of the whole Canyon- only these that occur either on the Bright Angel or the South Rim part of the Kaibab trails. I want to be as authentic and therefore interesting as possible, of course.

Mary Colter's indelible mark on American architecture has been acknowledged by architectural historians. Perhaps, the highest praise came from the 1917 Grand Canyon Working Plan which said, "As long as the (Fred Harvey) Company's work is passed on to Miss Colter, its present architect, its appropriateness can be considered assured."

From 1901 through 1935, the Harvey Company and the Sante Fe built twenty three hotels of which only the following are still in operation: El Tovar and the Bright Angel Lodge in the Grand Canyon, La Fonda in Sante Fe and La Posada in Winslow, Arizona.

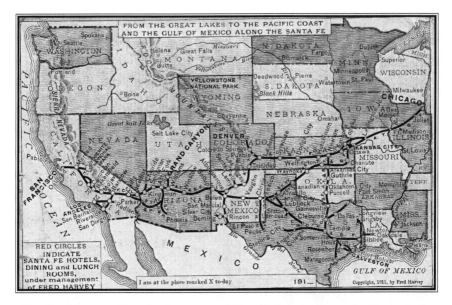

The Fred Harvey Hotels, Dining and Lunch Rooms from the Great Lakes to the Pacific Coast and the Gulf of Mexico along the Sante Fe Railroad route in 1911.

In 1945, Metro-Goldwyn-Meyer made a movie called "The Harvey Girls" based on a novel by Samuel Hopkins Adams. The musical film featured Judy Garland, Preston Foster, Angela Lansbury and Cyd Charisse. It had songs such as "The Atchison, Topeka and the Santa Fe," "Wishing on a Load of Hay" and "In the Valley Where the Evening Sun Goes Down," Naturally, the movie idealized an unrealistic image of the Harvey Girls but did stress the civilizing influence of the Harvey Houses and the Sante Fe Railroad.

The famous humorist Will Rogers wrote about the Harvey Girls:

> "In the early days, the traveler fed on the buffalo. For doing so, the buffalo got his picture on the nickel. Well, Fred Harvey should have his picture on one side of the dime and one of his waitresses with her arms full of delicious ham and eggs on the other side, 'cause they have kept the West supplied with food and wives."

SOURCE MATERIALS

Christine Barnes, *Great Lodges of the National Parks*, W.W. West Inc., Bend, Oregon, 2002

Arnold Berke, *Mary Colter: Architect of the Southwest*, Princeton Architectural Press, New York, 2002

Lesley Poling-Kempes, *The Harvey Girls: Women Who Opened the West*, Marlowe & Company, New York 1991

Bill McMillon, *Old Lodges and Hotels of Our National Parks*, Icarus Press, South Bend, 1983

Marta Weigle and Barbara A. Babcock, Editors, *The Great Southwest of the Fred Harvey Company and the Santa Fe Railway*, The Heard Museum, Phoenix, 1996

Ernest Henderson (1897-1967):

SHREWD NEW ENGLAND INVESTOR AND FOUNDER OF THE SHERATON CORPORATION OF AMERICA

The person who built the largest chain in the world never took any real interest in designing a hotel or building one, never managed a hotel or probably never thought of himself as a hotelman. As his son, Ernest Henderson, III put it. "My father had been bumping around from one industry to another. He got interested in buying common stocks in companies which had more bonds outstanding than the value of the property, and in doing so, acquired four hotels: the Lee, Wayland Manor, the Stonehaven and the Sheraton. So in 1941, he had four hotels. The Statler was the great company at that time in the hotel industry. It had the same name on all of its properties. My father felt that he should have the same name on all of his hotels. On the roof of the Sheraton in Boston was a big sign saying Sheraton, so he selected this as the name of the hotel chain".

Mr. Ernest Henderson, Sr. of the Sheraton Hotel Corporation speaking at the Cornell School of Hotel Administration in 1955 said:

> As recently as two or three decades ago the stature of a hotel man was often measured by the extent of his personal charm, the degree of his individual popularity and by the number of people he could greet by name. Today the axis is shifting. Maybe we are sacrificing some of the industry's picturesque glamour on the altar of hard facts, know-how, and a familiarity with the tools of scientific management. But it is these latter that pay off when the monthly statement or annual report is issued. A hunch sometimes pays off, but facts and

knowledge pay bigger dividends. Modern competitive conditions demand a scientific approach.

Ernest Henderson was forty-four years old when he got into the hotel industry. Twenty-six years later, at his death, Sheraton had 154 hotels and grossed more than $300,000,000 annually. Henderson's greatest strengths were his financial and organizational skills, his down-to-earth and hard-bitten New England common sense about investments and profits. By any evaluation, he was not a hotelman's standard of a charming and outgoing hotel executive. He was a capitalist who thrived on hard work, energy, skepticism and shrewdness. He had no romantic notions of the role of "Mine Host". Henderson was an opportunist in the best sense of the word, ready to buy or sell a hotel if the right deal could be negotiated. While Conrad Hilton worked for years to acquire the Plaza and Waldorf-Astoria hotels with single-minded energy, Henderson bought and sold many lesser-known hotels. In Henderson's scheme, the tax base against which depreciation could be taken was much more important. Some hotels were bought and sold as many as four times by the Sheraton Corporation.

The contrast between Ernest Henderson and Conrad Hilton could not have been greater. While the splendid Hilton headquarters were located in Beverly Hills, California, Henderson maintained modest offices on the Boston waterfront at 470 Atlantic Avenue. Ernest Henderson was born in 1897 in Chestnut Hill, a suburb of Boston. The family, comprised at the time of five children, moved to Washington, DC but spent summers in Dublin, New Hampshire. Henderson's mother, born in England, was three-quarters British and one-quarter German. His father came from Staten Island, New York, graduated from Harvard in 1883 and acquired in Berlin both a Ph.D. and a lovely wife who, in her early years, commuted between Germany and the western borders of England.

In the fall of 1914, Henderson became a freshman at Harvard where his roommate was Robert Lowell Moore who became a lifelong friend and business partner. Henderson and Moore bought old second-hand Fords, substituted new bodies that were available because some ambitious firms bought new Fords, removed unused bodies, welded in place heavier rear axles, mounted a truck body on the reinforced classics and sold them at a premium. This was lucrative because Ford had not yet started to manufacture trucks.

After completing two and a half years of college, Henderson enlisted in the Navy just before World War I as a radio operator and electrician third class. Later he earned his wings as a Navy pilot in Pensacola, Florida. Henderson served in Italy and France before the armistice in 1918. As a World War I veteran, Henderson married Mary Stephens of Wheeling, West Virginia who changed her name to Molly Henderson.

With brother George and his former roommate, Bob Moore, Henderson embarked on various business ventures including foreign exchange, banking, importing and do-it-yourself radio manufacturing. They did business with merchant Eli Siegel and entrepreneur Carl Canner. During the depression of the nineteen thirties, Henderson and Moore created the Investment Trust of Boston to buy and sell undervalued shares of other investment trusts listed on the Stock Exchange. Their first introduction to the hotel business was shortly after the 1933 banking holiday when Franklin D. Roosevelt had just become president. Henderson and his partners acquired the Continental Hotel in Cambridge which ultimately became the most profitable hotel of its size in the country. Later, they acquired the 200-room Stonehaven Hotel in Springfield and, with it, Elmer Boswell, the resident manager who became one of Sheraton's top executives. In Henderson's own words,

> It was at this time, early in 1939, as possessors of three small hotels, that we began to develop some ambitious ideas. Perhaps we might someday have a large chain of hotels. Cherishing this somewhat nebulous dream, we began considering the advantages of a single name for the prospective empire. In addition to the Springfield property we had the Lee House in Washington and a hotel known as the Sheraton on Boston's Bay State Road. The latter, with an expensive electric roof sign, left us little choice in the selection of the new name for our future domain, for it would have cost a small fortune to change the letters of the sign. Our hotels in Springfield and Washington thus became Sheraton hotels... Many celebrities had permanent

accommodations at this original Sheraton Hotel. One of these was Ted Williams of Boston Red Sox fame. One time, I remember, a pretty young seventeen year-old from nearby Concord had reached the conviction that nothing really mattered more in this difficult world than getting a genuine autograph of the famed baseball hero. Realizing how important such things can be, I inquired of our general manger if her desire could be gratified. Soon a regulation baseball appeared, bearing the authentic inscription, "With greetings to Sally", followed by the coveted signature. It was to no avail. Someone previously had played on Sally's gullibility by presenting her with a spurious note from Ted, and she was sure the baseball likewise could only be a hoax. Calmly she tossed the offending "fraud" into the Concord River, aggrieved that any one should trifle with her deep emotions. I never heard what happened later when Sally learned that the treasure so lightly cast aside was really quite authentic.....

Henderson did make contributions to hotelkeeping. As an expert in real estate and the use of leveraged money, he demonstrated how a hotel organization can rapidly acquire numbers of hotels, expand its equity ownership in hotels and motels, and yet show only a modest profit for tax purposes. Chain hotelkeeping, as conducted by the Sheraton Corporation, was as much a real estate venture as it was bedmaking, salad making, food service and advertising.

There is a time to buy a hotel, and a time to sell it, the timing dependent upon the tax base which is left for depreciation in a property, general business conditions and whether or not he cash might not be put to better use in another property. Henderson put into practice a theory of maximizing-minimizing costs to predict the return on one's investment. He felt that he himself should earn at least $10,000 a day for the Sheraton Corporation.

Undoubtedly he did not feel that he could earn this sum by being a corporate manager. Rather his contribution lay in recognizing opportunities, investment and otherwise. He quoted H. L. Mencken as saying, "It is not the things we do but rather what we don't do that we eventually regret." Opportunities for him as an expert in real estate were the purchase and sale of properties at the right moment.

He believed in the use of leveraged money whenever possible and perhaps used it more successfully in the hotel business than anyone else. His son Ernest Henderson, III, cited an example of how far Mr. Henderson would go in leveraging his cash position. Suppose the Sheraton Corporation was interested in buying a motel which had a $100,000 income each year. The Corporation might be willing to buy at eight times the income, or $800,000. Henderson's objective was to get the property using a minimum amount of cash. He knew that he would borrow half of the $800,000 from a bank or insurance company at 6% interest. If the owner would agree to take a second mortgage for $500,000, Sheraton Corporation might raise the offer for the hotel from $800,000 to $1 million. With a first mortgage of $400,000 and a second mortgage of $500,000 Sheraton could take possession of the property for a cash outlay of only $100,000. This is an extreme example of how to gain control of an $800,000 property with only $100,000 in cash. Mr. Henderson was well aware of the "Discounted Dollar", the fact that $1 borrowed today is paid back with $1 worth something less than $1. Inflation has become a way of life in America. Inflation works to the advantage of the debtor. A certain amount of inflation is countenanced by the Federal Government and thought necessary for the continued growth of the economy.

A price rise at 1.5% a year means that in 10 years a debt of $1 can be paid off with money worth only 86.2¢. If the price rise is 2.75% a year, the same $1 can be paid off with a $1 worth only 76.2¢. Real property like hotels and motels tend to grow in value, especially if well located and maintained. Even if the hotel itself does not gain in value, the land which it occupies may well appreciate more than enough to compensate for a loss in the value of the hotel building. Of course, there are many instances to the contrary.

Henderson felt that one of the most effective management tools was the guest questionnaire. Letters sent to Sheraton headquarters were answered promptly, compliments and complaints were passed on to the manager concerned. The traveler, said Henderson, can run hotels better than the management. When the voluntary flow of complaints to the head office ran low, questionnaires were left in hotel bedrooms.

All complaints were classified: failure to honor confirmed reservations; delay in the appearance of a breakfast tray; ringing the wrong room for the morning wake-up call. Henderson felt that when the proportion of complaints to compliments was more than 50%, management was slipping. If the complaint ratio rose to 60%, drastic action was necessary. On the other hand, if there were too many compliments concerning a particular manager, the suspicion arose that the manager might be giving away the profits.

Henderson was actively engaged in operations. His office in the Sheraton Building was very much the nerve center of the Sheraton Corporation and he took an active interest in day-to-day operating problems. He believed in a lean organization. In naval terms, he ran a taut ship. Belt tightening programs could be expected every year to clear away unnecessary people and programs. He was no friend of bureaucracy and did not believe in a large headquarters staff. The training department was one man. The personnel department hardly much larger. Every Sheraton employee, but especially staff executive level personnel were expected to contribute, every day.

Mr. Henderson was definitely sales minded. Though the Sheraton Sales Blitz idea was originated by Bud Smith, head of the sales department, Henderson strongly favored and encouraged the plan. The sales blitz was a campaign to saturate a city with the promotion of Sheraton Hotels. Sales people from other Sheraton hotels in a wide area converged on a city and in team effort called upon hundreds of potential Sheraton customers. Sheraton credit cards were distributed in quantity and group business was solicited and booked. Franchising the Sheraton name brought in additional revenue but of more importance to Henderson was the fact that each franchise added another unit to the Sheraton referral system.

Mr. Henderson will probably be remembered largely for his ability to increase the equity value of the Sheraton Corporation from an estimated value of about $50,000,000 in 1947 to close to $400,000,000 in 1967. The increase was brought about with very little speculation in the usual sense of the word. Constant attention was given to avoiding financial over-extension.

Henderson wrote "A number of troublesome ills often plague our corporation. To ward off a few of these, we have sought at times to build up a degree of corporate immunity to at least some of the more insidious ones. For this we have devised a company "Decalogue", a collection of "thou shall nots" dedicated to all those connected with Sheraton. We believe fewer guests would visit our hotels each year had we not sought actively to discourage many transgressions by formulating our own private Ten Commandments:

1. Thou shalt not throw thy weight around, however irresistible may be the urge to do so.

2. Thou shalt not take presents from those seeking thy favors. Beware of those who bear gifts.

3. Suffer not thy wives to gratify a yen to decorate Sheraton hotels. May wives render unto their husbands what is rightfully theirs, but unto Mary Kennedy (Sheraton's corporate designer) that which is in her domain,

4. Thou shalt not dishonor a confirmed reservation, lest thy days be short in the job thy company giveth thee.

5. Thou shalt not give orders to an underling without making fully clear the exact purpose thereof.

6. Thou shalt duly recall that the virtues of those running small hotels may be the vices of those guiding larger establishments

7. Thou shalt not demand the last 'drop of blood' when effecting a business transaction.

8. Thou shalt not permit the escape of those fleeting degrees of Fahrenheit so essential to a customer's delight when he is exposed to delicacies on a hotel menu. May unending torture pursue a kitchen staff that suffers beans to be boiled beyond a specified limit.

9. Thou shalt not make decisions based on a 'feeling' that some action may be called for.

10. Thou shalt not explode like a firecracker when an underling falleth into error, last perchance it be thou who erred by not providing proper guidance."

Few hotel people have time for hobbies. Henderson collected coins, was an avid ham radio operator, a song writer, a dabbler at poetry, a story-teller, a staunch family man, and still found time for being a director of Northeastern University, Boston College, and of Boston University. He served as a director of the Boston and U.S. Chambers of Commerce; founding member of the World Affairs Council, and Chairman of the World Trade Center in New England. No other hotelman has so extended himself in civic commitments.

In light of his tremendous range of activity, it would be easy to picture to man who was trying to overcome serious social or financial drawbacks; such was not the case. His family was not wealthy but well enough off for his father to acquire a Ph.D. in Berlin and to maintain a home in Cambridge and a summer home in Dublin, N.H. Mr. Henderson was proud enough of his ancestry to include a chapter about them in his biography and to name his middle daughter Penny after a distant relative who was the wife of Lord Llanover. Grandfather Henderson founded Henderson and Company, a New York Stock Exchange firm; and left "something of a nest egg for the surviving children". Real estate and investing were part of a family tradition which Ernest enthusiastically continued.

What lasting contributions did Henderson make to the hotel industry? Henderson brought no new standards of comfort or luxury to hotelkeeping, no innovations in design or operation. Although Sheraton Corporation operated in ten countries, the company was tardy in expanding internationally. Hilton International and InterContinental Hotels were far ahead of Sheraton in this respect. Henderson was a capitalist in the best sense of the word, believing that there were few virtues greater than those found in ownership and creation of new wealth. Energy, hard work, keen analysis were combined with skepticism and shrewdness. He was an opportunist in the best sense of the word, ready to buy or sell a hotel if the right deal could be worked out.

A major blindspot was his intense dislike for President Franklin Delano Roosevelt. Henderson wrote in his autobiography:

> Despite a feeling that Roosevelt used businessmen as political scapegoats, my 1936 ballot was cast for him. Later I regretted this indiscretion, but not because of his domestic policies.

> It was Roosevelt's international program which troubled me most. I was never convinced that France, Britain and the United States might not have escaped the Second World War and its very painful ravages had F.D.R. exercised the restraining hand of statesmanship, rather than pursuing what may have been an unnecessarily belligerent policy that seems to have made a world war inevitable. I felt that Roosevelt's dislike for, and lack of understanding of, Germany actually encouraged at least some of the evils that developed under Hitler, and that Communism in Russia was really world enemy number one.

In the 1950s, Sheraton acquired the six-hundred room French Lick Springs Hotel for a million dollars for 1700 acres of land, the makings of an artificial lake, a shooting range, bridle paths, sulphur baths and two championship golf courses. After extensive remodeling, air-conditioning and modernizing, Henderson wrote that the renovated resort is definitely "one of the brighter stars in the Sheraton constellation." However, despite hotel-inspired Jazz and Music Festivals featuring Duke Ellington and Arthur Fiedler conducting the Boston Pops, the Sheraton French Lick Springs Hotel never fulfilled Henderson's prediction. Some 50 years later in 2006, the French Lick Springs Resort reopened after a two-year historic renovation of its 443 guestrooms, restaurants, casino, spa and golf course. The first hotel built on this site opened in 1845 to take advantage of the natural sulphur springs and Pluto mineral water. The original hotel burned down in 1897 but was rebuilt on a grander scale by Thomas Taggert, the mayor of Indianapolis (and later a U.S.

Senator). The Monon Railroad built a spur directly to the hotel grounds with daily passenger service to Chicago. Casino gambling, although illegal, flourished at the resort. In its heyday in the Roaring Twenties, the surrounding Spring Valley had 30 hotels and 15 clubs. At the time, it was a lively community for gamblers, politicians, sport figures, entertainers and gangsters. The town got its name from the French traders who founded it and the salty mineral deposits that attracted wildlife.

The French Lick Resort's new casino is apparently as luxurious and as big as the original. The 84,000 square-foot casino features 1,200 slot machines and dozens of blackjack, roulette, craps and poker tables. The Resort has eight new restaurants, six-lane bowling, indoor tennis, riding stables and promenade shops. The casino is built in the shape of a riverboat and is surrounded by a moat (in accordance with a 1993 state law which permits gambling only on riverboats). French Lickers call it the Boat in the Moat.

During the Prohibition years, French Lick had 13 casinos, all of them illegal. Famous guests who visited French Lick included Franklin D. Roosevelt, Harry S. Truman, Adlai E. Stevenson, the Marx Brothers, Joe Louis, Bob Hope and Bing Crosby.

The Donald Ross golf course at the French Lick Resort reopened in September 2006 unveiling a $4.6 million restoration of the famed course where Walter Hagen won the PGA championship in 1924. Hagen closed out Englishman James Barnes on the 36th and final hole of the two-round match-play championship. Similarly, Betsey Rawls walked off the 72nd hole in 1959 with an LPGA Championship defeating Patty Berg. Mickey Wright won the tournament there a year later.

In 1958, Sheraton acquired the Hotel Ambassador at 345 Park Avenue at 51st Street and renamed it the Sheraton-East. Coincidentally, it was on the roof of the Ambassador that the silent-film heartthrob Rudolf Valentino had staged a boxing match with sportswriter Frank O'Neill in an attempt to counter slurs on his masculinity (Valentino knocked him down). After collapsing in his hotel suite- the collapse was unrelated to the fight- on August 15, 1926, Valentino was taken to Polyclinic Hospital, on West 50th Street, near Ninth Avenue, where he had surgery for appendicitis and gastric ulcers. He died of peritonitis on August 23.

In 1959 Sheraton, in a stroke of genius by Henderson and his chief financial officer, Richard Boonisar, bought all of the Waikiki hotel properties owned by the Matson Navigation Company including the Moana Hotel, the Surfrider, the Royal Hawaiian and the Princess Kaiulani. Matson's involvement in Hawaii began in 1882 when Captain William Matson sailed his three-mastered schooner Emma Claudina from San Francisco to Hilo, Hawaii, carrying 300 tons of food, plantation supplies and general merchandise. That voyage started Matson's ventures into hotels and tourism, oil exploration, military service during two world wars and the movement of freight between the Pacific Coast and Hawaii. As commerce increased, a corresponding interest in Hawaii as a tourist attraction caused Matson to add steamships with guest accommodations. Immediately after the December 7, 1941 attack on Pearl Harbor four Matson passenger liners and 33 freighters were called into military service. In the 1950s two new Matson hotels were built on Waikiki, the Surfrider and the Princess Kaiulani. They joined the Moana Hotel, known as the "First Lady of Waikiki" which was originally built in 1901 by the wealthy Honolulu landowner, Walter Chamberlain Peacock, in accordance with a design by architect Oliver G. Traphagen. The Moana's architecture featured Ionic columns and intricate woodwork and plaster detailing. Some of the 75 guestrooms had telephones and bathrooms. The Moana contained a library, saloon, billiard room and the first electric-powered elevator in the islands. In Hawaiian, moana means "open sea" or "ocean". Peacock sold the hotel to Alexander Young who operated the Moana until the Matson Navigation Company bought the property in 1932 for $1.6 million.

The Royal Hawaiian Hotel, known as the "Pink Palace of the Pacific" was built by the Matson Navigation Company and opened in 1927. It cost $4 million and had 400 rooms. It was designed by the New York architects, Warren & Wetmore. Its first official registered guest was Princess Abigail Kawananakoa who would have been queen of the kingdom of Hawaii had the monarchy survived. Duke Kahanamoku, the legendary Olympic swimmer and popularizer of the sport of surfing created the famed group the Waikiki Beach Boys at the Royal Hawaiian

Hotel. In 1969, Sheraton added the 16-story Royal Tower to the Royal Hawaiian Hotel for a total room count of 526 rooms.

The Royal Hawaiian Hotel, Waikiki Beach, Hawaii opened in 1927 and is known as the "Pink Palace of the Pacific." It was built by the Matson Shipping Lines with 400 rooms in Spanish-Moorish style with a California mission influence. In 1959, Matson sold the Royal Hawaiian Hotel to Sheraton, who added the 16-story Royal Tower shown above.

In 1969, Sheraton built a new hotel on the Moana's west side. This new tower was named the Sheraton Surfrider Hotel and the old Surfrider building was made into a wing of the Moana Hotel. Finally, in 1989, a $50 million restoration (designed by Hawaii architect Virginia D. Murison) restored the Moana to its 1901 appearance and incorporated the two adjacent buildings into one beachfront resort with a common lobby, renaming the entire property the Sheraton Moana Surfrider. Sheraton also built the 31-story, 1900-room Sheraton Waikiki Hotel which opened in 1970. It was designed to allow the maximum number of guestrooms possible a view of the Pacific Ocean.

In 1974, Japanese businessmen and brothers Kenji and Masakuni Osano purchased the Royal Hawaiian Hotel, the Moana, the Princess Kaiulani, the Surfrider and the Sheraton Waikiki for $105 million and gave the management to the Sheraton Corporation.

From 1962 to 1967, Sheraton stock prices decreased from $22 to $9 per share despite Ernest Henderson's valiant but unsuccessful attempts to explain Sheraton's true financial condition. In addition to reporting revenues, net income, profits, depreciation and cash flow, the company reported an "estimated value" of each share of common stock, estimated net asset value and adjusted earnings. The financial marketplace never accepted Henderson's explanations.

Meanwhile in 1966, the International Telephone & Telegraph Corporation acquired the Airport Parking Company of America (APCOA) which owned eight Holiday Inn franchises in the Midwest. ITTs chairman Harold Geneen wrote,

> The future potential of hotels and motels looked extremely promising because a good deal of the whole operation had just become computerized, particularly the reservation system. Holiday Inns had a central computer which handled all reservations for its facilities across the country with one toll-free reservation number. The computer also monitored the occupancy rate of each hotel and motel, so that the company could plan future expansions with considerable accuracy. However, negotiations to buy the Holiday Inn chain fell through. We then approached Hilton, which had sold off its European hotels to Trans- World Airlines. Conrad Hilton escorted me around the Palmer House in Chicago, describing the operations of his successful hotel chain. But his price was too high. So we turned to the Sheraton Corporation of America, whose earnings on a percentage basis were the lowest in the industry. Its hotels were ancient, with an average age of thirty years, and in dire need of repairs. Even worse, the Sheraton hotels were located in depressed city core areas, and few people saw any way of improving Sheraton's overall situation. Against the advice of some of our own people,

we bought the Sheraton chain in 1968. We thought we
could turn it around.

For seventeen years, Harold Sydney Geneen was commander-in-chief
of ITT, the most complex corporation in the world, operating in every
major country not behind the Iron Curtain, employing at its peak more
than 375,000 men and women. Geneen had taken the old-fashioned
and stagnant ITT corporation with sales of $765.6 million and profits
of $29 million in 1959 to annual sales of $16.7 billion and earnings of
$562 million in 1977. In the interim, Geneen had bought or merged
with some 350 different businesses in eighty countries.

Meanwhile at Sheraton, in 1963 Robert Moore retired as chairman.
Henderson took that title and his son, Ernest F. Henderson III, became
president. Although forty-two years old, the son was universally called
"young Ernie". Henderson and Moore wanted to get their estates in
order and CFO Richard Boonisar was instructed to negotiate with
potential buyers. Boonisar was a tough, self-made man from South
Boston with a Harvard education. When Henderson died of a heart
attack on September 6, 1967, Boonisar was named chairman and
commenced serious negotiations with ITT. When an ITT executive
came to visit Sheraton in Boston, Boonisar greeted him with, "Who the
f--- are you?" and then wanted to know how many push-ups the visitor
could do. In October, 1967 Geneen met with Boonisar at Boston's
Somerset Hotel and struck a deal for $35 per share, which was $10
more than the recommendation of APCOA's hotel people. After the
acquisition, ITT fired Ernest Henderson III, gave out a half million
dollars in raises, installed Philip L. Lowe, an ITT product line manager
(PLM) for financial services, as president. For a non-hotel man, Lowe
had some striking successes:

- with president of Sheraton International Claude Feninger,
  many sites for new Sheraton hotels in South America,
  Europe and the Mideast were identified and acquired.

- reduced Sheraton's bad debt loss of $5 million a year
  by institutioning credit policies that required positive
  identification for credit cards or checks.

- ended the BBD&O Sheraton advertising campaign that featured a businessman with a large key stuck in his back saying "keyed-up executives unwind at Sheraton."

- with Sheraton's marketing director, William Morton, came up with single-number room reservation system to replace the more than 200 phone numbers Sheraton listed nationwide. With the help of ITTs telephone experts and a psychologist, the national, one-call, magical, toll-free number was 800-325-3535. By winter 1970, a new advertising campaign broke with saturation TV, full page magazine and newspaper ads, incessant repetition of eight, oh, oh, three -two-five, three-five, three-five. The number was set to a catchy tune and it was recorded by the Boston Pops, a singing dog performed it on Johnny Carson's NBC show, it was a cocktail-lounge background music on a TV drama and was played everywhere including at skating rinks. Reservations increased enormously and continuously.

- expanded the Sheraton franchise department and hired Irving Zeldman to head the effort with Joseph McInerney as his assistant. The new franchises soon surpassed the number of owned and managed hotels and became a major profit center.

Lowe's efforts were undermined by Dick Boonisar's personal dislike. Boonisar was rough, Lowe was smooth; Boonisar was Lebanese, Lowe Jewish. Boonisar was soon bad-mouthing Lowe all over Boston, telling everyone how badly Sheraton was being run and what fools ITT people were. Nothing ITT did could stop Boonisar from him impolitic public criticism of ITT and its appointees. Finally, Philip Lowe was replaced by Howard 'Bud' James, a sportsman with a degree in hotel management from Denver University who had risen to be president of the Sahara-Nevada chain.

There is dispute as to how much James should get credit for Sheraton's recovery. Former ITT controller Herb Knortz says, "Bud claims to have invented 'get out of real estate', but Hilton was doing it before we were and so were other chains; it's just the sensible way to operate a hotel business." Sheraton continued to lose money under James and did not become profitable until 1978. Meanwhile, James vetoed and prevented Sheraton's acquisitions of some world-famous hotels that could have enhanced Sheraton's reputation: the Greenbrier Resort Hotel, White Sulphur Springs, West Virginia; the Gotham Hotel on Fifth Avenue, New York; the Fontainbleau Resort, Miami Beach, Florida; and the Halekulani Resort Hotel, Honolulu, Hawaii.

I was recruited by ITT soon after the acquisition of Sheraton as assistant to Howard Miller, Group Vice President for Consumer Service Companies. One year later, I was promoted to Product Line Manager ITT Hotel/Motel operations. Here is the job description:

POSITION SUMMARY

Develops short – and long term business plans of ITT motel/hotel operations monitors performance and takes steps to insure accomplishment or improvement of planned growths and profit targets. Studies marketing methodology and organization to maximize market potential of motel/hotel operations and related consumer service activities in both the U.S. and abroad. In conjunction with other ITT functional responsibilities, develops organization and management programs designed to promote growth and profits of the ITT motel/hotel business. Evaluates sites, develops pro formas, conducts negotiations with governments, promoters and owners of sites and hotels/motels, and develops financing programs. Develops preliminary physical layouts for potential facilities.

MAJOR DUTIES AND RESPONSIBILITIES

1. Develops short-and-long-term business plans of ITT motel/hotel operating units. Coordinates these plans between different areas to optimize growth and profit potential of ITT in motel/hotel operations worldwide.

2. Establishes criteria and standards for ITT motel/ hotel operations in (a) quality of service offered (b) image to the consumer (c) return on sales target.

3. Guides motel/hotel units in the preparation of their individual and coordinated business plans to be submitted for Group and ITT World Headquarters review and approval.

4. Monitors operating performance against planned growth and profit objectives and recommends such actions as are necessary to accomplish objectives or improve upon them.

5. Coordinates operation of the ITT motel/hotel business with other activities in the ITT Consumer Services area so as to maximize growth and profit potential for the entire consumer services product line.

6. Examines marketing methods and techniques so as to develop a strong marketing organization to promote ITT motel/hotel opportunities.

7. Directs market research and studies designed to expand ITT motel/hotel operations in the U.S. and to accomplish penetration of new markets overseas for this type of business.

8. Evaluate operations and problems of potential acquisitions and planned construction.

9. Plan and evaluate physical layouts of planned construction.

10. Establish pro formas for potential acquisitions and planned construction.

11. Conducts negotiations with government, promoters, and owners of sites and hotels/motels and develops financing programs.

12. Plans, negotiates and monitors construction activities.

13. In conjunction with ITT Organization, plans and develops a streamlined organization which will operate the ITT motel/hotel business on a controlled and minimal cost basis.

14. Institutes and supervises management development and training program designed to attract management talent to the ITT motel/hotel business and insure maximum performance to their level of skills.

15. Works closely with ITT Treasurer's Department in exploring potential acquisition in the motel/hotel field. Once an acquisition is made, coordinates entry and integration of the acquired unit into the ITT motel/hotel business.

16. Supervises programs of acquisitions of new properties and leases for motels/hotels. Coordinates these programs as required with the ITT Treasurer's Department

17. Develops delegations of authority which provide guidelines of control between the units and Group and ITT World Headquarters.

18. As required, streamlined legal entity structure at the point of maximum operating efficiency concurrent with minimum administrative expense.

SOURCE MATERIALS

1. Harold Geneen with Alvin Moscow, *Managing*, Avon Books, New York, 1984

2. Ernest Henderson, *The World of "Mr. Sheraton"*, David McKay Company, Inc., New York, 1960

3. Donald E. Lundberg, *The Hotel and Restaurant Business*, Institutions/ Volume Feeding Management Magazine, Chicago, 1971

4. Anthony Sampson, *The Sovereign State of ITT*, Stein and Day, New York, 1973

5. Robert J. Schoenberg, *Geneen,* W.W. Norton & Company, New York, 1985

6. Jerome J. Vallen, *The Art and Science of Modern Innkeeping*, Ahrens Publishing Company, New York, 1968

7. Moana Hotel and Royal Hawaiian Hotel, Wikipedia, the free encyclopedia

Conrad Nicholson Hilton (1887-1979):

FLAMBOYANT KING OF THE INNKEEPERS

From 1938 through 1954, Conrad Hilton, in a brilliant series of transactions, acquired a large group of hotels at cut-rate, post-Depression prices. The Palmer House which cost nearly $26 million to build in 1929 was purchased by Hilton for $19.4 million in 1945. The 2,673-room Stevens Hotel, now the Chicago Hilton and Towers, built in 1925 for $30 million was acquired for $7.5 million in 1944.

Conrad Nicholson Hilton was born in San Antonio, Socorro County, New Mexico to Augustus Halvorson "Gus" Hilton (August 21, 1854 – January 19, 1919), a Norwegian immigrant, and Mary Genevieve Laufersweiler (December 3, 1861 – August 26, 1947), a German-American.

Conrad's father was the son of Halvor Nilsen Hilton and Karoline Hansdatter "Kari" Holum. Gus was born on the Hilton family farm near Klofta in Ullensaker, Norway, where relatives still live. Gus emigrated to the United States in 1870. Conrad's mother was born in Fort Dodge, Iowa, the daughter of a German-born merchant, Conrad Laufersweiler. Conrad's parents were married on February 12, 1885 in Fort Dodge.

Conrad's siblings were:

- Felice A. Hilton (1885-1968)
- Eva C. Hilton (1889-1979)
- Carl H. Hilton (1892-1957)
- Julia Hilton (1895-1897)
- Rosemary J. Hilton (1898-1995)
- August H. "Boy" Hilton (1901-1929)
- Helen A. Hilton (1906-2003)

Conrad was educated at the New Mexico Military Institute, at St. Michael's College (now the College of Santa Fe), and at the New Mexico School of Mines (now New Mexico Tech). In his early twenties, he was a representative in the first legislature of the newly formed State of New Mexico. Hilton spoke Spanish fluently.

Shortly after the United States entered World War I in 1917, Conrad Hilton enlisted in the U.S. Army and was sent to Officers' Training Command, Presidio of San Francisco. 2nd Lieutenant Hilton arrived in France, February 14, 1918. His unit, the 304th Labor Battalion, saw limited combat. On February 11, 1919, Conrad Hilton was discharged at Fort Dix, New Jersey. While Conrad was in the army, his father was killed in a car accident.

In 1919 the oil business in Ranger, Texas was booming. People from all around wanted a piece of the action. Hilton came to Cisco area of Texas to "launch big ships" and he went where the "water was deep". He wanted his business to be near the rich oil fields of Ranger and the business opportunities which were within his planned financing. Hilton originally planned to purchase a Cisco bank, but when the bank owner raised the promised sale price he gave up the effort. Hilton was frustrated and went looking for a place to sleep for the night. He found that there were no rooms available and that the owner of the Mobley Hotel, Henry L. Mobley, was renting all beds for eight hour shifts. He saw that there were more opportunities in business here than just banking. Hilton and Mobley quickly struck an agreement, since Mobley wanted to get out of the hotel business and seek his fortune in oil. So Hilton purchased the Mobley for $5000. Cisco was a boomtown short of hotel rooms and Hilton found himself many nights sleeping in a leather chair in his office, having rented all of his hotel's rooms. As Hilton's experience and confidence grew, he decided that he wanted to expand into other Texas cities. He left a business partner, Mr. Drown, to manage the Mobley while he went to Fort Worth to renovate and open the Annabel Hotel. In 1924 he sold the Mobley to his mother, Mary Hilton, where it stayed in the family until 1931, when it was sold to J.M. Radford of Cisco.

Through the years the old Mobley Hotel has been a boarding house, nursing home, and a private residence. The Hotel remained vacant for many years and it continued to deteriorate. The Hilton Foundation put up $1.2 million dollars for the restoration of the Hotel which is now used by the Cisco Chamber of Commerce as a museum, park, and community center. The Mobley has also earned its place in the National Register of Historic Buildings.

In 1929 Hilton consolidated his properties into Hilton Hotels, Incorporated. Despite advertising in national magazines, the firm came close to bankruptcy in 1931 as the nationwide Depression lessened nationwide travel. Hilton recovered only with the help of William Lewis Moody, Jr., of Galveston, and a number of other investors. He merged his hotels with the Moodys' operations to form the National Hotel Company, for which he served as one-third owner and acting general manager. After the merger failed, Hilton resumed his independent operation in 1934 with five hotels, and in 1938 he acquired the famed Sir Francis Drake Hotel in San Francisco, his first hotel outside of Texas. Hilton was 51 years old at this critical moment in his career.

In 1942 Hilton established his corporate headquarters in Beverly Hills, California. Hilton Hotels was incorporated under Delaware laws in 1946 and was listed on the New York Stock Exchange by 1947. The company began to expand abroad, starting in Mexico, and in 1948 Hilton formed Hilton Hotels International, a wholly owned subsidiary. One of the first employees of Hilton International Hotels, Curt R. Strand was president of the company from1968 until his retirement in 1986. In the June 1996 issue of the <u>Cornell Hotel and Restaurant Administration Quarterly</u>*, he wrote the following thorough and thoughtful memoir:

> Hilton International started small in 1947, but I was endowed with a great asset. It is a wise parent who does not bestow money on his children, just a good education. The parent, Conrad Hilton, was a consummate dealmaker. He had an intuition about hotels as real estate that was unmatched in his time.

* "Lessons of a Lifetime: The Development of Hilton International." Copyright Cornell University. Used by permission. All rights reserved.

Strand went to work at the Plaza Hotel in New York after World War II but didn't know that it was owned by Hilton. While Hilton owned the Stevens and the Palmer House in Chicago, he had not yet put his name on his hotels.

Curt Strand continued,

> Conrad Hilton had the vision of what we now call globalization back in 1947, but he did not have the means to achieve such a vision because his board of directors wanted no part of it. At that time, with so much of world's economy inoperative, expansion meant taking financial risk. The genesis of Hilton's—and the industry's—globalization was a confluence of three factors, almost historic accidents. Those factors were demand, an entrepreneur and financing. Most of Europe and much of Asia lay devastated by war in 1947. Every country had a critical need to earn hard currency but was incapable of producing much for export, since industry and agriculture were in ruins. Tourism was one of the few prospects and it was a good one....

Coincidentally, Hilton's first hotel outside the continental United States was in the commonwealth of Puerto Rico, a destination practically unknown in the United States. The island was intent upon attracting business organizations to investigate the opportunities of its newly-established tax haven. Government officials realized that they needed a first-class hotel and solicited proposals from the major U.S. hotel companies, including Hilton.

Strand reported that Hilton came up with a novel idea: he would design, lease and operate a new hotel that the government would finance it through bonds. The Caribe Hilton achieved high occupancy and become profitable for the investors, the management firms and for Puerto Rico.

> The rent was not to be fixed and could not therefore be considered a financial obligation. Instead the rent was based on operating profits (two-thirds of GOP, if you

can believe it). Today, this type of proposal would be commonplace, but at the time it was a revolutionary twist that had never been tried with hotels or any other real-estate deal. All Hilton put up was $300,000 for operating equipment and initial working capital. By no coincidence this was the total amount of cash Hilton's board grudgingly gave him to invest in his new subsidiary, Hilton International....

Strand's recollections of the difficulties faced by Hilton International all over the world are worth reporting.

At least for the company's first ten years (from 1947), hotel demand grew everywhere but even in Europe much travel was primitive and most other areas were not ready for development. In Madrid, for instance, streetcars competed with donkey carts, even downtown. Berlin was a field of recently cleared rubble. Hong Kong had just three hotels, and its water service operated for two hours every other day. In Cairo, a hotel was constructed by 6,000 women carrying cement mix on their heads up 12 stories because there was no crane. (This was considered normal women's work, but when that Cairo hotel opened, all the waitresses had college degrees because there were not enough jobs for college-educated women.) In all of Addis Ababa there was not a single shop. Criminals often met justice in the form of a public hanging, unfortunately in a spot on the road to the airport. (I personally asked the emperor to relocate the gallows, and he did so.) In Rome it took our owners, the largest construction company in Italy, ten years to get a building permit, due to politics and bureaucracy. The independence date of Barbados depended on completion of our hotel-both delayed, of course. In Nigeria, the priorities were reversed. Six months before it was completed, our hotel had to open for a week to accommodate 14 heads of state for a summit meeting....

After opening, these new hotels were extraordinarily beneficial to the sponsoring countries. They created new jobs which required extensive training in new skills. Hilton was savvy enough to design hotels which featured the national culture and utilized local arts, crafts, paintings and sculpture. Still, many locals felt ignored by the foreign managers who sometimes did not adapt quickly to the local customs and bureaucracies.

Strand reported that ten years after its start in Puerto Rico, Hilton International had opened just eight hotels.

> We had a big name but a small base..... Our goal was to get into Europe, because that was the place with the greatest demand for rooms both for business people and for tourists, particularly with the introduction of jet planes in the late '50s..... Our strategy became one of establishing an outer perimeter of locations where demand for our evolving experience was particularly strong. Spain (under Francisco Franco at the time), for example, was desperate for a Western link.

> Turkey was developing into a 20th-century state based on its magnificent history and culture. Berlin was isolated and still recovering from the strangulation of the Soviet embargo (overcome by the Western air lift of supplies). Egypt was just emerging from colonialism, once again an independent power.

> We also strengthened our reputation by operating properties in the New World. Cuba (before Fidel Castro) wished to emulate Puerto Rico's success and that of the newly developed gambling mecca of Las Vegas.

> In Montreal, the Canadian National Railway was building a huge convention hotel but realized belatedly that it had no organization to market it. Mexico discovered its tourist attractions but had no hotel-management knowledge....

Strand described Hilton International's strongest competition.

> We were regarded as successful pioneers. Our earliest competition came from InterContinental Hotels, a subsidiary of PanAmerican Airways, at the time a well-respected international airline. PanAm operated guest houses to accommodate its passengers and crews on overnight stops on South American routes.....
>
> Our next strategy involved two different contractual arrangements at once. We would use operating leases in established major cities- even fixed- rent leases in sophisticated places like London and Paris. In less-established locations, we would use a relatively new and risk-free arrangement, now universally known as the management agreement.
>
> Japan was a special case in that strategy. When we opened our first hotel in Tokyo in 1963 we did so with our standard profit-sharing operating lease, signed with a major Japanese railroad even though there would be no chance to renew the lease if the hotel was successful. Our Japanese investors were planning their own hotel chain, and the Tokyo Hilton would be their flagship. The Japanese took our technical assistance seriously. In fact, they published a book about it- a sort of guide to hotel construction and management-and then they went on to do a superb job of building and managing hotels, possibly to the world's top standard (despite high labor costs).....
>
> In 1963, only ten years from the opening of our first European hotel in Madrid, we opened eight major hotels in eight countries, from Tokyo to Rome- all in one year. We were stretched!

Strand then described the development and maturation of the management contract.

With our competitive advantage, we fought hard to gain the best terms possible in our management agreements. Terms extended up to 50 years, management fees were 3 to 5 percent of revenue plus 10 percent of GOP. Contracts did not allow for earnings tests or cancellation clauses, let alone forecast guarantees. The idea of sharing management with owners we felt to be analogous to driving a car with two steering wheels. If a prospective owner felt that we should give him our name and he would exercise his managerial judgment on budgets and key staff, we felt we would be better off to pass on that opportunity.

In order to expand, Hilton International had to build a staff of architects, engineers, interior designers, project managers, kitchen and back-of-the-house planners. Strand said that Charles Anderson Bell was in charge of that difficult function for many years.

We paid considerable attention to food and beverage facilities and quality. Our experience was that 80 percent of all room reservations were made locally. How do locals form an impression of a hotel? From attending functions there, from the coffee shop and from the restaurants. Somebody can always make a case for closing a hotel's dining room. The savings are easy to calculate but not the loss in standing and reputation. While concepts do have to change, a full-service hotel is not full service without a credible food-and-beverage operation. There is no excuse for building a five-star hotel in a two-star location, and that fundamental mistake cannot be corrected by closing the restaurant....

The sale of Hilton International to TransWorld Airlines in 1964 for $86 million looked like a good return on the initial $800,000 investment even when compounded over 20 years. Strand believed at the time that the sale was a serious mistake for Hilton.

The acquisition turned out to be an excellent for TWA for the best of reasons: Hilton International was successful. Shortly after TWA's peak year in 1969 (one year after the Hilton acquisition), TWA suffered substantial losses that were covered by Hilton International's earnings.

Hilton International remained with TWA for 18 years, until the era of corporate raiders who made fortunes by breaking up conglomerates. In 1986, after I had retired as president and CEO, Ed Meyer was CEO and Helmut Hoermann was COO. I was still acting part-time as chairman of the board and a consultant to these two executives. By this time TWA had transformed itself into a holding company with four essentially unrelated businesses. Investor Norman Perlman took a position in the holding company and wanted to raise the value of its stock. To appease him, the directors needed to sell one of the parts, and Hilton International was the most salable. United Airlines attempted to buy it, but that deal did not close. Likewise, KLM made an offer, but that deal did not close either. Finally, United Airlines did close a deal (as Allegis), but that conglomerate was itself broken up in short order, and Hilton International was again for sale.

This time the chain was purchased by Ladbrokes, a British conglomerate whose strongest business at the time was off-track betting shops. Ladbroke also owned a chain of small- and medium-size hotels in England, which meant the firm had interest and expertise in the hotel business. The sale netted TWA more than $1 billion above its $86 million investment 18 years earlier.

In the summer of 1949, a writer named Thomas Ewing Dabney readied for publication a book-length biography of hotelier Conrad N. Hilton. The book traced the story of Hilton's rise from obscurity in New Mexico, his entry into the hotel business in Cisco, Texas, and his celebrated purchases of Chicago's Palmer House and New York's Plaza Hotel. The book, titled *The Man Who Bought the Plaza*, was finished and in the hands of printers when the publishers suddenly ordered work to halt. Title pages were destroyed, dust jackets discarded, and the author called in to revise the text. Conrad Hilton was a good subject for a biography but, as Dabney had learned, a very poor sitter for a portrait. Hastily updated, the book was released to bookstores in 1950 under a new title, *The Man Who Bought the Waldorf.*

Why had Hilton, who had already won hotel fame and earned enough money to live on comfortably for several lifetimes, decide to buy the Waldorf-Astoria? It was famous property with a lustrous history, a vast 'city within a city' with nearly unlimited revenue-producing possibilities. It was a handsome structure that could profitably be operated in conjunction with Hilton's growing chain of large hotels in other cities. All these reasons, and more, were summed up in a single phrase scrawled by the ambitious hotelier across a photograph of the Waldorf-Astoria on his desk: "The greatest of them all". Because it was the greatest, Hilton was determined to own it. On October 12, 1949, the Waldorf became a Hilton hotel. More than 59 years later, it continues to carry that designation.

Did you ever wonder about the hyphen between Waldorf and Astoria (Waldorf-Astoria). Here's how it came to be. On March 14, 1893, William Waldorf Astor opened the world's most luxurious hotel on 33rd Street and Fifth Avenue, the current site of the Empire State Building. Despite poor weather, a kitchen workers' walkout and a serious accident, the hotel opened with a fund-raising event for the St. Mary's Free Hospital for Children. George Boldt, the hotel's proprietor along with thirty-seven year old Oscar Tschirky (destined to become Oscar of the Waldorf) greeted each guest at the door. The hotel was designed by the noted architect Henry Hardenbergh who later designed the Plaza Hotel in 1907.

William Waldorf Astor had decided to demolish his great mansion at the corner of Fifth Avenue and Thirty-third street only twenty years after it was built by his father. New hotels were being built on and near Fifth Avenue: the Holland House, Brunswick, Windsor, Buckingham, Grand Union, Park Avenue and the Fifth Avenue Hotel.

The new thirteen-story Waldorf Hotel opened on March 14, 1893 with 450 guestrooms and 350 bathrooms, each of these with an outer window- a feature which apparently made a tremendous impression upon the high-grade traveling public of the nineties.

The grand opening presented the New York Symphony orchestra under the direction of Walter Damrosch playing Liszt, Bruch, Bizet, Tschaikowsky, Rossini and Wagner. No New York hotel had ever opened with such pomp and circumstance. The New York Sun wrote about the Waldorf,

> To American enterprise is due most of the movement abroad in the world today toward luxurious hotels.... In few palaces of the Old World can such costly and artistic surroundings be found. Those who came found private suites, dining-rooms, salons and bedrooms such as kings could not excel... There were more wonders than could be seen in a single evening- magnificent tapestries, paintings, frescoes, wood-carvings, marble and onyx mosaics, quaint and rich pieces of furniture, rare and costly tableware... one sees throughout the hotel a mingling of foreign and American improvements... The owner has made the hotel the natural abode of transient and houseless fashion and wealth. He has made its café the rival of Delmonico and Sherry.

George Boldt was the great leader of this wonderful new hotel. Perfection – the perfection of hotel keeping– was his religion. Boldt introduced many innovations at the Waldorf: "room service" that enabled guests to have breakfast in bed; relaxed the rule that prohibited men from smoking in the presence of women, installed an orchestra in the hotel lobby, hired Turkish waiters to serve coffee, placed plenty of ash trays at strategic locations among the potted palms.

Among the regular tenants, one of the most notable was the self-made millionaire and big plunger, John W. "Bet-a-Million" Gates who was later to become one of the backers of the Plaza Hotel. The professional services which attracted millionaires was due in large part to the suave and affable Oscar Tschirky, who rose from headwaiter to maitre d' hotel and an unofficial position as chief lieutenant to General Manager George Boldt. A famous attraction was a long corridor that ran through the Waldorf connecting two of the most popular restaurants, the Palm and the Empire rooms. It was a sparkling hall with soaring Corinthian columns, mosaic floors, and upholstered benches along the sides. Almost from the opening, the corridor was a popular promenade for ladies of fashion to display their gowns, jewels and gaudiest plumage. The society editor of the <u>New York Tribune</u> called it "Peacock Alley". It was reported that it was not unusual for twenty five thousand people to stroll the length of Peacock Alley on a single day.

In 1895, John Jacob Astor IV (a cousin of William Waldorf Astor) demolished his mother's mansion brownstone mansion on the corner of 34th Street and Fifth Avenue adjacent to the Waldorf Hotel. He built the Astoria hotel and struck a deal with his cousin William Waldorf and George Boldt to manage both hotels jointly.

The new structure was seventeen stories with "perpendicular railways" (elevators) and an indoor driveway on the thirty-fourth street side, a grand ballroom seating 1500 and a roof garden. Between them the two hotels had 1000 rooms, three floors of banquet and meeting rooms and common management. After it was named Waldorf-Astoria, New Yorkers would tell their friends, "Meet me at the Hyphen." 'Where's that?', the friends would ask. 'Between the Waldorf and the Astoria.' As a nickname for the hotel "the Hyphen" did not stick but the hybrid name Waldorf-Astoria did and now is a most valuable intangible asset for exploitation in the Waldorf-Astoria collection. For the next twenty years the Waldorf-Astoria was operated as a single hotel until George Boldt died in 1916 and the hotel was acquired in 1918 by Lucius Boomer and Senator Coleman Du Pont. Boomer was a hotelier who had been trained in Henry Flagler's Florida hotels and earned his reputation in New York's McAlpin Hotel in Herald Square just one block from the Waldorf-Astoria. The value of property in the area had grown enormously in the thirty years since the Waldorf opened. New hotels like the Plaza, Savoy, Netherland, Pierre and St. Regis reflected the inexorable uptown movement to the fifties and sixties.

The original hotel's reign lasted until 1929, when, after four decades of hosting distinguished visitors and society balls, the Waldorf-Astoria was demolished to make way for The Empire State Building. But the Waldorf-Astoria tradition did not end then; two years later, in 1931, a new Waldorf-Astoria opened at Park Avenue between 49th and 50th Streets under Lucius Boomer's direction. The Art Deco style hotel, under scaffolding for months, dazzled thousands of onlookers when it was unveiled. With 42 stories and 2,200 rooms, the building was the largest hotel in the world at the time of its opening.

The original Waldorf-Astoria, New York, NY was built in two stages on 33rd Street and Fifth Avenue on the site of the Empire State Building. It was rated as one of the finest hotels in New York until it was demolished in 1929.

On September 30, the night before the official opening, thousands of New Yorkers gathered in the great ballroom as Lucius Boomer raised his hands in a gesture of silence and a voice from far-away Washington squeaked through a radio loud-speaker. It was Herbert Hoover, the first

President of the United States to speak at the opening of a hotel. "Our hotels have become community institutions," said Hoover. "They are the central points of civic hospitality... The erection of this great structure," he continued, mindful of the awful Depression that had settled over the nation, "has been a contribution to the maintenance of employment, and an exhibition of courage and confidence to the whole nation."

Oscar of the Waldorf was on hand for the opening, his smile as broad as ever, his palm still discreetly but unmistakably upturned. Those who remembered the old Waldorf were as pleased to see the broad hallway which paralleled Park Avenue and was entered from the main foyer. Its walls were paneled with French burl walnut inlaid with ebony, its pilasters faced with French rouge marble and topped with capitals and cornices of nickel bronze. Along the walls, at intervals rested maple vitrines fronted with glass in which leading New York merchants displayed their wares. It was a handsome corridor which captured the spirit, though it did not duplicate the appearance, of the fabled promenade in the old Waldorf. But it bore the same name, Peacock Alley, and that fact was enough to warm the hearts of nostalgic guests.

Even during the bleak years of the Depression, the Waldorf-Astoria was widely acclaimed as the world's greatest hotel. Top-name entertainers appeared regularly in its Empire Room. Important balls and banquets were held in its ballroom. One of the remarkable features of the hotel was a private railroad siding beneath the building where guests in private cars could come directly to the hotel via the New York Central tracks. In a Waldorf-Astoria advertisement (Fig. 14) which is reproduced in Lucius Boomer's authoritative book *Hotel Management: Principles and Practice*, Harper & Brothers, Publishers, New York, (1938), the following words appear under a Waldorf-Astoria photograph:

> The Waldorf-Astoria is definitely something more than a hotel. For more than forty years, the great figures of the earth have chosen the Waldorf-Astoria as the one hotel compatible with their political dignity, their economic importance, or their artistic fame.

In another advertisement in Boomer's Hotel Management book (Fig. 14A) for The Towers of the Waldorf-Astoria, these words appear under a photograph of a "Living-Room of an apartment in 18th Century English.":

> The very fact that no expense was spared in creating the superb period apartments in the Towers is proof of a very large expense spared to you! You are spared a costly investment in such a home as only your private fortune could otherwise build! You are spared concern for the custody and protection of that investment! And you are spared domestic cares by a service that has for 40 years been unique! Apartments are available by the day, month or year. 50th Street just off Park Avenue, New York.

The Waldorf Towers with its own private entrance and elevator lobby on Fiftieth Street is exclusively for long-term tenants. Hundreds of notables, ranging from European kings to Indian maharajas, bedded down in its luxurious tower suites. President Hoover, after his departure from the White House, made his home in the Waldorf, as did General of the Army Douglas McArthur, the Duke and Duchess of Windsor, publishers Henry Luce and William Randolph Hearst, Jr., song writer Cole Porter, Elizabeth Taylor, Bob Hope, the Sultan of Brunei, etc. The Towers has 115 suites and 90 rooms on the 28th to 42nd floors.

A plaque in the Presidential Suite reads:

> The Waldorf-Astoria Presidential Suite.
> A few of the famous occupants
> Every President of the United States since 1931
> Queen Elizabeth II, England
> King Hussein, Jordan
> King Saud, Saudi Arabia
> General Charles de Gaulle, France
> Chairman Nikita Khrushchev, Soviet Union
> Prime Minister David Ben-Gurion, Israel
> Prime Minister Menachen Begin, Israel
> Premier Giulio Andreotel, Italy
> President Valery Giscard D'estang, France
> Emperor and Empress Hirohito, Japan

King Juan Carlos I, Spain
President Nicolai Ceausescu, Romania
King Olav V, Norway
King Faisal, Saudi Arabia

Lucius Boomer introduced such U.S. hotel business "firsts" as the six-day work week, a floor reserved exclusively for women guests, a floor with Spanish-speaking clerks and maids to cater to guests from Latin America (which might not seem a novelty in New York today, but was unheard of in the 1929's) and the employment of women as front desk receptionists and clerks. Boomer laid great stress on modern management techniques softening the harsh carrot-and-stick methods of Henry Ford and the father of scientific management, Frederick Taylor. New institutions guided this shift to a kinder, gentler form of scientific management. On June 26, 1947, Lucius Boomer was killed in an air crash while vacationing in Homar, Norway. He was sixty-seven years old.

In his autobiography, *Be My Guest*, Hilton wrote "We have no secrets, nothing up our sleeves as to how we run hotels":

> My hotel philosophy agrees with that of Boswell as expressed in his *Life of Dr. Johnson*: "There is nothing which has yet been contrived by man by which so much happiness is produced as by a good tavern or inn".
>
> First: In any system of hotels we have found that each must be an individual personality, geared to the demands of its particular city and country. To ensure this means, among other things, to select good managers, and then entrust to them the authority they need.
>
> Second: Forecasting. A manager must be able to make an accurate forecast. By the first of each month every hotel in our system has forecast the day-to-day business for that month based on reservations on hand and the experience of the same month in previous years. A good hotel manager knows exactly how many maids, bellmen, elevator operators, culinary experts and waiters he requires for each and every day of the year. If he

does not, he either wastes money by being overstaffed or provides poor service by being understaffed. Similarly with food supplies which are perishable. Except for some entirely unpredictable "act of God" condition, our actual performance and forecasts are remarkably close together.

Third: Mass Purchasing. This is a decided advantage to the system with several hotels. Certain purchasing, of course, must be done at the local level, but there are twenty-one items such as matches, china, bar soap, carpets, to mention a few, where direct purchasing in large quantities from the manufacturers results in substantial savings—and the willingness of the manufacturer to test and develop products to meet exact standards.

Fourth: "Digging for Gold." This is the term we use for the procedure that came to me in a nightmare at the old Mobley in Cisco and resulted in our making the dining room into bedrooms and cutting the main desk in half, to make room for a newsstand. It means utilization of every possible foot of space for the production of maximum income.....

Fifth: Training good men is a common requirement in any industry if it is to keep its standards and progress. In our business, there are hotel schools such as those at Cornell and Michigan State, plus on-the-job training experience.

Sixth: Sales efforts, a point which needs absolutely no explanation to the average American. It includes good advertising, promotion, publicity and the intelligent booking of parties, conventions and the like.

Seventh: Inter-hotel reservations are an advantage which grows along with the number of hotels in the system. We handle thirty-five thousand inter-hotel reservations per month whereby guests leave one Hilton hotel to book into another in a different city or country. We can, we hope, one day book our guests around the world, always under a Hilton roof.

In 1943, the Plaza was sold to Conrad Hilton for the bargain-basement price of $7.4 million after thirty-six years of continuous original ownership. Hilton made important physical changes:

- Removed the brokerage firm of E. F. Hutton from its ground-floor office (monthly rent $416) and converted it to the Oak Bar

- Converted a basement storage area (once the Grill Room) into the Rendez-vous supper club

- Mezzanine writing rooms overlooking the lobby were converted into private meeting rooms

- Vitrines were installed throughout the lobby.

- The leaded-glass dome over the Palm Court was removed.

Hilton continued on his large hotel-buying program, acquiring the Hotel New Yorker for $12.5 million in 1953 and the Shamrock Hotel, the showplace of Houston, in 1954. Also, in 1954 Hilton heard that William Zeckendorf, president of Webb & Knapp, had made a $111 million offer for the Statler Hotels chain. Hilton asked his right-hand man, Joseph Binns to keep Mrs. Alice Statler in New York City for twenty-four hours until he could get there. Hilton later reported on their meeting, "Mrs. Statler was a hotel man's wife, a fine lady and a straight-talking one. "Yes", she admitted quite openly, "I would like to see our hotels in the hands of hotel people. A great deal of my life as well as my husband's is wrapped up in those hotels". I told her honestly that I admired their hotels, their methods of operation, their fine reputation. Our idea would be to change nothing, to perpetuate what you have built up, including the name. "I would like that," she said simply."

The Nile Hilton, Cairo, Egypt was constructed by 6000 women carrying cement mix on their heads up 12 floors because there was no crane. When the hotel opened, all the waitresses had college degrees because there were not enough jobs for college-educated women in Cairo. Its 400 air conditioned rooms overlook the ancient Pyramids at Giza.

Conrad had a hard time convincing his own Board of Directors who thought that the purchase price of $111 million was too high. But, finally, on October 27, 1954 the Hilton Hotels Corporation officially acquired control of the Statler Hotel system. It consummated the greatest merger in hotel history, the largest real estate transaction the world had ever known. It brought the number of Hilton-operated hotels in the United States and abroad to twenty-eight comprising 26,600 rooms.

This action resulted in a suit by the United States Justice Department alleging violation of the Clayton Antitrust Act. In 1953, in response to the Justice Department, Hilton sold the Plaza Hotel to the Boston industrialist and hotel pioneer A.M. Sonnabend.

The son of company founder, Barron Hilton was named chairman of the board of Hilton Hotels Corporation after Conrad N. Hilton died in 1979. He started his career at the company in 1951 as an elevator operator and held numerous positions before being named president and chief executive officer in 1966, a position he held until February 1996. In his role as president and chief executive officer, Hilton was instrumental in originating the universal Carte Blanche credit card system and developing the Hilton Inns franchise program. He also led the way when Hilton Hotels Corporation became the first New York Stock Exchange company to enter the casino gaming business in 1971.

In 1996 the Hilton Hotels Corporation purchased the Bally Entertainment Corporation and in 1998 spun off the casinos into a new company, the Park Place Entertainment Corporation. In 1997, the Hilton Hotels Corporation lost the bidding for the IT&T Corporation (Sheraton) and in 1999 for Wyndham International, Inc. (formerly Patriot American). However, in September 1999, Hilton acquired the Promus Hotel Corporation for $3.1 billion, creating one of the largest hotel companies in the world. The deal combined Hilton's 275 luxury hotels in North America with Promus's Doubletree Hotels, Embassy Suites and Hampton Inns. This critical acquisition brought Hilton to 1,900 hotels with approximately 350,000 rooms in 50 countries.

In 2006, the Hilton Hotels Corporation finally acquired Hilton International reuniting the two arms of the Hilton brand for the first time since 1964. This $5.7 billion deal rectified the poor judgment of Conrad Hilton when he sold Hilton International to TransWorld Airlines 42 years earlier. During those years, Hilton was precluded from expanding into regions outside North America. "This is one of the most noteworthy days in the history of our company, as Hilton is once again a global hotel company for the first time in over 40 years," said Stephen F. Bollenbach, the brilliant co-chairman and chief executive officer of Hilton Hotels Corporation. "As the world's largest and most geographically diverse hotel company with the industry's most talented and dedicated team members, we look forward to an exciting future." The challenge for the future is to launch Hilton's mid-market brands: Hilton Garden Inn, Hampton Inn, Doubletree, Embassy Suites and Homewood Suites all over the world. In addition, Hilton will continue its focus on the luxury segment by expanding the Waldorf=Astoria Collection and Conrad Hotels internationally.

On July 3, 2007, Hilton Hotels Corporation announced that it has entered into a definitive acquisition agreement with The Blackstone

Group's real estate and corporate private equity funds in an all-cash transaction valued at approximately $26 billion. Under the terms of the agreement, Blackstone acquired all the outstanding common stock of Hilton for $47.50 per share which represented a premium of 40% over the closing stock price.

Blackstone currently owns more than 100,000 hotel rooms in the U.S. and Europe, ranging from limited service properties such as La Quinta Inns and Suites to LXR Luxury Resorts and Hotels. The LXR collection includes such upscale properties as The Boulders Resort and Spa (Arizona), The El Conquistador Resort (Puerto Rico), The Boca Raton Resort (Florida), The Golden Door Spa (San Diego), and The London NYC (New York). Blackstone's holdings seem to complement Hilton's unparalleled family of brands, which include Hilton, Conrad Hotels & Resorts, Doubletree, Embassy Suites, Hampton Inn, Hilton Garden Inn, Hilton Grand Vacations, Homewood Suites by Hilton, and The Waldorf-Astoria Collection.

Stephen F. Bollenbach said: "Our policy has always been to maximize shareholder value. Our Board of Directors concluded that this transaction provides compelling value for our shareholders with a significant premium. We are delighted that a company with the resources and reputation of Blackstone fully appreciates the value inherent in our global presence, strong brands, industry leading marketing and technology programs, and unique portfolio of hotel properties." It remains to be seen whether Blackstone will serve as a worthy owner of the Hilton legacy.

Curt Strand told me in 2008, that Conrad Hilton said to him that he made three major mistakes in his life:

1) the sale of Hilton International in 1964

2) the failure to acquire the Plaza Hotel in New York permanently

3) marrying Zsa Zsa Gabor

SOURCE MATERIALS

Whitney Bolton, *The Silver Spade: The Conrad Hilton Story*, Farrar Strauss and Young, New York, 1954

Eve Brown, *The Plaza*: 1907-1967, Duell, Sloan and Pearce, New York, 1967.

Albert Stevens Crockett, *Peacocks on Parade*, Sears Publishing Company, Inc. New York, 1931

Thomas Ewing Dabney, *The Man Who Bought The Waldorf: The Life of Conrad N. Hilton*, Duell, Sloan and Pearce, New York, 1950

Albin Pasteur Dearing, *The Elegant Inn: The Waldorf-Astoria Hotel*, 1893-1929, Lyle Stuart Inc. Secaucus, 1986.

Curtis Gathje, *At the Plaza: An Illustrated History of the World's Most Famous Hotel*, St. Martin's Press, New York, 2000.

Conrad Hilton, *Be My Guest*, Prentice-Hall, Englewood Cliffs, 1957

Edward Hungerford, *The Story of the Waldorf-Astoria,* G.P. Putnam's Sons, New York, 1925.

Sonny Kleinfield, *The Hotel: A Week in the Life of the Plaza*, Simon and Schuster, 1989.

James Remington McCarthy, *Peacock Alley*, Harper & Brothers, New York, 1931.

Howard Dearing Johnson (1896-1972):

HOST OF THE HIGHWAY AND THE ORANGE ROOF

Ice cream, fried clams and hot dogs were the staples of his menu, and the orange roof and a weather vane the signature fixtures of his stores. But Howard Dearing Johnson probably was best known for being one of the first to introduce the restaurant industry to the world of franchising. Before franchising became the target of franchisee/franchisor disputes, Johnson used the business tool for what it was intended – a uniform system of operations and procedures that provided rapid expansion opportunities. "He was the first person to realize there was very limited food service on the U.S. highways," said his son, Howard B. Johnson. "He also realized early on you should develop a product line that was consistent so people would trust it."

And that is exactly what Johnson did. From a simple soda- fountain menu, he built his reputation on manufacturing and selling high-quality ice cream. Johnson spent 15 years with his father's cigar company and eventually became one of the company's top salesman, reportedly earning $25,000 in his first year. Following his father's death, Johnson developed a new line of cigars that were not accepted in the marketplace because cigarettes were becoming more popular. The failed product created a sizable debt and a loss of pride for Johnson, who closed the business and went to work in a small drugstore in Wollaston, Massachusetts.

But shortly after Johnson began to work there, the proprietor died and the surviving son asked Johnson to take over the shop. In 1925, with a $2,000 loan, Johnson set out to pay off his $42,000 debt as the owner of the Howard D. Johnson Co. "patent medicines and toilet articles" shop. It sold patent and over-the-counter medications but Johnson quickly noticed that the marble soda fountain was the busiest part of the drugstore. It was said that his "secret formula" for ice cream was based on his mother's recipe with twice the normal butterfat and all natural ingredients. The super-premium ice cream was an immediate sensation and led Johnson to open a beachfront ice cream stand where he sold $60,000 worth of ice cream cones in the first year at 5¢ per cone. By 1928, he had created 28 flavors which became his trademark. He advertised it as "New England's Best Ice Cream" which reinforced his early guiding business principle, "Quality Sells."

Over the next few years, Johnson did for the hot dog what he had done for the ice cream cone. Instead of the normal greasy hot dog on a stale bun, Johnson clipped the frankfurters at both ends, notched them lengthwise and grilled them in pure creamery butter. He used only the highest quality meats, relish and lightly toasted, buttered fresh rolls. The results were amazing: the hot dog was elevated to a gourmet food status and became a public favorite all over the country.

Johnson's success was noticed by some local bankers who lent him the funds to open a restaurant in Quincy, Massachusetts in a ten-story Art Deco building. This first Howard Johnson restaurant featured chicken pot pie, baked beans, fried clams and, of course, those delicious hot dogs and the now- famous Howard Johnson ice cream- all 28 flavors. In 1929, unexpected circumstances boosted the restaurant's popularity. Boston's Mayor Nichols banned an upcoming production of Eugene O'Neill's "Strange Interlude". Rather than dispute the mayor, the Theatre Guild moved the production to a theatre in Quincy which was close to the Howard Johnson restaurant. The five-hour play was presented in two parts with a dinner break in between. Hundreds of influential Bostonians ate in the Howard Johnson restaurant for the first time. Soon thereafter the stock market crashed and Johnson could not borrow any construction money. It was the monetary crisis that led Johnson to utilize a remarkable new idea called franchising. In 1935 Johnson convinced a business acquaintance to open a Howard Johnson restaurant in Orleans on Cape Cod. Johnson's organization designed the restaurant, set the service standards, created the menu and provided the ice cream and specialty food items. Franchising was not original with Johnson. A&W Root Beer, a California company, sold their first franchise to J. Willard Marriott in 1925 when he founded Hot Shoppes. By the end of 1936, there were 39 franchised Howard Johnson restaurants and 107 by the end of 1939. By the time World War II started in 1941, Howard Johnson directed a franchise network of more than 10,000 employees with 170 restaurants, many of which served one and a half million people a year. It was Johnson's foresight on quality and consistency, unique architectural design, curbside marketing, brand awareness and selection of high-traffic locations that expanded the company from a single ice-cream shop to a full-service national chain.

All were operated according to the "Howard Johnson Bible"- a set of quality standards that left nothing to chance. Johnson himself wrote the manuals on how to operate, how to handle customers courteously and how waitresses should dress ("Howard Johnson Waitresses- Your Appearance from Head to Toe"). Johnson planned menus, recipes, operating methods, regimens for cleanliness and rules of courtesy. He decreed that customers must always find a friendly and welcome experience when they visited Howard Johnson's.

World War II brought gas rationing, food stamps and a sharp reduction in automobile travel. Johnson's restaurants were particularly hard hit. By 1944, only twelve remained in business. The Johnson company survived by preparing and serving commissary food to shipyards, the military and war factory workers. Johnson's survival was helped because his pre-war production of ice cream gave him large wartime quotas of sugar and cream. Those quotas were valuable since sugar and cream were strictly rationed.

The post-World War II period was characterized by a huge burst of economic activity stimulated by the GI Bill of Rights, pent-up demand for new housing, availability of cheap gasoline, new automobiles, creation of suburbia and improvement of state and interstate highways. By 1947, 200 new Howard Johnson restaurants were opened throughout the Southeast and Midwest. By 1954, aided by company-owned turnpike restaurants, there were 400 Howard Johnson's in 32 states. In the 1950's and 60's , the company bought out those franchisees who were not maintaining Howard Johnson standards.

It would be the roadside restaurant, however, that would propel Johnson to fame and fortune. Johnson seemed to have a keen eye for what Americans like, and was able to combine elements of various styles of roadside dining into one package that would be appealing to the greatest number of people.

From the early days of motoring, establishments sprouted along the roadways to feed travelers, but each of these had some drawback that hindered their growth. There were tea rooms, whose homey atmosphere appealed to women, but in this era it was usually men who were driving the car. There were diners, which men liked, but women were not likely to want to sit on a counter stool in the days before booth service was common. Finally, there were hot dogs stands and other casual food stops, often operating out of shacks or other unsavory looking buildings, where the quality of the food was open to question.

For his creation, Johnson borrowed a building type that was well-known and loved throughout New England; the large Colonial home. In the early years, there were some variation in the size and detailing of the buildings, partly because many of them were built by franchisees. As the 1930s came to a close, however, the style became refined and more uniform: a Colonial building sided in clapboards painted white, multi-paned windows, three dormers, and a cupola with a clock mounted on the front. This handsome style fit well in the New England towns where Johnson opened his restaurants, but Johnson added a twist of his own; a brilliant orange roof, guaranteed to catch the eye of the passing motorist. The cupola was also topped off with a weathervane featuring an outline of Simple Simon and the Pieman, a trademark developed for Howard Johnson's by artist John Alcott.

As the company entered the 1960s, the company had a successful formula in place, and there were plenty of new interstate highways being built providing prime locations for Howard Johnson's Restaurants and Motor Lodges for years to come. In the mid 1960s, Howard Johnson's was at the top of its game. In 1965, the company's sales exceeded that of McDonalds, Burger King, and Kentucky Fried Chicken combined. By 1965, the Howard Johnson name was to be found on 770 restaurants and 265 motor hotels.

Here's the combination of the Howard Johnson's restaurant and motor lodge which were advertised as "nestling together at strategic locations on all major highways where you may expect the utmost in cleanliness, hospitality, service and comfort."

Meanwhile, motel operators recognized the extraordinary benefit of locating next door to a Howard Johnson restaurant. They copied the architectural features of white clapboards and roof cupolas. The success of these motor inns ultimately caused the Johnson company to get into the lodging business. It was a natural extension of the Johnson reputation along the highways of America. The first Howard Johnson Motor Lodge was opened in 1954 in Savannah, Georgia. Meanwhile, new toll roads and highways opened in Pennsylvania, New Jersey, New York, Connecticut, Massachusetts and Indiana. Many of them featured service plazas with Howard Johnson restaurants.

In 1957, President Dwight D. Eisenhower instituted the system of interstate highways which, in turn, triggered the greatest road and home building boom in the history of the United States. The federal legislation set very specific standards, one of which prohibited service plazas on the new highways. Not to be thwarted, the Johnson company acquired sites near the exit ramps with land enough to include a Howard Johnson Motor Lodge as well as a restaurant.

In the fifties, Johnson pioneered convenience frozen foods. Quietly and without publicity, he built commissaries in Boston and Miami where many of the Howard Johnson menu items were produced and frozen on a production line basis. Huge refrigerated trucks left the Miami commissary carrying frozen turkey pies and other pre-proportioned and pre-cooked foods as far south as Texas and as far north as North Carolina. At the time frozen foods were considered by many to be inferior to freshly prepared ones. On the cutting edge of technology, Johnson went quietly about distributing his frozen foods while others were debating the merits, the economics and feasibility of serving frozen meals. Incredibly, the most successful restaurant chain in the world froze and reconstituted food years before the idea of the frozen entrée was broadly accepted. The Howard Johnson company pioneered large-scale commissary freezing which permitted impressive economies in restaurant labor. As early as 1953, Howard Johnson revolutionized restaurant kitchen operations by restricting food preparation to griddling, frying and baking. No intricate recipes were needed for preparing food. Instead of paying for an expensive chef on site, only minimum wages were paid for kitchen preparation staff. If a "food warmer" decided to leave, he could easily be replaced.

The Company continually sought to simplify equipment, standardize preparation methods and control portions. When Clyde Weithe put together a continuous conveyor belt dish machine in his garage in Adams, Massachusetts, he took it to the Howard Johnson Company. It was not long before all new Howard Johnson restaurants were installing the Adamation machine. One person could operate the machine both loading and unloading. Waitresses could rack soiled ware in the racks from the dining room. A teenager could operate the machine, keep the restrooms clean and, if necessary, fill in on the food preparation station. In the New England Division, all of the coffee making machines were leased from one company who also contracted to maintain them. The Howard Johnson menu was aimed directly at the American middle class traveling public. No frills, just solid American food. The food was served in comparative luxury with décor which was contemporary in the fountain area, carpeted and chandeliered in the table service area.

What kind of a manager was Howard Johnson? He able to accomplish so much because, as Mr. Johnson himself said, his business was his life and his only hobby. Whether he was at a party or a family gathering he ended up talking business. His major method of motivation was to consistently urge his employees to greater effort. At any time, at any place, Johnson might be found driving up to a restaurant or motor lodge, observing it from a distance, then inspecting it closely inside. He missed nothing, not the hand print on the front door, the discarded newspaper in the parking lot or the stained uniform on the waitresses. Johnson was instantly and loudly critical of these shortcomings.

The Howard Johnson Company developmental program was not a favorite for young interns of hotel schools, even less for University business school graduates. The only successful employees were those followed the strict Johnson guidelines with energy, persistence and without attention to the number of hours worked. Therefore, few college graduates were happy in the Howard Johnson organization. There was practically no home office or any need for staff personnel. Each restaurant and lodge manager was his own personnel manager who followed the ideas and programs set forth by Mr. Johnson and his few close associates.

Restaurant managers could not be distinguished from restaurant workers. They wore the same little hat and white coat as the fountain personnel and could be found dishing up ice cream, unloading supplies or operating the cash register. The pressure was forever on to cut labor cost. The working manager was one way to achieve a lower labor cost. Bonuses were paid on the basis of labor and food cost, little else. Managers were expected to work until the job was done, six- and seven-day work weeks were commonplace.

Salaries for Howard Johnson store managers weren't particularly good as compared with salaries paid unit managers of other chains. Supervisors who had responsibility for several stores were expected to step in and relieve unit managers whenever necessary. Most of the higher echelon unabashedly stood in some fear of Mr. Johnson while giving him grudging respect.

In the 50's the Company had the Northern and Southern Division. Howard Cummings, a soft spoken genteel relative of Mr. Johnson by marriage, headed the Southern Division while Victor Nelson, executive vice president, operating out of Boston led the Northern Division. All executives knew that, regardless of rank or salary, they could expect to hear from Mr. Johnson by telephone and frequently. When abroad, Mr. Johnson called his executives daily to check on operations, costs and new developments.

Johnson continually standardized food service to a greater extent than had ever had been done before on large scale. Ellsworth M. Statler standardized the food services of Statler Hotels but Johnson produced commissary-prepared food, a method of reheating frozen food and of serving it which was standardized in all Howard Johnson restaurants. In about 1955, a hotel student at the Florida State University did a study which showed that the average ice cream cone being served in Florida Howard Johnson restaurants costs the company 88¢. The fact that they were being sold for 10¢ meant that the 10¢ cone was a loss leader. Cone prices were raised shortly thereafter and the dippers used were of a size which made it difficult to serve a larger-than-called-for portion. The number of seats in a Howard Johnson restaurant varied as new stores were built. But gradually there evolved a standard building with standard seating and equipment. The design and operation became more and more standardized so that each Howard Johnson store might have rolled off an assembly line. Every year between 1961 and 1979 annual sales increased. During that period, the Johnson family sold nearly two million shares of stock worth an estimated $125 million.

The Howard Johnson Motor Lodges were a sharp improvement in quality over the many poorly maintained motels on the highways. They featured modern facilities with large guestrooms, fresh linens, a bathtub and shower, air conditioning and television. Each motor lodge had an orange roof and an adjoining Howard Johnson restaurant. Although Howard Johnson kept expanding to more than 1000 restaurants and 500 motor lodges in 42 states and Canada by 1975, the original Johnson concept was coming to an end. Over 85% of the company's revenues depended on automobile travel. The oil embargo and gasoline shortage of 1974 reduced the number of automobiles on the road drastically.

In 1959, Howard Johnson passed the chief executive reins to his son, 26 year-old Howard Brennan Johnson, a graduate of Andover and Yale who said, "I knew from the age of five that I wanted to join the company. It was all we talked about at home and my father was the kind of person you almost couldn't let down." Howard Johnson, Sr. continued to serve as chairman and treasurer but paid more attention to his art collection and his sixty-foot yacht. When Howard Johnson died in 1972 at 76 years of age, his name was the best-known brand on Americas highways.

The younger Howard Johnson assumed control of a company that had become large in a relatively short time, and the field supervision was weak and inadequate. In the early days, Howard Johnson, Sr. would often pay surprise visits to his restaurants to make sure his standards were being kept, but the chain had grown so large that this was no longer possible. Also, most Howard Johnson's restaurants drew their customers off the highway rather than local repeat business, so this allowed some of the less scrupulous managers to let the standards slip. Unfortunately, regional management and oversight were not implemented. But, as more and more travelers experienced mediocre meals in deteriorating surroundings served by indifferent help, this ultimately hurt the reputation of the Howard Johnson name.

Young Johnson missed the fast food phenomenon that was sweeping the country. The company assumed that its traditional Howard Johnson restaurants would continue to have exclusive control of the highways. But McDonald and others began to win contracts and increase roadside locations. Even the Marriott Corporation whose Hot Shoppes competed with Howard Johnson's, entered the fast food segment with its Roy Rogers chain.

As more of the Interstate Highways system neared completion and the nation became saturated with orange roofs, the company looked to other restaurant concepts for continued growth, tacitly admitting that maybe the Howard Johnson's restaurant was not all things to all people. Red Coach Grill, an upscale steakhouse similar to the Steak and Ale chain, was often located next to a Howard Johnson's Motor Lodge to tap business travelers and their expense accounts, but ultimately the concept did little for the company. More successful was the Ground

Round, a casual restaurant chain that survives today under separate ownership.

One restaurant segment that saw phenomenal growth in the 1960s went little noticed by the company: fast food. The company assumed that the traditional Howard Johnson's Restaurant would remain the standard in roadside dining even as McDonald's and their imitators added locations at a rapid pace. Even traditional rival Marriott Corporation, whose Hot Shoppes restaurants competed with Howard Johnson's in some places, entered the fast food segment with its Roy Rogers chain.

At the same time, new competition delivered a one-two punch that hit the existing restaurant and lodging business, and it nearly was a knockout blow. America had become a nation in a hurry, and fast food restaurants met the new demand for a good, quick meal at a good, low price. Suddenly everyone was singing. "You Deserve a Break Today" and "Have It Your Way at Burger King." Howard Johnson seemed like yesterday's news. Changing times overtook the hospitality business as well. Somehow the spanking new Holiday Inn, Ramada Inn and Marriott hotels that were springing up everywhere made those once-modern Howard Johnson's Motor Lodges look not so modern anymore.

In 1980, Howard Johnson's was sold to the Imperial Group, a British concern. Imperial continued to operate the still-large chain of restaurants and hotels with few changes. But, with the Interstate Highway System largely complete, the opening of new Howard Johnson's restaurants all but stopped. In fact, many franchised HoJo's sought greater fortunes in converting to the company's newer Ground Round casual restaurant concept, or by painting over the orange roof and going independent.

Howard Johnson's was no longer alone on the commercial strips at highway interchanges, and appeared to be slowly losing the battle for traveler's road food dollars. However, on the older toll highways that preceded the Interstates, it seemed as though things hadn't changed since the 1950s. Howard Johnson's enjoyed exclusive long-term contracts to operate the restaurants on many of these highways, and the traditional HoJo's with counter and booth service still ruled the toll road, although some locations had cafeteria lines for quicker service. This, too, was about to change.

The original 1940 contract that had granted Howard Johnson's the exclusive right to operate restaurants on the Pennsylvania Turnpike had come up for renewal. The Turnpike Commission used this opportunity to bring fast food chains to the Turnpike on a trial basis, and they were an immediate success. Seeing the handwriting on the wall, Howard Johnson's secured the rights to Burger King on toll highways and former HoJo locations on roads such as the New York Thruway and Massachusetts Turnpike became Burger Kings.

In the mid 1980s, the Howard Johnson's logo was redesigned, tossing aside the distinctive Howard Johnson's lettering for simple block letters proclaiming "HOWARD JOHNSON." The apostrophe-S was inexplicably deleted. But the biggest change of all came shortly afterward in 1985, when the Imperial Group sold the assets of the Howard Johnson Company, except for the Ground Round chain, to the Marriott Corporation.

Unlike the Imperial Group, Marriott had little interest in maintaining Howard Johnson's the way it was. The Howard Johnson's Motor Lodges did not fit Marriott's more upscale image in the lodging business, so they were sold to Prime Motor Inns. The lodging chain kept the Howard Johnson name, and continues today as a unit of Wyndham Worldwide. A new logo was unveiled in 1997, keeping familiar blue and orange colors but putting the Howard Johnson name in script-like lettering. Most interestingly, the top of a dormer peeks out above the name, a subtle nod to the chain's early three-dormer restaurant style. Possibly the portion of Howard Johnson's of most interest to Marriott was their toll road food service operations. Marriott was already a big player in this field, and folding the Howard Johnson's operations into their own created an industry giant. Travel Plaza by Marriott (later Host Marriott) operated some locations under the Howard Johnson's name for a while, but eventually all were remodeled and by the 1990s the Howard Johnson's name had disappeared from toll highways. The Howard Johnson's acquisition also enabled Marriott to add Burger King to a growing stable of brands it operated on toll roads, including Big Boy, Roy Rogers, and Sbarro.

Marriott had similar intentions for the remaining Howard Johnson's restaurants, wanting to convert them to Big Boy rather than continue the Howard Johnson's brand. This plan met with resistance from many Howard Johnson's franchisees, who had built their reputation on HoJo's (and likely did not want to incur the remodeling costs of switching to another restaurant brand.) The franchisees formed a new company, Franchise Associates, and successfully acquired from Marriott the rights to the Howard Johnson's restaurant business, including the trademarks, recipes, and rights to sell Howard Johnson's food products, such as ice cream and macaroni and cheese.

Franchise Associates brought the old familiar logo out of retirement to represent their organization: Simple Simon and the Pieman, which had been around since the 1930s but retired in the 1970s. And at the restaurants themselves, there were hopeful signs that things were moving in the right direction. As restaurants came up for repainting, many locations ditched the dreadful tan and brown "environmental" colors imposed in the 1970s and went back to the original white and turquoise trim. Inside, nostalgia was the drawing card: the menu covers featured images from HoJo's glorious past such as the 1939 World's Fair "World's Largest Restaurant," and ice cream was promoted with signs proclaiming, "Tastes as good as you remember!"

Amid the hopeful signs were signs of trouble, though. Franchise Associates seemingly did little to actively promote the Howard Johnson's brand or add new locations while the restaurant business became increasingly competitive. Meanwhile, the existing Howard Johnson's restaurants were aging, and sometimes not very gracefully. If somebody remodeled a Howard Johnson's, chances are it was to convert it to a Denny's or some other restaurant brand. Others simply closed and were demolished or converted to non-restaurant uses.

In 1990, the Howard Johnson name and lodging system were sold to HJ Acquisition Corp., later to become known as Howard Johnson International, Inc. This new company was a subsidiary of Hospitality Franchise Systems Inc., or "HFS". After years of turmoil, it was now time to find business and marketing focus for this grand old brand name. HFS (which merged to become Cendant in 1997) quickly made it clear that from now on Howard Johnson would again be positioned as a mid-price hotel chain catering to family and business travelers. Fried clams and ice cream represented the past. And that went for the orange roofs as well. Bigger and better hotels were the future for Howard Johnson International.

Instead of rushing to add new properties and new concepts, the new owners sought a sharper focus for Howard Johnson. A plan to upgrade all Howard Johnson hotel properties was put in place, and a strict quality rating system was established.

Gradually, Howard Johnson was moving down the road to recovery. But by 1997 it was clear that the brand still had a long way to go. And competition in the mid-price hospitality world was becoming fiercer than ever. That is when the management decided to take dramatic bold steps to make Howard Johnson more relevant for today's family and business travelers and to make it a major international travel brand. The first step was a research study to determine the current strengths of the Howard Johnson brand, to find out how people really felt about Howard Johnson, and to assess the qualities that set Howard Johnson apart from other travel brands.

It was this study that revealed the hidden magic in the Howard Johnson brand name. The brand might have briefly lost its way, but it had not lost its soul. It was there, deep down, perhaps ignored for too many years by too many owners. Howard Johnson represented solid American values. The very same values that built the brand back in the thirties taking care of families; solid quality, clean, comfortable surroundings; good, honest value, a name travelers could trust- were the values that American consumers echoed 75 years later. Remarkably, in spite of all the changes and all the disruptions, the underlying strengths of Howard Johnson, the very soul of Howard Johnson had not changed. Howard Johnson, it turned out had always stood for a lot more than an orange roof.

After reviewing the findings, management decided to rebuild the Howard Johnson brand based on those solid values- and to do so on a global scale. A new marketing and advertising initiative was launched under a theme that clearly expressed the solid values concept: "Howard Johnson Makes You Feel at Home."

On April 28, 2005, in the <u>New York Times</u>, the famous chef Jacques Pepin wrote the following poignant recollection:

> "When word spread that the last Howard Johnson's restaurant in New York City in Times Square would probably close, there was something of an uproar. Though plans are uncertain, brokers say it is likely that a big retail chain will replace it. The idea that this icon of American dining will disappear from the city landscape made me particularly sad, since it was at Howard Johnson's that I completed my most valuable apprenticeship."

Pepin reports that he had only been in America eight months when he started working at Howard Johnson's. He moved there from Le Pavillon, the temple of French haute cuisine, where he had been working since his arrival in the United States in 1939. Howard Johnson, who often ate at Le Pavillon, hired him and his fellow chef, Pierre Franey.

> "It was Mr. Johnson's contention that I should learn about the Howard Johnson Company from the ground up. I worked a few months as a line cook at one of the largest and busiest Howard Johnson's restaurants at the time, on Queens Boulevard in Rego Park. I flipped burgers, cooked hot dogs and learned about the specialties of the house, among them tender fried clams made from the tongues of enormous sea clams whose bodies were used as the base for the restaurants' famous clam chowder. Other specialties I became familiar with included macaroni and cheese, hash browns, ice cream sundaes, banana splits, and certainly, apple pies."

Pepin worked for Howard Johnson for more than nine years mostly in the Queens Village commissary where he and Franey learned how to mass produce Howard Johnson specialties such as beef stew, scallops in mushroom sauce, beef burgundy, clam croquettes, etc. Pepin recalled making fresh stock in large batches requiring 3000 pounds of veal bones, carving 1000 turkeys and making 10 tons of frankfurters. Apparently,

Howard Johnson would visit the test kitchen to ask questions and make suggestions.

Pepin recalled,

> "Albert Kamin, the famous Swiss pastry chef, soon joined us, working to set up a pastry department that produced 10 tons of Danish pastries a day for the hundreds of restaurants in the chain and thousands and thousands of apple, cherry, blueberry and pumpkin pies each day. This was my first exposure to mass production. I developed products for the Red Coach Grill, which was the Cadillac of the Howard Johnson chain, as well as the Ground Round, and the grocery division of the company, which supplied supermarkets, schools and other institutions."

Today there appears to be a new momentum behind Howard Johnson. Revenues are on the rise and new hotels are joining at the fastest rate ever in countries all over the world. To sustain this momentum, management has initiated a series of specific programs to raise the standards for performance, quality and growth. Together, these programs represent an extensive effort to assure the highest quality standards, franchisee profitability and growth of the brand.

At a recent Howard Johnson International Conference, Rui Barros, Howard Johnson senior vice president, told attendees that the brand is helping to create a more enjoyable guest stay by improving the sleep and shower experience. The new brand standards were developed in conjunction with the Howard Johnson strategic plan, which also focuses on system growth, property performance, leveraging the scale of Wyndham Hotel Group and enhancing the brand's marketing campaign. To generate interest in the chain and grow the system, the brand team will work closely with the franchise sales team to promote Howard Johnson's successes and meet regularly with developers, lenders and brokers.

This year, the brand introduced a new awards program, Heroes of Hospitality, designed to recognize Howard Johnson property owners and their staffs. "The new program builds upon the legacy of good customer service and solid value started by our brand founder, Howard Dearing Johnson, more than 80 years ago," said Barros. "The Heroes of Hospitality program celebrates our greatest assets: our innkeepers and their teams."

The Howard Johnson story began 75 years ago. It has been a long road with more detours than the founder and namesake could ever have envisioned. Few brands have seen more change over the years than Howard Johnson. But that only serves to underscore the extraordinary strength of this great brand name. It's a name that stands for honest quality and solid value.

Throughout the 1940s, '50s and '60s, Howard Johnson's was an icon of popular culture. The orange-roofed buildings were as identifiable as McDonald's arches today, the slogan "28 flavors" more familiar than Baskin-Robbins' later 31. Howard Johnson's typified the best features of the national, uniform, standardized chain restaurant. A family on a trip looking for a place to eat in an unfamiliar area could always find a Howard Johnson's.

To the founder's credit, Howard Johnson's lived up to its longtime slogans, "Host of the Highways" and "Landmark for Hungry Americans." In fact, its domination for turnpike locations and service plazas was so complete that people began to think of its as a place where they ate while on road trips because they had to, not a place that they went to at home because they wanted to. The nickname "HoJo," eventually officially adopted by the company, was as familiar as it was affectionate.

In 2007, the Howard Johnson name was on nearly 500 hotels in 14 countries and more than 15 million people visited Howard Johnson Hotels.

Today, Howard Johnson International currently franchises hotels in the United States, Argentina, Canada, China, Colombia, Curacao, Dominican Republic, Ecuador, Guatemala, Israel, Malta, Mexico, the United Arab Emirates, the United Kingdom and Venezuela.

SOURCE MATERIALS

Howard Johnson's, Wikipedia 2007

Donald E. Lundberg, *The Hotel and Restaurant Business,* Institutions/ Volume Feeding Magazine, Chicago, 1971.

Making People Feel At Home For 75 Years: Howard Johnson Company booklet

The New York Times, April 28, 2005

J. Willard Marriott (1900-1985):

From Hot Shoppes to the Worldwide Marriott Hotel Company

One of the best descriptions of J. Willard Marriott was written by Mark Evans Austad, famous Washington radio commentator, who called Marriott, a "twentieth century Horatio Alger":

> Evidencing that he is also very human, Bill is a bundle of contradictions- both gentle and tough; devoutly religious, and yet fun-loving; demanding yet tolerant; half pessimistic, half optimistic; penurious, yet philanthropic. All he wants of family, employees and friends is perfection. Though he is a worrier, he knows no fear. He has no use of laziness, dirtiness, dishonesty, social climbing or wasting time.

John Willard Marriott was born to Ellen Morris and Hyrum Willard Marriott at Marriott Settlement, Utah on September 17, 1900. He was the first son and second of eight children, all of whom pitched in to raise sugar beets and sheep on the family's small farmstead. Marriott remembered many years later, "My father always gave me the responsibility of a man. He would tell me what he wanted me to do, but he never told me much about how to do it and he never sent anyone along with me to show me how. It was up to me to find out for myself."

Hyrum's father, John Marriott, convert to Mormonism and founder of the Marriott Settlement, came to Utah in 1854 with the second wave of Mormons to flee the persecutions in Ohio, Illinois and Missouri. Hyrum was born on December 6, 1863, twin brother to Esther Amelia, the only twins fathered by John who had 29 other children. J. Willard was one of 135 grandchildren.

At the age of 13, Bill Marriott became aware of several acres of unused land and asked his father if he could farm them. As the story came down through the family, Will answered, "You sure can, but whatever you make from them, I'll take half." Bill said, "you can have it all." Bill borrowed money from Will to buy lettuce plants and several cases of soda pop. He enlisted his younger siblings to help plow the land, plant the seeds, harvest and wash the crop. Six weeks later Bill sold the lettuce and presented a check for $2000 to his Dad and Mom.

The next year, Hyrum sent Bill to San Francisco by rail to sell a herd of 3000 sheep. After arriving and delivering the sheep, Bill stayed for a week in a hotel on Market Street opposite the new City Hall which was under construction. This visit, his first out of Utah, was an eye-opener for young Bill, especially the big Panama-Pacific Exposition and its Palace of Fine Arts, exhibit pavillions, formal sunken gardens, the Buddhist Temple, sideshow tents, the Turkish mosque, barkers and hawkers.

When he was 18 years old, he went to New England to serve a mission for the Church of Jesus Christ of Latter-Day Saints. Bill attended early morning study sessions in Brooklyn and street-corner gospel meetings in Manhattan. After three weeks, he headed by train to Burlington, Vermont where he preached to taciturn Vermonters with little success. Bill spent the next year in Connecticut ringing doorbells, getting rebuffed, explaining Mormon doctrine, preaching on street corners, studying the life of Joseph Smith and the history of the Church, the Bible and the Book of Mormon.

After completing his mission in New York, he stopped in Washington, D.C. on his 21st birthday. Bill later reported that as he watched the tourists in sultry Washington, he couldn't get over the sight of a pushcart peddler selling so much lemonade, soda pop and ice cream that he'd be sold out as quickly as he stocked up with a new supply.

When Bill returned home during the post-World War I economy, he discovered that the bottom had fallen out of the livestock market.

His father was $50,000 in debt to the Ogden State Bank and was unlikely to become solvent. Bill realized that he couldn't compete in the marketplace without a college education. He was twenty-one years old and didn't have a high school diploma. He enrolled in Weber Junior College in Ogden, Utah which offered four years of high school and two years of college. Bill graduated in June 1922 just a few months before his 23rd birthday.

During his next three summers, Bill sold warm woolen goods, spun from the fleece of Utah and Nevada sheep in the mills of Utah to the lumber camps in the Sierra Nevada mountains north of Lake Tahoe. During these years, Bill attended the University of Utah living at the Phi Delta Theta house, the fraternity that he joined in his junior year. He worked part-time for the White House Caterers run by his friend, Franklin Richards, who had served in the Eastern States Mission with Bill and later became head of the Federal Housing Administration in 1935. Marriott graduated from the University in 1926 when he was twenty-five years old and then spent the following year teaching theology and English at Weber College where he became secretary and treasurer.

While working at Weber College, Marriott hatched plans for starting a business of his own in Washington, D.C. Bill remembered the pushcart peddler selling lemonade, ice cream and soda pop and thought he could do the same with A&W (Allen and Wright) Root Beer. He acquired the A&W franchise for Washington, D.C., and headed east in the spring of 1927. Marriott partnered with Hugh Colton, Congressman Don B. Colton's brother, to buy equipment and rent space for their tiny operation. The A&W franchise was one of the first ever sold (and possibly the first ever). For $2000, Allen gave Marriott and Colton the exclusive right to sell A&W root beer in a given location. The purchaser agreed to buy all the root beer concentrate, cooling equipment and other supplies from Allen and to sell nothing but A&W root beer. On May 20, 1927, the duo opened their nine-stool root beer stand at 3128 14th Street, NW in Washington, D.C.

The root beer formula had been put together by Roy Allen of Sacramento. In contained the unlikely ingredients of wintergreen leaves, wild cherry bark, dandelion root, althea root, anise seed, sarsaparilla root, angelica root, sassafras root and birch bark. The A&W store in Salt Lake City store sold 5,000 mugs of root beer every day during the summer months.

Bill and Hugh looked for "drive-up" locations but, because of costs, settled on two small walk-in stores in Washington, D.C. where they installed a large orange barrel in the window and began selling root beer. Bill had figured that Washington, D.C., since it was hotter than Salt Lake City, was good for 20,000 glasses a day. The catch was that in Washington it isn't the heat, it's the humidity. Washington, D.C. was hotter than Salt Lake, but also muggier. Root beer sales were brisk in the summer but in the fall sales dropped sharply.

To a greater extent than most hotel and restaurant chains, Marriott is family oriented. Except for periods when her children were small, Alice Marriott was active in the business. Alice Sheets Marriott (1907-2000) was born October 19, 1907, in Salt Lake City, Utah to Alice Taylor and Edwin Spencer Sheets. She graduated with honors from the University of Utah in 1927 at the age 19. She was a member of Phi Kappa Phi Honor Society and Chi Omega sorority.

Two weeks later Marriott raced back to Utah and on June 9, 1927, one day after Alice graduated, the pair got married in Salt Lake City at a beautiful marriage ceremony performed by Bishop Joseph H. Christensen. The couple's honeymoon consisted of a long, hot, bumpy drive back to Washington, D.C., in Bill's Model T Ford.

Bill and Alice worked as a team, beginning at 8:30 in the morning and often working through until 2:00 the next morning. Alice monitored the cash and kept the books. Bill did everything else that needed to be done. By winter they realized that they would need something other than cold drinks in order to keep the business running. Since it was prohibited to sell food in A&W franchises, the Marriotts received permission from Allen and Wright to add hot food to the menu. When they decided to specialize in Mexican and Southwestern food, the chef at the Mexican embassy graciously supplied them with a few recipes. Because the Marriotts were worried about the risk of losing their patronage if they closed the shop to make the changes needed for food service, they made preparations ahead of time so that it took only one night to convert the store. They finished just in time to open the next morning as The Hot Shoppe.

Bill bought out Hugh Colton in 1928, and when spring came opened one of the first drive-in restaurants in the nation. He literally built the restaurant, taking up hammer and nails himself; he had no architect. The design was a simple rectangle, the building painted orange with black trim.

Employees did not just cook or serve food. They painted, washed windows, did carpentry and, on occasion, acted as bouncers. The drive-in was built in a high density, Jewish neighborhood and turned into one of the most successful restaurants ever built. Profits from the place were used to finance other restaurants. At one time, as many as 150 carhops were employed.

In 1930 there were five Hot Shoppes and ten years of depression ahead. Profit margins were small, but with full value given to customers the business prospered. The Marriotts began laying plans for expansion. Characteristically, they had an unshaken belief that prosperity would return.

The 1930's were at time of tremendous growth for the company and the Marriott family. The Marriotts' first child, J. Willard Marriott, Jr., was born in 1932. By 1934 the corporation had added drive-in restaurants with "running boys" that provided customers with in-car service. In 1939 the Marriott's second son, Richard Edwin Marriott was born.

Hot Shoppes Drive-In Restaurants advertised "Convenient locations, No parking problems, Drive in and dine in your car or in our beautiful dining rooms. Double rich milk shakes, A&W root beer, barbecues, hamburgers, Hot Shoppes ice cream".

In 1930, Alice Taylor Sheets, Mrs. Marriott's mother, married United States Senator Reed Smoot and with that marriage came the Marriott's inclusion in the political circles of Washington, D.C. In addition to these social activities, Mrs. Marriott continued to be very involved with the business, even after the birth of their sons. She was instrumental in key decision-making which affected the company's growth and success, and even helped design and decorate company restaurants and hotels and scouted out new locations for company expansion.

In 1933 Bill became desperately ill with what was diagnosed as Hodgkin's Disease. Five doctors were unanimous in telling him that he had but one year to live. Frightened, he took a much needed vacation trip and amazingly on his return the disease was found to be gone. It was at this time, Marriott states, that he realized the importance of having an organization of people behind him, one that was not dependent upon any single individual.

Diversification came early but was introduced in measured steps. In 1934 the sandwich menu was enlarged to include full course meals. In 1937 the company became the first airline caterer, putting up meals in cardboard boxes for American and Eastern Airlines passengers out of Washington, D.C. Thirty years later, Marriott Flight Services, biggest of the air caterers, served 50 airlines from 20 domestic flight kitchens and 19 overseas airports.

Much of the company's food service expansion efforts came to fruition in the 1940s and 1950s. The corporation built several new restaurants and opened numerous industrial, defense plant, and school cafeterias. A corporate recipe card system was developed and a test kitchen was built to standardize food preparation and portions.

Bill Marriott bought the Robert C. Wian Enterprises of Los Angeles which owned 23 Big Boy fast food restaurants in Southern California and franchised more than 600 others in 38 states. Included in the package was Big Boy Properties, a real estate firm owning several other restaurants. Soon thereafter, Bill suffered a heart attack which sidelined him from the business and from the presidential campaign of George Romney, a fellow Mormon and governor of Michigan. When Romney's presidential campaign foundered, Marriott was disappointed. However, there was no disappointment in Bill Marriott, Jr.'s assumption of the leadership of the Marriott Company. At the annual shareholder's meeting just before Thanksgiving, the company announced record earnings up 18% over the previous year. Operating units increased from 150 to 206 including 12 new Hot Shoppes Jr.'s; 22 Big Boy restaurants plus 600 Big Boy franchise units: acquisition of Bill's favorite hotel, the Camelback Inn, the first existing hotel acquired; a new $10 million central supply and quality control facility called Fairfield Farm Kitchens; and the beginnings of Marriott's international In-Flite service with new flight kitchens in Caracas, Venezuela, St. Croix in the Virgin Islands and San Juan, Puerto Rico.

Before working at the family business, Bill Marriott Jr. polished his father's shoes so that they would be ready for church on Sundays. On Saturday he had to rigorously scrub the shoes to remove a gummy substance that his father had picked up during work from the previous week. It took the boy hours to properly clean the shoes so that he might pass his father's grueling inspection. In *Spirit to Serve: Marriott's Way*, Marriott Jr. wrote about his father, "Perfection was one notch below the desired result". The younger Marriott learned a valuable lesson from that early experience: to stick with any job until it was done right.

In 1941, at the age of 14, Bill Marriott Jr. was old enough to learn about the family business from the ground floor; he took his family company job stapling invoices together for the accounting department. He quickly learned that his father used a hands-on management approach and that both parents were very conservative and never took anything for granted, especially success. Marriott Jr. was fond of quoting his father (who was quoting Winston Churchill) as saying, "Success is never final".

Marriott Jr. continued working at his parents' Hot Shoppes while attending the prestigious St. Albans Prep School in Washington, D.C. He cooked hamburgers, washed dishes, and mopped floors. Through this work and exposure to his parents' work he learned some of the skills that he would need later in his career with the company. Marriott Jr. recalled on the company website, "When I was a kid, we used to sit around the table at home and all we would talk about was the business." While attending the University of Utah, Marriott Jr. worked at the fountain and in the dish room, cleaning counters and floors, serving customers and cooking, at a Hot Shoppe restaurant in Salt Lake City.

After receiving his bachelor's degree in banking and finance in 1954, Marriott Jr. became a lieutenant with the U.S. Naval Reserves, spending two years as a ship's service supply officer aboard the U.S.S. Randolph. In 1956 he returned full-time to his parents' company. By that time, the Marriott's food-service customers included hospitals, schools, and highway rest stops, in addition to the expanding divisions of Hot Shoppes and In-Flite, an airline catering service.

Upon Marriott Jr.'s return to the family business, an exciting and promising new development was taking place: the building of the company's first motel, Twin Bridges Motor Hotel, in Arlington, Virginia. As the company's first venture into the lodging industry, the hotel would become very important to Marriott Jr. Eager to manage his own piece of the family enterprise, Marriott Jr. asked his father to place him in charge of the small hotel division. The senior Marriott agreed, even though his son had been back in the business for only eight months. Marriott Jr. immediately faced the challenges and hurdles of running a new business. He was responsible for everything from hiring architects and securing general contractors to preparing last-minute details for the grand opening of the new hotel. He applied the lessons he had earlier learned from his father; part of his ethic was to understand every facet of the business by using a hands-on approach to management.

Marriott Jr. enjoyed every aspect of his work, completely immersing himself in the job-amassing ideas and slowly building the newly-formed hotels division as well as the systems needed to run them from the ground up. He was instituting the Marriott "badge of quality" from a solid foundation of hard work, dedication, and old-fashioned common sense.

Alice Sheets Marriott's political activities were varied and extensive throughout her life. From 1955 to 1957 she served as assistant treasurer for the League of Republican Women for the District of Columbia, and in 1957 was appointed vice president of the organization, a post she held for two years. She continued to affiliate with the League of Republican Women, serving in numerous positions in subsequent years. In 1959 she was named to the District of Columbia Republican State Executive Committee. She was a member of the Republican National Committee from 1959 to 1976, and during those years she served as vice chairman and as an executive committee member. She served on the Arrangements Committee for the Republic National Conventions of 1960, 1964, 1968 and 1972, and was treasurer of the conventions in 1964, 1968, and 1972. She was vice chairman of the1969 Inaugural Committee and honorary chairman of the 1973 Inaugural Committee.

The nation's arts community has benefited greatly from Mrs. Marriott's service and philanthropy. In 1971 she was appointed chairman of the Advisory Committee on the Arts for the John F. Kennedy Center for the Performing Arts, and in 1972 was appointed to the board of trustees. She was now an honorary trustee, having served two 10-year terms on the board and executive and finance committees. She also served on the board of directors of the National Ballet Society, and was a former member of the Women's Committee of the National Symphony Orchestra.

Mrs. Marriott's dedication to academic excellence has been manifest not only in her college years, but throughout her life. She held two honorary Doctor of Humane Letters degrees, one from Mount Vernon College and one from the University of Utah. The University of Utah has been the recipient of the Marriott's support and generosity for many years. In 1989 the new dance building was dedicated as the Alice Sheets Marriott Center for Dance in recognition of her particular interest in the arts. In 1988 for the Marriott Library's twentieth anniversary, Mrs. Marriott made a sizeable donation, and the tradition of the family, her son, J. Willard Marriott, Jr., chaired the university's capital campaign which far exceeded its goal of one hundred and fifty million dollars. At the conclusion of the campaign, the Marriott's made a significant donation to the library.

On April 17, 2000 Alice Sheets Marriott passed away at the age of 92. Mrs. Marriott's counsel and advice had been sought by various individuals and organizations throughout her life. She served as a member of the National Arthritis and Musculoskeletal and Skin Diseases Advisory Council and was on the board of directors of the Arthritis Foundation. Mrs. Marriott was director emeritus of Marriott International Incorporated and Host Marriott Corporation, having served one of the longest periods of active board service in American business history.

In 1964 John Willard Marriott Sr. appointed his son, at the age of 32, president and a member of the board of directors of Marriott-Hot Shoppes. At this time Marriott Jr. convinced his father that to achieve growth within the company they needed to take on debt from the equity they had built up. He told his father that to bring about fundamental internal change- that is, to complete the evolution from a handful of local businesses into a global enterprise- they would need three Ds: development, deals and debt.

During the next three years, Marriott Jr. turned Marriott-Hot Shoppes into an international company by purchasing an airline-catering kitchen in Venezuela and expanding its restaurant operations to include the Big

Boy and Roy Rogers restaurant chains. In its 40th anniversary year, the company changed its name from Marriott-Hot Shoppes to the Marriott Corporation.

In 1972 at age 40, Bill Marriott Jr. assumed the role of CEO, replacing his father but maintaining the latter's conservative business practices. Marriott Jr. had learned that the hotel business depended on balancing excellent customer service and clean, comfortable accommodations with controlled costs. As quoted by Logan Rochelle in her book of business biographies, Marriott continued operating under his father's basic philosophy: "to make sure our associates are very happy and that they enjoy their work, so they go the extra mile to take care of customers and have fun doing it. A lot of companies go through the motions, but they don't go the extra mile".

Marriott Jr. began to implement his dream for the business: expanding the lodging division through acquisitions and development of new brands. Under his discretion, the company quickly established complex financing techniques and built an effective in-house construction capability. By the early 1980s Marriott Jr. had transformed the company into one of the world's largest real-estate developers, building more than $1 billion in hotel properties annually.

As the number of the company's full-service hotels increased, Marriott Jr. continued his aggressive plans to develop a series of lodging brands. Beginning in 1983 with Courtyard by Marriott, the company introduced new hotel lines ranging from economy to luxury accommodations; these innovations in the hospitality industry were often far ahead of what the competition was doing- or even planning. In 1984 Marriott entered the vacation time-share business.

Bill Marriott stepped into the role of chairman following his father's death in 1985. He immediately took charge of the entire company's operations, traveling globally to manage what had become the world's largest hotel chain-by that time, an average of two Marriott hotels opened each week. Marriott Jr. narrowed Marriott's focus on lodging, senior accommodations, and contract services by divesting the company of its fast-food and family restaurants.

Marriott Motor Hotel- Twin Bridges (with a Hot Shoppes Restaurant) was the first Marriott Hotel. With the logo "Quality Courts", it was advertised as the world's largest motor hotel (345 rooms). Located on the shores of the Potomac only 5 minutes from downtown Washington at Twin Bridges on U.S. 1, Arlington, Virginia, it advertised "Swimming Pool in summer, Ice Skating in winter."

In 1981 Bill Marriott, Jr. became intrigued with the idea of revitalizing Times Square in New York City. During the term of mayor Ed Koch, architect/developer John Portman proposed an atrium-style hotel design to the Urban Development Corporation. Since Times Square was rife with pornography shops, prostitutes, panhandlers and homeless people, it seemed like a ridiculous idea and an enormous risk. Against all odds, Bill Marriott. Jr. made the commitment and investment to build the 1946- room Marriott Marquis. After its grand opening in 1985, success was five years in coming. Three historic theaters were demolished to make space for the hotel, prompting some members of the theater community to fight the planned hotel including actor Tony Randall who was arrested while protesting. Finally, cooler heads prevailed and the Times Square Business Improvement District set about enhancing street lighting, developing a dedicated security force and a Times Square uniformed cleaning service.

The larger-than-life fusion of signage, noise, traffic, and humanity in the Times Square and Broadway's Theater District is quintessential New York City. Skyscrapers peppered with impossibly huge billboards block much of the sky and a giant stock ticker adds further urgency to the vibrant intersection of Broadway and 7th Avenue.

At the center of this revitalized location stands the Marriott Marquis, which, at 1,946 rooms, was Marriott's largest property for many years. With its spectacular 37-story atrium, rows of shining marquis lights, and glass-enclosed elevators, it is a property well-suited for its vibrant location. It is within close proximity of the Javits Convention Center and in the heart of Times Square.

In recognition of the turnaround in Times Square, Mayor Rudolph Giuliani named September 5, 2000, "New York Marriott Marquis Day" and issued a proclamation in honor of the property's 15th anniversary. The Marriott Marquis now stands as one of the busiest hotels in New York City and has hosted numerous high-profile events including the Daytime Emmy Awards, the Tony Awards Supper, the Heisman Trophy Dinner, and the NFL Draft. It is home to the View, the city's one revolving restaurant, and Encore, which recently was remodeled and remains one of Marriott's busiest restaurants. The success of the Marriott Marquis can be attributed to the foresight and business acumen of Bill Marriott, Jr.

Respect within the hospitality industry was growing for the very successful company. In 1988 Chief Executive magazine named Bill Marriott "CEO of the Year" and Fortune magazine included him on its list of the "25 Most Fascinating Business Leaders." One of the reasons given by experts as to why the Marriott family ran such an impressive business was their attention to detail. For example, over the years the Marriotts collected information on how to clean a room properly in a consistent and high-quality manner, eventually developing an instruction guide that laid out 66 separate steps such that each hotel room would be cleaned in less than 30 minutes. Every aspect of the business was based on such natural and logical methods of performing tasks and services.

In 1993 Marriott Jr. helped to split the former company into two separate companies: Marriott International, a lodging and services management company and Host Marriott Corporation, focusing on real-estate and airport concessions. The acquisition of the Ritz-Carlton Hotel Company expanded Marriott International's growth into the luxury hotel segment.

Despite industry concerns, Marriott has enhanced and supported the Ritz-Carlton five-star image. Those hotels are not Marriott plus, they are opulent and luxurious. No Marriott Hotel looks like them. For example, step into the imposing neoclassical marble lobby of the Ritz-Carlton, Philadelphia, and you'll feel like you've stepped into another era. Inside the Rotunda, a replica of the Pantheon in Rome, Ionic marble columns soar 140 feet to a dome of grandiose dimensions. Intricate exterior and interior carvings and reliefs echo a gracious Imperial past inside this new incarnation of the former Girard Trust Company/Mellon Bank building. Marble staircases carry guests to the open mezzanine and Grand Ballroom on the concourse level, where vaults once held the jewels and other valuables of high society. Thirty floors up, the mahogany-paneled former executive boardroom offers club-floor guests dramatic city views, along with delicious food and drink.

In 1997 Marriott named William J. Shaw, a 22-year company veteran, to the posts of president and chief operating officer. Also that year Marriott Jr. coauthored a book with Kathi Ann Brown about his business philosophy, *The Spirit to Serve: Marriott's Way*. Therein, Marriott Jr. talked openly about all of the many facets of his business life, including the mistakes he had made. He realized that failures were just as important as successes in learning over a lifetime how to develop a successful business. Marriott Jr. remarked frequently on the virtues of taking care of employees, listening well, and not wasting time on regret. He attributed the company's rapid expansion in part to early standard operating procedures and internal training programs; noting that if they had had to create a new hotel each and every time without the use of standard procedures, they would not have been so successful.

Marriott Jr. cited the competition's lack of reliability and uneven standards, as compared with Marriott, in referring to the company's developing and maintaining superior quality across the spectrum of its businesses. He was proud to point out that the original hands-on, personal-inspection management approach- which had been first used more than 75 years prior in a small root-beer stand- was still a part of Marriott's philosophy and culture. As of the early 2000s Marriott Jr. continued to travel an average of 150,000 miles each year in visiting Marriott sites. In *Spirit to Serve*, he said, "If you're in the service business and your name is above the door, it's important for people to be able to link a face to a name. I want our associates to know that there really is a guy named Marriott who cares about them, even if he can only drop by every so often to personally tell them so". Marriott Jr.'s oldest son, Steve said of his father, "He loves to go through a hotel, greeting people. He told me once that he'd rather be doing that than anything else". Marriott Jr. himself admitted at the end of the 20th century, "The truth is, I'm still having fun after 40 years".

In spite of his busy travel schedule, Marriott Jr. serves on several boards, including the National Geographic Society, the Naval Academy Endowment Trust, and the National Urban League. He also volunteers each week with The Church of Jesus Christ of Latter-Day Saints and supports a number of community organizations.

Bill Marriott Jr. and his wife, Donna, who were married in 1955, have three sons (Steven, John, David) and one daughter (Deborah). The Marriott's four offspring gave them 12 grandchildren. Following in their father's footsteps, the Marriott children all worked in various positions within the family company; the three sons all work full-time for Marriott International.

As reported in his biography, *Marriott: The J. Willard Marriott Story"* there is an epilogue entitled "Reminiscing". On a perfect afternoon in February 1976 in the paneled living room of Jackrabbit Casa in Scottsdale, Arizona founder J. W. Marriott, Sr. (recovering from three recent heart attacks) talked to his biographer Robert O'Brien about things he was proud of, good times, exciting times, his feelings about work and religion. These reminiscences are worth quoting verbatim:

About his survival

"I am certain that the power of prayer made it possible for me to come through these heart attacks alive. Many friends and church members were praying for me all the time, especially the Council of the Twelve Apostles in the temple at Salt Lake City. President Kimball called Allie twice to see how I was getting along, and the last time, when all the doctors had just about given up hope, he said, "We had a prayer circle for Bill. Tell him that he is going to live and fill out his mission on earth."

I never worried after that. I know he was a prophet of God and was speaking with authority. I also felt I had constructive things to do with the rest of my life-to give guidance to my sons and their great staff with its 60,000 employees; to see them and their families mature as respectable, worthwhile individuals capable of bringing to the affairs of their community and nation a renewal of the kind of spiritual character that made this country great.

About the restaurant and hotel business

The service business is very rewarding. It makes a big contribution to society. A good meal away from home, a good bed, friendly treatment from those who come in contact with our customers—these are all so important. It's important to make people away from home feel at home and feel that they're among friends and are really wanted. When they come to our restaurants and hotels, we try to treat them well enough that they'll come back, and I think most of them do.

About Allie

My wife, Allie, is undoubtedly the most important asset in my life. She has had the same faith and ideals that I've had, I must give her credit for rearing my two sons. I've had such a busy life in business and civic work and church affairs that I had little time for our family. But she's taken care of our home admirably- always with the boys when they were at home, teaching them, helping them build the kind of character she has herself.

By now the fire was burning low. Bill poked it up, sending showers of sparks snapping into the chimney. The sun had gone down. One at a time, the quail and the rabbits were leaving the back lawn. Allie turned on a bridge lamp, so she could continue her needlepoint.

Bill said one of the things he missed the most since being laid up was horseback riding. Ironic, wasn't it, he said that here he was in Arizona, in the great open spaces, and he couldn't ride a horse because the doctor told him not to. The doctor didn't think his heart could take it- not now, anyway. He used to go on hunting and fishing trips almost every year, either in Utah or the Jackson Hole country, he and Hugh Colton, with Roland Parry or Ken Garff.

A day or so later, at about the same time of day, maybe a little earlier, Bill and I went for a walk. We walked down Mummy Mountain Road to Desert Fairways Drive and then cut through somebody's yard, scattering quail as we went. It was chilly, in the high fifties. Bill wore a turtleneck, a heavy shirt, and a sweater over that. I asked him if he'd started out with the idea or the ambition to make a million dollars or build an empire:

> No, not at all. I just had three general ideas in mind, all equally important. One was to render friendly service to our guests. The second was to provide quality food at a fair price. The third was to work as hard as I could, day and night, to make a profit.

> Also, I wanted to grow for other reasons. I wanted to reap the rewards of growth: jobs for more employees, money to take care of my family and to contribute to good causes. On top of that, we needed to diversify, and for this we needed different kinds of food service to satisfy a larger segment of society. There's a lot to be said for diversification. "Don't put all your eggs in one basket," they say. There's wisdom in that. If business slumps in one division, there are other divisions to carry

it through. All businesses fluctuate. Diversification takes care of it.

Whatever I did, I'd figure on doing a first-class job. I'd work day and night. I don't have much use for anyone getting by on a 40-hour week, as I've said before. The man who wants to build and make a contribution in the business world mustn't neglect his family or his church, but he can't lead a "vacation life."

A man should keep on being constructive, and do constructive things, until it's time to die. He should take part in the things that go in this wonderful world. He should be someone to be reckoned with. He should live life and make every day count, to the very end. It takes push and discipline. Sometimes it's tough. But that's what I'm going to do."

SOURCE MATERIALS

Rochelle Logan and Julie Halverstadt, *100 Most Popular Business Leaders For Young Adults: Biographical Sketches and Professional Paths*, Libraries Unlimited, Greenwood Village, Colorado, 2002.

J. Willard Marriott, Jr. and Kathi Ann Brown, *The Spirit to Serve: Marriott's Way*, Harpercollins, Publishers, New York, 1997

Robert O'Brien, *Marriott: The J. Willard Marriott Story*, Deseret Book Company, Salt Lake City, 1979

Answers.com, J. Willard Marriott

Marriott Website, www.Marriott.com

Wikipedia, J. Willard Marriott

Kanjibhai Manchhubhai Patel:

A WONDERFUL AMERICAN IMMIGRANT SUCCESS STORY

In 1923, Mr. Kanjibhai Manchhubhai Patel of Digas who was on his way to Trinidad, decided to disembark from his ship on the California coast and make San Francisco his home. He apparently was an illegal immigrant who became involved with operating a small residential hotel called the Goldfield Hotel on 4th Street near Howard Street in San Francisco. Kanjibhai's benevolent nature and genuine desire to help others became a guiding light for other immigrants. This is the first reported Patel who was responsible for providing newcomers to the United States with shelter and help in learning how to operate hotels. According to the skimpy evidence available, Kanjibhai was hard-working, ambitious and resourceful. Like the pioneers who followed him, he was entrepreneurial and persistent.

Some twenty-six years later in 1949, another Asian American of Indian descent came to the United States from his home near the city of Surat during the first wave of legal immigration from India. Bhulabhai V. Patel picked apricots and grapes in Northern California and worked at various jobs until he saved enough to purchase the 108-room William Penn Hotel in San Francisco in 1960. By 1996, Bhulabhai owned nine properties in Northern California with his son, Raman and grandson Pramod. At the time, he was amazed by the rapid growth of the Indian American lodging community. "It started with one hotel", he said, "Now we've got thousands".

By 2006, a remarkable revolution had taken place: members of the Asian American Hotel Owners Association (AAHOA) acquired 20,000 hotels with more than one million rooms. This represents 50 percent of the economy lodging properties and almost 37 percent of all hotel properties in the U.S. If you bear in mind that Indian Americans constitute less than one percent of America's population, the achievement appears extraordinary. The market value of these hotels totals about $40 billion. It is estimated that the hotels employ almost 800,000 people and pay some $700 million in real estate taxes annually. Incidentally, there may be an additional 4,000 hotels owned by Indian Americans who are not AAHOA members.

How did this happen under our noses?

To find out, we must travel back in time to 2,000 years before the birth of Jesus. The Gujarati, descended from Aryan nomads, settled in what is now the Indian State of Gujarat on the Arabian Sea between Bombay and India's border with Pakistan. More than 40 million people live in Gujarat, India's most populous state. Mahatma Gandhi, the 20th century's greatest Indian, was a Gujarati.

The British sent thousands of English-speaking Indians to their other colonies in the 19th and 20th century as civil servants to be laborers, tea traders and plantation managers. Indians built the railways that linked Indian Ocean ports like Zanzibar to East Africa. Throughout British Africa, they became tradesmen, operated general stores, ran transportation companies and worked as coffee traders. In Trinidad and Guyana, they were shopkeepers, civil servants and bank managers.

The political instability and racial tensions of post-colonial Africa had a dual effect: It made the Indians some of the shrewdest businesspeople in the world and it forced them out of Africa. For example, in 1972, General Idi Amin expelled 70,000 from Uganda, most of whom settled in Great Britain because they had British passports. The Gujarati faced racism from South Africa to Kenya. They later migrated to the U.S. from Great Britain and all over the African subcontinent including Zimbabwe, Tanzania, Uganda, Zambia, Malawi and Kenya.

"Patel" means farmer or landowner in Gujarat where the Patels are the original and largest clan. In order to facilitate tax collections, the British delineated, reassigned and renamed some of them "Amin" (the farm managers) and others "Desai" (those who kept the books). It is said that the Patels have a commerce gene in their blood and the anecdotal evidence seems to bear this out.

In the mid-1970's, Patels from Africa and Asia began to emigrate to the United States where any immigrant willing to invest $40,000 in a business could apply for permanent residence, the first step to citizenship. There were limited opportunities for such an investment. Restaurants required the Hindu Gujaratis to handle meat, an uncomfortable activity. Furthermore, a restaurant required one-on-one interaction with guests, confusing for newly-arrived immigrants. But distressed roadside motels could be acquired outright for $40,000. In addition, the motel industry was slumping badly because of the oil embargo and the resultant nationwide shortage of gasoline.

One Patel pioneer reported that a motel "… is easy to run. You don't need fluent English, just the will to work long hours. And, it's a business that comes with a house- you don't have to buy a separate house…."

The new owners brought their business expertise and their families to operate these motels. They instituted modern accounting techniques to monitor the all-important cash flow. Four times cash flow became the mantra of the Patels. If the distressed motel produced $10,000 per year in revenues and could be acquired for $40,000, it was profitable to a hard-working family.

They renovated and upgraded the rundown motels to improve cash flow, sold the properties and traded up to better motels. This was not without difficulties. Conventional insurance companies wouldn't provide coverage because they believed these immigrant owners would burn down their motels. In those days, banks were unlikely to provide mortgages either. The Patels had to finance each other and self insure their properties.

In a July 4, 1999 *New York Times* article, reporter Tunku Varadarajan wrote, "The first owners, in a manner consistent with many an emergent immigrant group, scrimped, went without, darned old socks and never took a holiday. They did this not merely to save money but also because thrift is part of a larger moral framework, one that regards all nonessential expenditure as wasteful and unattractive. It's an attitude buttressed by a puritanical aversion to frills and frivolities, one that has its roots as much in the kind of Hinduism that the Patels practice as in their historical tradition as commercial perfectionists."

They bought, renovated, operated and resold motels mostly along the interstate highways. Soon, the name "Patel" became synonymous with the hotel business. Patels own motels all over the U.S., including Canton (Texas, Mississippi, Michigan and Ohio), Burlington (Vermont, Iowa and North Carolina), Athens (Georgia, Tennessee and Alabama), Plainview (New York and Ohio) and Longview (Texas and Washington).

Reportedly, at least 50 percent of all new franchisees since 1992 are Indian-owned. Typically these motels are not fleabag properties but EconoLodges, Days Inns, Holiday Inns, Comfort Inns, Quality Inns and Super 8s. These are economy/budget properties with no food, conference facilities, guest laundries or room service. Gradually, the second generation Patels own and franchise a growing number of full-service hotels like Marriott, Hilton and Sheraton.

Author Joel Millman writes in *The Other Americans:*

> Patels took a sleepy, mature industry and turned it upside down- offering consumers more choices while making the properties themselves more profitable. Motels that attracted billions in immigrant savings turned into real estate equity worth many billions more. That equity, managed by a new generation, is being leveraged into new businesses. Some are related to lodging (manufacturing motel supplies); some related to real estate (reclaiming derelict housing); some simply cash seeking an opportunity. The Patel-motel model is an example, like New York's West Indian jitneys, of the way immigrant initiative expands the pie. And there is another lesson: as the economy shifts from manufacturing to services, the Patel-motel phenomenon demonstrates how franchising can turn an outsider into a mainstream player. The Gujarati model for motels might be copied by Latinos in landscaping, West Indians in homecare or Asians in clerical services. By operating a turnkey franchise as a family business, immigrants will help an endless stream of service providers grow.

As investment and ownership expanded, the Patels were accused of a wide variety of crimes: arson, laundering stolen travel checks, circumventing immigration laws. In an unpleasant burst of xenophobia, *Frequent Flyer* magazine (Summer 1981) declared, "Foreign investment has come to the motel industry.....causing grave problems for American buyers and brokers. Those Americans in turn are grumbling about unfair, perhaps illegal business practices: there is even talk of conspiracy." The magazine complained that the Patels had artificially boosted motel prices to induce a buying frenzy. The article concluded with an unmistakable racist remark, "Comments are passed about motels smelling like curry and dark hints about immigrants who hire Caucasians to work the front desk." The article concluded, "The facts are that immigrants are playing hardball in the motel industry and maybe not strictly by the rule book." The worst visible manifestation of such racism was a rash of "American Owned" banners displayed in certain hotels across the country. This hateful display was repeated in post- Sept 11 America.

In my article, "How American-Owned Can You Get", (Lodging Hospitality, August 2002), I wrote,

> In post-Sept. 11 America, signs of patriotism are everywhere: flags, slogans, God Bless America and United We Stand posters. Unfortunately, this outpouring sometimes oversteps the boundaries of democracy and decent behavior. After all, true patriotism encompasses the best features of our founding documents, and the very best of America is reflected in its diversity. Conversely, the worst is reflected when any one group attempts to define "American" in their own image. Unfortunately, a few hotel owners have attempted to describe their own peculiar version of "American." When at the end of 2002 the Hotel Pennsylvania in New York City installed an entrance banner saying "an American-owned hotel," the owners attempted to deflect criticism by explaining, "The issue of American-owned is basically not disparaging toward other hotels. We want to provide our guests with an American experience. We want people to know they are going to get an American

experience. We are not really interested in what the other hotels are or what they are not.

This explanation is as wrongheaded as it gets. What is an "American experience" in a country that prides itself on its cultural diversity? Is it only white bread, hot dogs and cola? Or does it encompass all the arts, music, dance, food, culture and activities that all the various nationalities bring to the American experience?

How much more American can you get?

The Asian American Hotel Owners Association (AAHOA) was originally founded to fight racism. As early as the mid-1970's, Indian Americans hoteliers faced discrimination from banks and insurance carriers. Around that time, after delegates to a regional fire marshal's convention reported that Patels had set fire to their motels and submitted phony claims, insurance brokers refused to sell insurance to Indian owners.

To fight this problem and other forms of discrimination, the Mid-South Indemnity Association was formed in Tennessee. It grew nationwide and eventually changed its name to the INDO American Hospitality Association. Another group of Indian hoteliers came together in Atlanta in 1989 also to address discrimination issues and to increase awareness of Asian Americans in the hospitality industry. With the help of Michael Leven, then president of Days Inns of America, they formed the Asian American Hotel Owners Association. By the end of 1994, these two groups merged with the following mission:

> AAHOA provides an active forum in which Asian American hotel owners through an exchange of ideas with a unified voice, can communicate, interact, and secure their proper position within the hospitality industry, and be a source of inspiration by promoting professionalism and excellence through education and community involvement.

As Joel Millman wrote in *The Other Americans*:

Instead of pariahs, Patels became the darlings of the lodging world. And just as the hospitality companies needed Patels, the immigrants needed the infrastructure of an established American corporation. To move beyond the drive-up trade, they needed the kind of steady business a toll-free reservation system creates. They needed to learn how to manage bigger properties. For immigrants, franchising provided instant training, with seminars and manuals to describe every motel nuance. Franchising also gave economies of scale in purchasing everything from disposable bathroom cups to towels, to television sets. It's no surprise, then, that as the hospitality chains grew, they attracted a disproportionate number of Patels. Today, of every hundred new low-service properties, about half of them are in the hands of Gujarati.

A recent AAHOA survey revealed that 80 percent of members have been in the hotel industry for five or more years. It also indicates that the greatest population of members have their primary holdings in the Southeast and on the West Coast with the third highest demographic in the Southwest.

In 1998, AAHOA Chairman Mike Patel announced to the hotel industry that the time had come to identify AAHOA's 12 Points of Fair Franchising. He said that the major purpose was "to create a franchising environment that promotes equality and is mutually beneficial to all parties."

In Spring 1999, Eric Pfeffer, the head of Cendant Corporation's hotel division was so annoyed with AAHOA's 12 Points that he yanked Cendant's AAHOA's sponsorship. In June 1999 I wrote a column in Lodging Hospitality entitled, "Cendant's AAHOA Decision: The March of Folly":

> When I read about Cendant's withdrawal of support as sponsor of the Asian American Hotel Owners Association (AAHOA), I thought: "This must be a misprint." No franchisor would willingly antagonize

a group of entrepreneurs that owns more than half of the properties in the economy sector, and nearly 35 percent of all hotels in the U.S., unless that franchisor was planning to go out of business.

Then I received a copy of Cendant's letter to AAHOA members dated March 12 and signed by 11 Cendant executives. The letter reveals a blatant attempt to control AAHOA's missions and agenda. It clearly reflects a sharp disagreement with AAHOA's campaign to seek fairer franchise license agreements.

When AAHOA first proposed changes in these license agreements, it seemed to me that the group's suggestions represented a logical sequence in the evolution of the franchise agreement.

Various commentators have described the AAHOA positions as revolutionary and militant, more demagoguery than negotiation. Nonsense. In our free enterprise system, it is just plain good business to use your strengths to negotiate better license agreements. Did you ever hear editorial criticism of a franchisor who imposed arbitrary and one-sided license provisions on its franchisees? Were these provisions labeled revolutionary? Militant? Demagogic?

I believe any franchise company that adopted the AAHOA recommendations would create a level of trust with its franchisees that does not now exist in the hotel business. It could be the sine qua non by which all others are measured and would be hugely successful.

It is distressing, therefore, to observe that Cendant's action was a short-sighted, self-serving march of folly.

One year later, Cendant reinstated its sponsorship after it agreed to form a Franchise Owners Council with AAHOA to hash out issues. Pfeffer subsequently praised the very organization he once accused of engaging in virtual collective bargaining.

At the end of 2006, Chairman Mukesh Mowji reported that "it is time to update AAHOA's 12 Points; it is time to provide the hotel industry with a current set of standards by which to judge their actions; it is time to build on our past points and let everyone know in no uncertain terms what AAHOA believes is fair franchising , and what is not ."

Mike Patel agreed. "This is a big step for AAHOA. I am honored to be part of it. We can use the updated 12 Points to further educate our members about important provisions in their franchise environment."

AAHOA president Fred Schwartz said, "In order to have a healthy franchise system, both parties must act in a fair and reasonable manner. The updated 12 Points will pave the way for franchisors and franchisees to build on their strengths and create relationships that will be conducive to an optimal franchise agreement."

AAHOA'S Updated 12 Points of Fair Franchising

Point 1:

Early Termination and Liquidated Damages

A. Voluntary Buyout Or Involuntary Termination and Liquidated Damages:

At the current time, if a franchise agreement is being terminated by either a franchisor or franchisee due to a voluntary buyout or involuntary termination, most franchisors are assessing liquidated damages (LDs) at unfair and unreasonable rates that penalize the franchisee. For example, many franchise agreements provide that the LDs will be calculated based on one of the following formulas: (1) by assessing a rate of $1,000 to $2,000 for each guest room of the facility, or (2) by multiplying the average monthly gross room revenues by the royalty fees payable in the remaining months of the franchise agreement, multiplied by the number of months until the franchisee could have terminated the agreement without penalty, not to exceed 36 to 60 months.

In the interest of fair franchising, a franchisee should only have to pay six months of royalty fees. Specifically the franchisee should be required to pay as LDs, and not as a penalty, the product of the average monthly royalty fees paid by the franchisee during the prior 12 full calendar months (or the shorter time that the facility has been in the system), multiplied by six months.

Further, in the event of an early termination, if a franchisor has paid any "incentive" money to a franchisee under the franchise agreement (including, for example, a development incentive advance, loan, or grant), the incentive money should be amortized over the total number of months of the term of the franchise agreement, and the repayment of any incentive money should be based on the number of months remaining under the agreement.

<u>Commentary</u>: *The current provisions relied on by franchisors for assessing LDs are punitive in nature, and not based on a reasonable estimate of the franchisor's probable losses from the early termination of a franchise agreement. Regrettably, most franchisors have been unwilling to negotiate or change such provisions to provide for a fair and reasonable method of assessing LDs based on, among other things, the actual amount of monetary losses franchisors have experienced in the past as a result of an early termination, or the average amount of time it will take a franchisor to replace a terminated facility.*

AAHOA's proposed method of limiting the LDs to six months of average monthly royalty fees for the subject facility is fair and reasonable because it does not provide one side with a windfall or an unfair advantage over the other, and it compels both franchisors and franchisees to work together to avoid an early termination. Indeed, under AAHOA's method of assessing LDs, a franchisor will have six months to locate replacement facility of the same or a similar brand name as the terminated facility before it faces the prospect of suffering any losses arising from an early termination. Moreover, a franchisee will still be required to pay a significant sum of LDs, but will not be unduly penalized in connection with a voluntary buyout or involuntary termination of its franchise agreement.

If a franchisor has given any "incentive" money to a franchisee, that should not be used as a means of penalizing a franchisee in the event of an early termination. Rather than requiring a full repayment, the amount should be amortized over the term of the agreement, and any monies that must be repaid should be based on the remaining months under the agreement.

B. Windows Provisions

Most franchise agreements contain "window" or "additional termination" right provisions, which allow the parties to terminate the agreement on specified anniversary dates (e.g., on the fifth, tenth or fifteenth anniversaries) after the opening date of the facility, without having to pay LDs. Regrettably, many franchisors have included "gotcha" clauses in their franchise agreements. These clauses preclude a franchisee from terminating early if the franchisee encountered monetary or operational problems at any time after the opening of the facility which resulted in an alleged uncured default or low scores on quality assurance (QA) inspections on two consecutive occasions.

Such "gotcha" clauses should be eliminated from the franchise agreements. A franchisee should have the ability to terminate its agreement, with or without cause, and as a matter of right, on the specified anniversary dates by giving at least six months' prior written notice to the franchisor. The only contingency for the exercise of the early termination rights should be that at the time of proposed termination, the franchisee is not in default, and has paid all fees due under the franchise agreement.

<u>Commentary</u>: *In franchise agreements containing "windows" or "additional termination right" provisions, the types of "gotcha" clauses that are most unfair are those that explicitly state a franchisee's rights will automatically terminate, without notice, if (1) the franchisee fails to cure any default under the franchise agreement within the time permitted, if any, in the notice of default sent by the franchisor, or (2) the facility receives a poor score on a QA inspection, and then does not receive a higher predetermined score set by the franchisor during a re-inspection of the facility.*

Consequently, in many situations, the fact that a franchisee experienced financial or operational difficulties that resulted in notice of default, or low QA scores, in the first few months or years after the opening of the facility will forever preclude the franchisee from being able to exercise its early termination rights without penalty. This is true even if the franchisee subsequently pays all of its fees on a timely basis, and receives excellent QA scores for many years, before attempting to exercise its early termination rights. These "gotcha" clauses give the franchisors an unfair advantage and should be eliminated from all agreements.

C. Early Termination for Underperforming Properties: *As discussed in Fair Franchising Point 3 below, franchisors should issue minimum performance guarantees to franchisees regarding the occupancy levels of their brand name hotels. In an attempt to address this issue, some franchisors have adopted a "policy" that allows a franchisee to terminate its franchise agreement without penalty if the facility is underperforming and certain conditions are met. At a minimum, franchisors should include the provisions of their fair franchising "policies" as contractual terms in their franchise agreements.*

These specific contractual terms should provide that the franchisor will allow a franchisee to terminate the franchise agreement without penalty if the property has achieved an occupancy rate (total occupied rooms divided by total available rooms) that is below 50 percent for a period of 12 months or more. There should be no restrictive or unnecessary conditions placed on a franchisee's ability to terminate the agreement early for low occupancy rates.

Point 2:

Impact/ Encroachment/ Cross Brand Protection

Franchisors should establish a fair and reasonable formula to protect a franchisee's assets, and the formula should be included as a contractual provision in their franchise agreements. The formula should include the following important terms:

A. Franchisors should grant each franchisee contractual rights to a protected area or geographic "area of protection" (AOP) in which the franchisor will not allow another facility with the same or similar brand name as the franchisee's hotel to operate. For example, if the franchisee owns an ABC Hotel, the franchisor will not allow another facility with the same name (i.e., ABC Hotel) or a similar name (i.e., ABC Hotel & Suites) to operate in the protected area or geographic AOP.

B. Franchisors should be prohibited from licensing not only other franchised hotels with the same or similar brand name to operate in the protected area or geographic AOP, but also company-owned hotels.

C. The franchisee's protected area or AOP should be maintained and recognized until such time as the franchise agreement between the franchisor and franchisee has been legally terminated.

D. In the interest of providing fair impact rights, franchisors should adopt a reasonable and unbiased formula to determine which of the brand name hotels within the franchisor's system are competing in the same marketplace. The formula for determining which hotels are competing in the same marketplace for purposes of determining impact rights should be based on objective market criteria developed and relied on by reputable national organizations, such as Smith Travel Research (STR).

E. Upon receipt of an application for a proposed facility, franchisors should give written notice to franchisees of all brand name hotels within the franchisor's system that are (i) competing in the same marketplace as the applicant's proposed facility – even if these other hotels are not he same brand name as the applicant's proposed facility and (ii) within a 15-mile radius of the proposed facility.

F. To the extent a franchisee has a brand name hotel that is both (i) competing in the same marketplace as an applicant's proposed facility and (ii) within a 15-mile radius of the proposed facility, the franchisor should permit such a franchisee to request an impact study, so long as the franchisee(s) requesting the study have not been subject to a notice of termination within six months of making the request.

G. Any franchisee who requests an impact study should be allowed to choose the person or company who will be conducting the study. The selection should be from a list of at least five individuals or companies that have experience in the hospitality industry conducting such studies. The list should be jointly compiled and agreed upon by the franchisor and the franchise advisory councils for the various hotel brands.

H. The costs of the impact study should be split equally between the franchisor and the franchisee(s) requesting the study (i.e., with the franchisor paying 50 percent, and the franchisee(s) requesting the study paying 50 percent), regardless of the outcome of the impact study.

I. To the extent an impact study concludes that the applicant's proposed facility will result in an incremental impact of three percent or more on a franchisee's existing hotel during the first three years of projections, franchisors should respond by (a) denying the application for the proposed facility, (b) offering the existing franchisee a first right of licensing for the proposed facility, and thereby allow the existing franchisee an opportunity to open a facility with the same or similar brand name in the same or a nearby location, (c) offering reduced rates to the existing franchisee to exit the system without paying LDs.

J. If the impact study concludes that the applicant's proposed facility will result in a less than 3 percent incremental impact on an existing franchisee's hotel during the first three years of projections, but within three years after the opening date of the proposed facility, the existing franchisee is able to establish that it has, in fact, experienced an incremental impact of three percent or more on its hotel, the franchisor should respond by offering reduced rates to the franchisee impacted by the new facility or allowing the impacted franchisee to exit the system without paying LDs.

Point 3:

Minimum Performance & Quality Guarantees

Franchisors should issue minimum performance guarantees to franchisees regarding the occupancy levels of their brand name hotels, and the number of reservations that will be delivered through the franchisors' reservation systems.

Franchisors also should commit to maintaining a certain level of quality in the franchise system, including, for example, the key characteristics of each brand name, the public image and reputation they will develop for each brand name, the minimum number of hotels they will maintain under each brand name, and the amount and type of advertising they will employ for each brand name.

Thus, if a franchisee's hotel is not able to maintain certain occupancy levels over a designated period of time as discussed in Fair Franchising Point 1 above, or if the franchisor allows the quality of a particular brand name to decline, the franchisee should be able to terminate the franchise agreement without penalty.

Point 4:

Quality Assurance Inspections/ Guest Surveys

Franchisors should have the same standards for each of their facilities operating under a specific brand name in the franchise system.

Franchisors also should conduct their quality assurance (QA) inspections in a fair, reasonable and unbiased manner, and use their best efforts to prepare QA reports that are accurate and complete.

If a franchisee fails a QA inspection and is given a punch list of items to repair, correct, or change, the franchisee should strive to complete all of the items on the punch list in a timely manner. During the subsequent re-inspection of the facility, the franchisor should only seek to confirm that, in fact, the franchisee has completed all of the items on the punch list. If so, the franchisor should give the franchisee a passing grade. During the re-inspection of the property, the franchisor should not create an entirely new punch list of items that were not previously mentioned, or give the property a failing score for items that were not included on the original punch list.

In the event of a dispute concerning a QA inspection or low scores arising from guest survey cards, franchisors should establish an appeals process whereby a franchisee can appeal the decision of an inspector, or challenge the low scores it received from the guest survey cards. In connection with the appeals process, the franchisee should be able to present evidence that it is in compliance with the standards of the hotel brand, or request that the director or supervisor of the franchisor's quality assurance department personally visit the property and re-inspect the facility to ensure it is satisfying the necessary standards.

<u>Commentary:</u> Franchisors should use their best efforts to work with, educate and train franchisees who have received one or more failing QA inspections, or low scores arising from guest survey cards, to ensure the franchisees understand and are doing whatever is necessary to cure the failing QA

inspections and/or improve the scores, and thereby avoid problems in the future.

In the interest of fair franchising, a franchisor should not terminate a facility based on one or more alleged failing QA inspections, or as a result of low scores from guest survey cards, unless and until each of the following has occurred:

- *The franchisor has thoroughly analyzed the facts and circumstances concerning the failing QA inspections, reports, and/or the low scores from the guest survey cards, and evaluated whether there are any valid reasons that the property received such failing grades or negative comments on the survey cards at the time they were issued; and*

- *The franchisee has been given a reasonable opportunity and an adequate amount of time to cure any failing QA scores, problems with the property, and/or improve the guest survey scores; and*

- *The director or supervisor of the franchisor's QA department has personally visited the property, and has issued a written statement verifying that the facility is not in compliance with the standards of the hotel brand and should be terminated.*

Point 5:

Vendor Exclusivity

In general, franchisees should be free to buy conforming goods from any vendor, not just those mandated by the franchisor. To the extent a franchisor believes it is necessary to mandate vendors for the purpose of establishing standards and specifications for the hotel brands, the franchisor should strive to ensure that the franchisees are receiving competitive prices by providing a list of three or more approved vendors from which franchisees can purchase conforming goods, or by allowing the franchisees to take advantage of the volume discounts arising from the franchisees' group purchases of goods and services.

In addition, because the franchisors receive a significant amount of revenues and commissions from the mandated vendors in return for requiring all franchisees to purchase certain goods and services only from such vendors, franchisors should return these revenues and commissions to the franchisees for the good of the franchise system.

Commentary: In the interest of fair franchising, franchisors should strive to ensure that the franchisees are receiving competitive prices on all goods and services that they are required to purchase from mandated vendors. This can be accomplished in a variety of ways. For example, franchisors should identify three or more approved vendors from whom franchisees can purchase the goods or services. Franchisors also can pass on the volume discounts on prices arising from the purchasing power of the franchisees.

Franchisors should not be allowed to pocket the entire amount of revenues and commissions they receive from mandated vendors in return for requiring all franchisees to purchase certain goods and services from such vendors. Franchisors should retain only that amount of revenues and commissions as is necessary for the franchisors to cover the administrative costs of managing the mandated vendor program. All other revenues, commissions and related benefits received from mandated vendors should be invested in programs that benefit the franchisees, including allocating the money to marketing and advertising campaigns for the hotel brands or reducing the franchisees' royalty fees.

Point 6:

Disclosure and Accountability

There should be greater franchisor disclosure and accountability concerning the expenditure of marketing and reservation fees collected from franchisees. On an annual basis, franchisors should disclose how the marketing and reservation fees are spent, including identifying the specific products and services that are paid for with the fees. A franchisor should not profit directly from the marketing and reservation fees it collects from the franchisees or use such fees to pay for marketing and advertising related to a franchisor's sale of hotels.

Point 7:

Maintaining Relationships with Franchisees

Franchisors should have their books and records audited on an annual basis concerning the collection and disbursement of marketing and reservation fees, and should share the results of the audits with the franchise advisory councils (FACs), or the designated audit committees of the FACs.

Franchisors should strive to maintain and build on their relationships with the franchisees by actively seeking feedback from the franchisees themselves, and by working with the various councils and associations that represent the franchisees, including the franchise advisory councils and AAHOA.

A. *Franchise Advisory Councils*

Franchisors should encourage and support the establishment of independent and democratic FACs, which are comprised of a representative group of franchisees themselves, and who can advise the franchisor on matters of importance to the franchise system. At least six months before implementing any changes to the franchise system, franchisors should seek feedback from the FACs, and use their best efforts to follow the recommendations proposed by the FACs on such matters.

- *Amenity Creep*

Amenity creep is a recognized problem in the hotel industry, and franchisees are concerned that they are not being heard on such issues. Franchisors should regularly seek input from the FACs concerning whether specific amenities should be added, eliminated or changed for the brand name hotels. Prior to mandating the addition of a new amenity, franchisors should submit the issue for a vote to the franchisees themselves and obtain a 66 percent vote of approval from all franchisees who vote on the matter.

- *Marketing and Advertising*

Franchisors should regularly seek input from the FACs concerning how best to market and advertise the various brand name hotels and their services. For example, franchisors should consult with the FACs concerning the annual marketing and advertising budgets, the annual marketing and advertising plans, the format and scope of the directors of hotels in the franchise systems, the franchise system Internet Web sites and the operational plans for the franchise central reservation system. As discussed in Fair Franchising Point 6 above, there should be greater franchisor disclosure and accountability concerning the expenditure of the marketing and reservation fees, including annual audits that are shared with the FACs on their audit committee.

B. *AAHOA Relations*

Franchisors should strive to work closely with AAHOA and its members to promote fairness in the franchise system, and to enhance their respective business interests. Franchisors also should seek ways in which they can increase and improve their communications with AAHOA and its members, obtain input and feedback from AAHOA and its members on issues concerning the franchise systems, and educate and train AAHOA and its members on matters that will improve the individual hotels and strengthen the franchise system on a global basis. Franchisors should attempt to meet with AAHOA personnel on a regular basis to discuss these and other related issues that are of importance to the AAHOA franchisee members.

AAHOA's CHO Program

The AAHOA Certified Hotel Owners (CHO) program is an innovative professional development program for hotel owners offered by the AAHOA Institute of Management (AIM). The CHO program involves an intense, eight-day comprehensive course taught by world-class instructors. At the conclusion of the coursework, attendees attend a CHO certification review and take a CHO examination.

Franchisors should recognize and support the AAHOA CHO program as a hospitality professional accreditation program, and CHO graduates should be given credit for successfully completing the CHO program in the same manner that, for example, the Certified Hotel Administrator (CHA) and Certified Lodging Managers (CLM) training courses have been supported and recognized by franchisors in recent years.

Commentary: The CHO Program was designed to recognize and certify the expertise of AAHOA's member hotel owners, and is the first program of its kind in the country. The CHO program covers a variety of topics, including Front Desk Operations & Reservations; The Laws Of Innkeeping;

Leadership; Hotel Sales, Marketing & Public Relations; Hotel Accounting & Business Ownership Structure; Technology For The Lodging Industry; Human Resource Management; and Housekeeping, Laundry, Engineering & Maintenance. The CHO program has several recognized sponsors, including Best Western International Inc., and was developed by Kapoor & Kapoor Hospitality Inc.

Point 8:

Dispute Resolution

In all franchise agreements, franchisors and franchisees should commit to establishing an independent and fair process for the resolution of any disputes concerning the terms of a franchise agreement itself, or the relationship between the parties. Specifically, franchisors and franchisees should agree in good faith to participate in an informal, in-person meeting between the authorized representatives of the parties in an attempt to resolve a dispute.

If the informal meeting is unsuccessful, the parties should agree to participate in a non-binding mediation, before a mediator who is neutral and mutually acceptable to the parties, including a mediator associated with the National Franchise Mediation Program. If the mediation is unsuccessful, the dispute should not be submitted to binding arbitration unless and until all parties agree to do so, including mutually agreeing on the arbitrator who will hear the dispute, the location of the arbitration proceedings, and the corresponding rules and procedures for the arbitration.

Absent an agreement by the franchisor and franchisee to use binding arbitration to resolve their dispute, any party should be entitled to pursue its claims against another party in a court of law. There should be no waiver of the right to a jury trial by any party. There also should be no caps or limits on the amount of damages that a party can seek or recover against another party, including a cap or limit on the amount of punitive damages that can be recovered against a party as allowed by law.

Point 9:

Venue and Choice of Law Clauses

In the event a dispute between a franchisor and franchisee has not been resolved by participating in an informal, in-person meeting with authorized representatives from the parties, or by participating in mediation proceedings, the party pursuing its claims in a court of law should do so in the county and state in which the subject facility is located. Further, any lawsuit or claims should be governed by laws of the county or state in which the lawsuit or claims are filed.

Franchisors should mandate fair and honest selling practices among their salespersons and agents.

Point 10:

Franchise Sales Ethics and Practices

Franchisors should use their best efforts to identify whether any of their sales agents, or any persons acting on behalf of the franchisors, made any oral or written representations or promises to any franchisee applicants, or reached any agreements with any franchisee applicants, that are not contained in the proposed franchise agreements. To the extent any salespersons or agents made any oral or written representations or promises, or reached any agreements with a franchisee applicant, they should be set forth in writing and attached as an addendum to the particular franchise agreement.

Franchisors should include contractual provisions in their franchise agreements that grant a franchisee all rights, title and interest in its own guest lists, and in all related information for guests that have stayed at the franchisee's particular facility, which survives the termination of the franchise agreement. Franchisors should not use any database developed from one hotel brand to market or sell their other hotel brands to the detriment of the franchisees.

Franchisors and their salespersons and agents should not engage in the practice of "churning" properties (i.e., seeking the early termination of an older hotel on the basis of low quality assurance (QA) inspection scores or otherwise, so the franchisor can then seek and approve an application for the conversion of a newer hotel, or the construction of a new hotel, with a particular brand name in the same geographic region or area of protection (AOP) as the older hotel for which the franchisor is seeking an early termination).

<u>Commentary</u>: It is an unfortunate situation in franchising that many first-time or "rookie" franchisee applicants do not fully understand that the salespersons or agents of the franchisors will sometimes make oral representations or promises about the facility, the franchise system, the franchise agreement. Regrettably, because these first-time franchisee applicants trust and believe that the franchisor's sales-person or agents will honor their oral representations and promises, the applicants do not read carefully the lengthy and sometimes complex franchise agreements to determine whether such representations and promises have been included in their own agreements.

In the interest of fair franchising, prior to the execution of the franchise agreement, a franchisor should ask a franchisee applicant to prepare a written document that identifies any oral or written representations or promises made by, or agreements reached with, the franchisor, its sales agents or any persons acting on behalf of the franchisor that are not contained in the franchise agreement. This written document should be attached as an addendum or exhibit to the franchise agreement.

If the franchise applicant does not identify any such representations, promises or agreements, the franchisor should ask the applicant to review carefully and initial the paragraphs in the franchise agreement which explicitly state that (1) neither the franchisor nor any person acting on its behalf has made any representations or promises on which the applicant franchisee is relying that are not written in the agreement, and (2) the agreement, together with the exhibits and schedules attached, is the entire agreement superseding all previous oral and written representations, agreements and understandings of the parties about the facility, the franchise system, the franchise agreement and the license.

Point 11:

Transferability

In situations in which a franchisee seeks to transfer its property to an unrelated third-party, the franchisor should not delay, withhold its consent or impose conditions on the transfer in an unreasonable, arbitrary or capricious manner. Transfer fees should be fair and reasonable (i.e., generally no more than $1,500), and based solely on the estimated administrative costs to process the transfer.

There should be no fees for a franchisee's transfer to a spouse, child, parent, sibling, niece, nephew, descendant, spouse's descendant or other family member, if the transferee is legally competent to assume the franchisee's obligations under the franchise agreement.

There also should be no transfer fees for a franchisee's buyout of other shareholders or partners who had an interest in the facility, or for the addition of any shareholders or partners who will gain an interest in the facility.

In the event of a requested transfer, franchisors should not condition the granting of the request on a requirement that the franchisee or new owner adopt an extensive renovation or modernization plan for the subject property in connection with a transfer should be limited only to those specific items identified in the last two quality assurance (QA) inspection reports for the subject facility that were issued prior to the requested transfer.

To the extent a franchisor approves a requested transfer, the franchisor should not seek liquidated damages (LDs) from the prior franchisee, or seek any increased fees from the new franchisee owner of the subject facility, because the franchisee sought to transfer its facility prior to the scheduled termination of its franchise agreement.

Within ten days of the completion of an approved transfer of a subject facility, franchisors should automatically release the prior franchisee from any and all obligations it had under the terminated franchise agreement and provide it with a written letter of release in connection therewith.

Point 12:

Sale of The Franchise System Hotel Brand(s)

If a franchisor sells one or more of its various hotel brands to another entity, the franchisor should promptly give notice of the sale to its existing franchisees, and pledge to work with them and the new franchisor owner to ensure the transition is as smooth as possible. To the extent possible, the prior franchisor owner also should continue to honor its guest loyalty or rewards programs for the guests who stayed at the hotels it is selling to the new franchisor owner. Alternatively, the prior franchisor owner selling the hotels should transfer the points or rewards earned by such guests to another existing guest loyalty program of the prior franchisor owner, or a new program it establishes for the benefit of such guests.

The new franchisor owner who purchased the hotel brand should similarly strive to ensure that the transition is a smooth one. Among other things, the new franchisor owner should work closely with the existing franchise advisory councils (FACs) for the hotel brand, or, if circumstances warrant, a newly created FAC, to address all issues involving its purchase and ownership of the hotel brand. The new franchisor owner should maintain the same or a higher level of quality and performance for the hotel brand as the prior franchisor owner.

To the extent a new franchisor owner desires to change any system requirements for the hotel brand, it should work closely with the FACs and the franchisees themselves before implementing any such changes and offer to pay or reimburse the franchisees for the costs of making such changes. The new franchisor owner also should honor the guest loyalty or rewards programs for the guests who stayed at the hotels it is purchasing. Alternatively, the new franchisor owner should transfer the point or rewards earned by such guests to another existing guest loyalty program of the new franchisor owner, or a new program it establishes for the benefit of such guests.

End of 12 Points of Fair Franchising

A majority of AAHOA members are multi-property owners: 61 percent owning multiple hotels and 39 percent have one or two properties. Sixty percent of survey respondents plan to construct new hotels. Most of these (71 percent) will be mid-sized properties of 51-100 rooms, while six percent are developing properties with more than 150 rooms. Among many that own ten or more properties include: ABC Investments & Management Company, Alliance Hospitality, Ashbury Suites & Inns, Avista Hotels, Buggsi Hospitality Group, Diplomat Hotels, Elite Hospitality, HMB Management, JHM Hotels, Kana Hotels, LTD Management Company, Noble Investment Group, Pattni Lodging Group, Pinnacle Hotels, SREE Hospitality Group, Tarsadia Hotels, Temple Hospitality, etc.

One of the most successful Asian American hotel companies is the Hersha Group, the parent company of a vertically integrated array of lodging enterprises that includes the Hersha Development Corp., Hersha Construction Services, Hersha Interiors & Supply, Hersha Hospitality Management and Hersha Hospitality Trust. The executive offices are in New Cumberland, Pa. Hasu Shah came to this country with less than $100, worked three jobs while attending college in Tennessee and New Mexico, moving to Pennsylvania for a state job that enabled him to buy homes at foreclosures. He fixed the homes up and then sold them. The profits enabled him to buy his first hotel. "I started the company with a 125-room hotel," says Hasu, who emigrated from Bombay in 1967. "At first, when it was not doing so well, I kept working as a chemical engineer in the evening. After a year, I quit my job, and we started working together, man and wife. We kept on acquiring two to three hotels a year." Hasu's sons, Jay and Neil, now run the company.

Another success story is exemplified by Hasmukh P. Rama who was the first Chairman of the Asian American Hotel Owners Association. In 1999, Rama was elected chairman of the American Hotel and Lodging Association, the national trade group representing America's $90 billion lodging industry. He is the first Asian American to head the 92 year- old organization. H.P. Rama was recently the recipient of the Pioneer Award from the prestigious International Society of Hospitality Consultants. Rama, a Malawi- born Indian, acquired his first motel in 1973, a 40-room independent in Pomona, CA. H.P. says "We bailed these old operators out. Most of the old small hotels, I'd say eighty percent, were sold by people whose kids weren't interested in running motels." Today, his Greenville, SC company, JHM Hotels, own 31 hotels in five states and one in India. In 1998, his family created the Rama Scholarship Fund for the American Dream with a donation of $1,000,001 (Hindus consider gifts of money ending in the numeral 1 to be particularly auspicious). The gift is intended to help minority students go to hotel management schools.

Clearly, Asian Americans will continue to have a major impact on the lodging industry. Many of their children who have been raised in the United States have completed their college studies in hospitality and are getting MBA's and law degrees. Just a few years ago, it would have been inconceivable that this community would become large-scale owners of upscale properties such as Hiltons, Marriotts and Embassy Suites.

AAHOA has become a mature, pro-active trade association with 8,300 members. Under President Fred Schwartz, AAHOA is professionally managed and is one of the leading forces in the hospitality industry. Its ongoing initiatives include:

- ☐ AAHOA Lodging Business magazine, a monthly publication

- ☐ Annual Convention with attendance of up to 4000 members. They are held in such cities as Las Vegas, Fort Lauderdale, Atlantic City, Grapevine, TX and Charlotte, N.C.

- ☐ Free educational seminars throughout the year for management and supervisory personnel

- ☐ Free regional trade shows featuring industry speakers, timely workshops, supplier exhibits and education courses

- ☐ Free youth conferences to alert young people to the opportunities and responsibilities of the industry

- ☐ Free women's leadership conferences designed to inform and motivate the women who are no longer just the "behind-the-scenes" family backbone.

- ☐ An ambitious scholarship fund to help defray the costs for qualified students who want to pursue a college education in the hospitality industry.

Chairman Mukesh J. Mowji outlined his goals for AAHOA at the 2006 annual convention:

1. Reach an AAHOA membership of 10,000 of which 1000 should be lifetime members

2. In 2007, transition to a membership-based relationship with partners and vendors

3. Revamp AAHOA's 12 Points of Fair Franchising and evaluate how the franchisor community is performing against these 10 year old standards.

4. Create a three-year marketing plan to invigorate the AAHOA brand on Capitol Hill

5. Establish a state-of-the-art member communication system with proprietary information

6. Train board members to be better leaders. Merge the Women's Conference and the Youth Conference into an AAHOA Leadership Conference.

7. Update current bylaws to eliminate conflict and wide interpretation. Plan now for the AAHOA we want in 2015.

SOURCE MATERIALS

"Accidental No More" by Harry Lister, Lodging, December 1996

Joel Millman, *The Other Americans*, Viking Penguin, New York, 1997, Chapter Five: Interstate Commerce

"Born to Last" by Harry Lister, Lodging, January 1999

"A Patel Motel Cartel?" by Tunku Varadarajan, New York Times Magazine, July 4, 1999

"All in the Family: AAHOA Comes of Age", Lodging Hospitality, by Carlo Wolff, February 2001

"Vested Interests" by Anne Willoughby, Lodging, September 2001

Henry Bradley Plant (1819-1899):
DEVELOPER OF FLORIDA'S GULF COAST

Like Henry Morrison Flagler, Henry B. Plant built hotels to encourage northerners to come to Florida on his railroad lines. His magnum opus was the 500-room, Moorish-style Tampa Bay Hotel, which opened in 1891. Immense by any standard, the $3 million property is one-quarter mile long and features a domed dining room, a music room, a solarium. Still standing, the building is used by the University of Tampa and includes the Henry B. Plant Museum.

In 1819, the year of Henry Plant's birth, Florida's population was estimated at 12,000, less than half of what it had been when the first Europeans came ashore in 1513. At that time, the native Indian tribes (Apalachee, Calusa and Timucua) had close to 30,000 population. Unfortunately, these tribes were systematically decimated between 1492 and 1650 by white man's diseases, the slave trade, and European wars of conquest. The destruction of the aboriginal tribes attracted other Indians to the Florida hunting grounds from Georgia and Alabama. Members of the Creek nation established farms, grazing lands and hunting villages in the more remote interior regions of Florida during the early 1800s.

Meanwhile, Florida's population was increased by the influx of runaway and fugitive slaves some of whom joined with or were taken into slavery by various newly-arrived Indian tribes. In 1845, when Florida became a state, the main body of native Americans were forced to relocate to Arkansas except for those diehards who hid out in the Everglades. Those former Indian hunting lands in central Florida became cowboy cattle kingdoms and agricultural farms where cotton and fruit crops were planted and harvested by labor gangs of black slaves.

Henry Bradley Plant was born in Branford, Connecticut on December 27, 1819. His ancestors had lived in Connecticut since 1639. Plant's parents were Betsey and Anderson Plant, farmers of modest success. When Plant was only six years old, his father died. After several years, his mother remarried and Plant lived with them in Martinsburg, New York and later in New Haven, Connecticut. Plant was proud of his New England origins and maintained memberships in the Sons of the American Revolution and the New England Society all his life. He also kept a residence and office in New York City after 1875 and a summer home in Connecticut. Plant's last bit of formal education ended in the eighth grade at the Lancastrian School in New Haven. At eighteen years of age, Plant declined his mother's offer to send him to Yale College and instead began his employment with the New Haven Steamboat Company as a "captain's boy". He worked hard to learn all aspects of the shipping business. He later worked for the Adams Express Company in various jobs in New York City and Augusta, Georgia. At age 23, Plant married Ellen Elizabeth Blackstone, daughter of a well-to-do state legislator, James Blackstone. The Plants had two sons, one of whom died at 18 months old. The second, Morton Freeman Plant, born in 1852, would later participate in his father's business. When Plant's wife developed congestion in her lungs, two physicians advised that she should go to Florida for a proper recovery. The Plants decided to leave New York on March 25, 1853 for a trip south by steamboat. When Plant and his wife arrived in Jacksonville, Florida, he noted that the city had inadequate wharf facilities and no vehicles to carry baggage or passengers to their hotel or local residence. After being warned about the condition of the hotels, Plant and his wife spent the first night in Florida in a private home and then traveled in a large dug-out canoe paddled by a crew of blacks to accommodations in a home at Strawberry Mills six miles distant on the St. Johns River. So poor was Mrs. Plant's recovery from the lung problem that she returned to Florida every winter during the remainder of her life and Henry did the same, spending thirty-nine winters in Florida. Over time, Mrs. Plant's health continued to decline and she died on February 28, 1861.

In Augusta, Georgia, the Plants lived in the following hotels: the Globe, Eagle, Phoenix and Planter's Hotel. When the oncoming Civil

War was imminent, the Adams Express Company sold its southern business to Plant and his associates for $500,000. Plant signed five personal notes for $100,000 each. The company gained good will when it carried all clothing packages for Confederate soldiers free of charge. The Southern Express Company transported mail and packages as well as supplies, medicine, and payrolls for the Confederate States of America. By the end of the century, under Plant's continuous leadership, Southern Express employed 6800 people in 15 states using 885 wagons and 1450 horses. In addition, the business utilized 24,000 miles of railroad lines. The company ended operations when it was acquired by the American Railway Express Company in 1918.

Plant was instrumental in restoring economic health to the south during the Reconstruction era after the Civil War. Porter King, the Mayor of Atlanta, said in the <u>Atlantic Constitution</u>, "Georgia, the South and Atlanta owe more to Plant than to any other man."

While living in Augusta, an incident occurred which resulted in the purchase of a slave by Mr. Plant. A black slave by the name of Dennis Dorsey was rented by Plant to act as porter in his office. One summer when Plant was about to go north, Dennis said that his master was going to sell him for $1500. Dennis said that "it is too much, I am not worth so much. You can buy me when you come back, as there is little danger of my being sold at that price." But Dennis was sold in Plant's absence. When Plant returned, he bought Dennis from a trader in Mobile, Alabama for $1800 and brought him back to Augusta.

In 1873, twelve years after the death of his first wife, Henry Plant married Margaret Josephine Loughman, who was the housekeeper of his home in Branford. Margaret, whose ancestry included nobility in Ireland, would later be a great help to Henry in the selection of furnishings for the Pullman palace cars, steamships and the Tampa Bay Hotel. After the Civil War, Plant expanded his Southern Express Company by acquiring the Texas Express Co. and then was able to serve all the major cities in the south: Atlanta, Augusta, Charleston, Memphis, Montgomery, New Orleans and Savannah. Plant also became familiar with the railroad business.

Starting in 1879, Plant acquired the following railroads: Atlantic and Gulf, Savannah and Charleston and other short lines with partners, stockholders and other investors. In 1883, Plant and a dozen other investors, including Henry M. Flagler, acquired three-fifths of the South Florida Railroad which linked Savannah and Jacksonville with Tampa. These railroads carried passengers, timber and produce and river freight. Plant owned and operated steamboats on the St. Johns River. By the 1880's his Plant Steamship Company was carrying passengers, freight and the United States mail between, Tampa, Key West and Havana.

The economic stimulant to railroad building in Florida was the Florida Internal Improvement Fund which in 1881 sold 4 million acres of land to Hamilton Disston, a Philadelphia industrialist for twenty-five cents an acre. This action and later state donations of land in return for construction triggered an avalanche of railroad building in Florida. Ultimately, 16 million acres of land were granted to companies building railroads, drainage districts and canals. The effect of this building, much of it by Plant, by the 1890s was to give Florida a railroad system, greater in proportion to population than almost every other state. When steamship and steamboat services were included, travel facilities were better in Florida than in most of the other states.

In 1885, Plant created the port of Tampa by building a causeway, a huge wharf and piers in deep water west of downtown Tampa at Port Tampa. The wharf accommodated steamships, trains, warehouses and a hotel known as the Inn at Port Tampa. The port ultimately had a capacity for berthing 26 ocean steamships, some of which provided steamship service to Key West, Cuba, other islands and Central America.

Most of Henry Plant's business interests were involved in the creation of railroad, steamboat and hotel services for the moving of people and goods for profit. Plant's mature water-based operations were widespread ranging from north-south steamboat service from Columbus, Georgia to Apalachicola, Florida for almost two decades and on the St. Johns River from Jacksonville to Palatka and Sanford using the "People's Line" name.

After he built the port, wharf and warehouse facilities at Tampa, he operated steamship lines on routes in the Gulf of Mexico from Mobile to Punta Gorda and Fort Myers. Plant also had extensive steamship service to Canada's maritime provinces. But the most important service was steamship service from Tampa to Havana, Cuba either via Key West or direct from Tampa. The "Federal Express/UPS" man of his time, Henry Plant owned a huge organization that included several steamship lines, 14 railroad companies and eight hotels.

At the end of the 19th century, the newly-created American leisure class began to travel extensively for pleasure. During this gilded age, Americans traveled on new and improved rail transportation made more comfortable with Fred Harvey's restaurants and resort hotels and George Pullman's Palace sleeping and dining cars.

Three national expositions broke attendance records mainly because of the reliable new railroad service: the 1870 American Centennial Exhibition in Philadelphia, the 1893 World's Columbian Exposition in Chicago and the 1895 Cotton States and International Exposition in Atlanta. Encouraged and informed by new guidebooks, illustrated magazine articles and railroad advertising, travelers vacationed in American resorts from the east coast to the Rocky Mountains. Many of these resorts followed the railroads and were located in spectacular and picturesque locations: Bar Harbor, Maine; Newport, Rhode Island; New Jersey shore; White Mountains, New Hampshire; Berkshire Hills, Massachusetts; Adirondacks and Catskills Mountains, New York; Saratoga Springs and Ballston Spa, New York; Hot Springs, Arkansas; Lake Geneva, Wisconsin; Aiken, South Carolina; Hilton Head, South Carolina; Thomasville, Georgia; Rocky Mountains; Colorado Springs, Colorado, etc.

The construction of new private lines was often followed by great new resort hotels. In Canada, Scottish-born American William Van Horne, president of the Canadian Pacific Railway, completed the construction of the CP railroad across the continent. In order to attract passengers, Van Horne hired New Yorker Bruce Price to design two spectacular hotels: the Banff Springs Hotel opened in 1888 and the Chateau Frontenac in Quebec in 1893. The CP also built Swiss-chalet-style hotels in eastern Canada.

In Florida in conjunction with their railroad construction, Henry B. Plant and Henry M. Flagler built five of the most successful of the resort hotels of the late 19th and early 20th century. Miraculously, Plant's spectacular Tampa Bay Hotel and his luxurious Hotel Belleview are still standing.

Henry Plant owned hotels in eight southwest Florida locations served by his railroad system. He developed and built three hotels: the Inn at Port Tampa (1888), the Tampa Bay Hotel (1891) and the Hotel Belleview (1897). He purchased the Hotel Kissimmee (1883), the Ocala House (1884), the Seminole Hotel (1886), the Hotel Punta Gorda (1887), and the Fort Myers Hotel (1897).

Some of these hotels had remarkable features and amenities for their time:

The Tampa Bay Hotel- with the success of Flagler's Ponce de Leon Hotel in St. Augustine, Plant decided that Tampa needed a spectacular new hotel. With the agreement of the town council for a new bridge across the Hillsborough River and for substantial real estate tax abatement, Plant chose New York City architect John A. Wood. The cornerstone was laid on July 26, 1888 and the 511 room hotel opened on February 5, 1891 with a 70 square foot lobby and a 23 foot high rotunda supported by thirteen granite columns. Florida's first fully electrified hotel contained the following features:

The Tampa Bay Hotel, Tampa, Florida in its opening promotion in 1891 declared itself to be 1100 feet long and the main hall more than 700 feet long. There were about 500 rooms with accommodations for nearly 1000 guests. Broad galleries extended on the south and north fronts from 16 to 76 feet in width, all under cover of roofs supported by ornamental columns, making a grand promenade.

1. Guest rooms: one bathroom for every three rooms (while the Ponce de Leon had shared bathrooms at the end of the hallways); carpets, soft beds, telephones, hot water heating, a fireplace and circular fifteen inch diameter mirror set in the ceiling of each room with three bulbs set below to throw out light to all parts of the rooms. In addition, there were two electric lights placed in the side of the dressing table.

2. Sixteen suites: each with double parlors, three bedrooms, sliding doors, two bathrooms and private hallways.

3. Public facilities included a cafe, billiard room, telegraph office, barber shop, drug store, flower shop and special ladies area for shuffleboards, billiards and cafe facilities. Also available were needle and mineral water baths, massages

and a physician. There were other small shops in an arcade area.

4. Recreation facilities included tennis and croquet courts, rickshaw rides, an 18-hole golf course, stables, hunting trips and excursions by electric launch on the Hillsborough River to observe alligators and mullet, and, after returning to the hotel, tea and crackers at 5:00 PM.

5. Evening meals served at 6:00 p.m. were formal with fancy dresses, jackets and ties. There was live music by the orchestra placed on the second level of the large dining room. After dinner, the guests separated- men to the bar for stories, cigars and after-dinner liqueurs; women to the sitting room for cool drinks and conversation.

6. Another service provided by the hotel were fifteen dog kennels for the accommodation of pets carried along by hotel guests during their stay in Florida. The kennels were located in a half-acre park with shade trees and enclosed by a six foot fence. The hotel's brochure claimed that it had "the most complete dog accommodations of any hotel in existence."

In the 1896-97 season, Plant built a casino/auditorium, an 80 x 110 foot exhibition building with a clubhouse in the front and a combined auditorium and swimming pool in the rear. The eastern end of the clubhouse contained two bowling alleys and a shuffleboard court. When needed as an auditorium, the tiled pool filled with spring water could be covered with a wooden floor. When the hall, which seated 1,800 persons, was not used as a theater, the dressing rooms of the actors became changing rooms for the bathers. The hotel had great wide verandas, beautiful gardens, arches of electric light, oriental ceramics, beautiful statues and paintings, Turkish rugs, chinese bronze vases. Mr. and Mrs. Plant took trips to Europe and the Far East to select and purchase articles to furnish the public rooms.

A hotel postcard of 1924 described the beautiful grounds as follows:

A jewel so magnificent should have an appropriate setting and so it has, in a tropical garden of rare beauty of foliage and species. The acreage surrounding the hotel should match its noble proportions and so it permits of orange groves, alluring walks, and enticing drives through long lines of palmetto and under live oaks trailing their gray banners of Spanish moss.

Alongside a small stream were planted many tropical plants and fruits including roses, pansies, bamboos, oleander, papayas, mangos and pineapples. Since occasional cold weather could damage tropical plants, a glassed-in conservatory was built to grow plants and flowers for guest rooms, public areas and dining room tables. After a trip to the Bahamas, head gardener Auton Fiche returned with a boat load of tropical plants. An 1892 catalogue of fruits, flowers and plants growing on hotel grounds listed twenty two kinds of palm trees, three varieties of bananas, twelve varieties of orchids and various citrus trees including orange, lime, lemon, grapefruit, mandarin and tangerine.

Even today, you can see why the Tampa Bay Hotel was the jewel of Plant's Florida Gulf Coast Hotels. Much of the original building is used by the University of Tampa and houses the Henry B. Plant Museum. When it opened on January 31, 1891, the journalist Henry G. Parker in the Boston Saturday Evening Gazette wrote,

> The new Tampa Bay Hotel: It was reserved for the sagacious and enterprising railroad and steamboat magnate, Mr. H.B. Plant, to reap the honor of erecting in tropical Florida the most attractive, most original and most beautiful hotel in the South, if not in the whole country; and it is a hotel of which the whole world need to be advised. The entire estate, including land and building, cost two millions of dollars, and the furniture and fittings a half million more. Nothing offends the eye, the effect produced is one of astonishment and delight.

Despite all the hotel's features, it was never a commercial success in Plant's time. He ignored the financial reports and claimed that the hotel was worthwhile if only to enjoy the great German pipe organ.

The Henry B. Plant Museum in the Tampa Bay Hotel (established in 1933) recalls the hotel's gilded age, when formal dress for dinner was standard and rickshaws carried guests through the hotel's exotic gardens. The Spanish-American War Room tells the story the hotel played in the 1898 conflict between the United States and Spanish-held Cuba. Because Tampa was the city nearest to Cuba with both rail and port facilities, it was chosen as the point of embarkation for the war. The hotel was designated a National Historic Landmark in 1977.

The Hotel Belleview, Bellaire- Four years after opening the Tampa Bay Hotel, Henry Plant decided to expand his hotel holdings and acquired 700 acres at Clearwater Harbor. Plant commissioned Michael J. Miller and Francis J. Kennard of Tampa to design and build a luxury winter resort hotel on the Gulf of Mexico. On January 15, 1897 the Belleview Hotel at Bellaire opened with 145 rooms, Georgia pine construction, swiss-style design, golf course and race track. The Belleview became a retreat for the wealthy whose private railroad cars were often parked at the railroad siding built to the south of the hotel.

The Belleview, named the "White Queen of the Gulf", is four and a half stories and the largest wood-frame building in Florida. In 1920, the Hotel was purchased from the Plant Investment company by John McEntee Bowman, owner of the Biltmore chain of hotels. For the past 87 years the hotel has been known as the Belleview Biltmore Hotel. It is listed on the National Registry of Historic Places and is famous for its Victorian charm and southern hospitality.

Many famous dignitaries have been guests at this hotel including presidents George H. W. Bush, Jimmy Carter, Gerald Ford, the former King of England, (the Duke of Windsor) the Vanderbilts, the Pew family of Sun Oil, the Studebakers, the DuPonts, Thomas Edison, Henry Ford and Lady Margaret Thatcher, baseball legends Babe Ruth, Joe DiMaggio, and entertainers Tony Bennett, Bob Dylan and Carol Channing. In 1985, a $10 million renovation of the resort took place in the guest rooms and in the construction of a luxurious spa.

The Mobil Travel Guide gave the Biltmore a four-star rating and the *World Tennis Magazine* gave it a five-star rating for tennis resorts. The Biltmore is one of the few hotels to have a waltz composed in its name, "The Belleview Waltz." The Belleview Biltmore Golf Club offers a beautiful 18 hole course designed by world-famous Scottish-born architect, Donald Ross in 1925.

The Belleview Biltmore provides 243 guest rooms in an intimate setting. In its better days, guests could enjoy a variety of guest rooms starting with a quaint one bedroom suite, all the way up to the 3,400 square foot presidential suite. Nearby residents of this Tampa Bay resort consider the Belleview Biltmore to be one of West Florida's most picturesque landmarks. Banquets, meeting rooms, conference services, gourmet dining, and weddings with attention top detailed service were offered at this exquisite hotel.

Despite its membership in the National Trust Historic Hotels of America, the Belleview Biltmore Hotel has been at risk of being demolished. Its current owners (DiBartolo and Urdang) have applied for a permit to raze all the buildings on this landmark resort and are planning to demolish seven buildings totaling 440,000 square feet including the removal of resort pools and tennis courts.

But, as I complete this chapter, there is good news to report. The Save the Biltmore Preservationists report that there is a contract to purchase the Belleview Biltmore by Legg Mason Real Estate Investors, Inc. Los Angeles who say that they intend to buy the resort and allocate $100 million to restore and improve the 110 year-old hotel.

Their announced plans include:

- a new landscaped grand entrance to the main hotel

- a fully restored 256-room main hotel structure with five ballrooms, meeting rooms, restaurants and retail shops.

- a new but architecturally consistent 174-room annex hotel adjacent to the main hotel structure.

- three restored Victorian cottages

- a new one-story spa facility with underground parking.

- removal of the existing "pagoda" structure at front entrance of the main hotel.

- a refurbished clubhouse, improved landscaping and parking at the Pelican Golf Club.

The Seminole Hotel- Two years before the opening of Flagler's Ponce de Leon in St. Augustine, the Seminole Hotel, a magnificent resort facility opened in Winter Park, Florida. It featured its own horse-drawn streetcar line, steam heat, a bowling alley, a billiard room, elevators, fire alarms, fire escapes, and a yacht basin. In the winter of 1888, the guest list included Ulysses S. Grant, Grover Cleveland, George Pullman, Charles F. Crocker and George Westinghouse. In 1891, Plant bought the Seminole Hotel and had it painted "Plant yellow" with white trim. The Seminole contained 200 rooms with connecting doors so that they could be rented as suites. The hotel housed its staff in a separate dormitory building and operated its own steam laundry. Seminole guests enjoyed tennis, croquet, fishing, horse-back riding and boating. According to hotel advertisements, parents were encouraged to leave their children under professional supervision while they traveled to Cuba on a Plant Line steamship. Three years after Plant's death in 1899, the Seminole burned down and was replaced ten years later in 1912 by a new Seminole Hotel which was ultimately demolished in 1970.

The Inn at Port Tampa- designed and built by architect W.T. Cotter on the new wharf some 2000 feet from the shore. The first building opened in 1888 with twenty rooms and the second structure added another twenty rooms in 1890. The Inn contained one large dining room and a smaller dining room for nursemaids and children. The Inn offered electricity, running water, comfort, convenience and entertainment. In a front-page article on January 29, 1891, the Tampa Journal described the Inn at Port Tampa as "colonial" and declared that the inn resembled a "cozy home" more than a hotel. It featured a large veranda on the ground floor which allowed guests to fish from the porch or from the windows of their rooms.

The Hotel Kissimmee- was built in 1883 with 125 rooms and opened as the Tropical Hotel on Lake Tohopekaliga. Isaac Merritt Mabbette, part-owner and hotel manager and George Bass built the hotel which was jointly owned by the South Florida Railway. Kissimmee was known as "The Tropical City" and in the 1870's featured a "ride-up bar" where horseback riders could drink their whiskey while sitting in their saddles. When Plant acquired the hotel, he added rooms and changed the name to the Hotel Kissimmee. It contained public rooms with open fireplaces, billiards, lawn tennis and boating. Good hunting included quail, duck, snipe deer, wild turkey and bear. A fire destroyed the wood frame Hotel Kissimmee in 1906.

The Ocala House- was built in 1884 and acquired by Plant in 1895. It was three-stories high with 200 rooms and with its extensive gardens and grounds occupied a city block. The guestrooms had working fireplaces, electricity, call bells and over-door transoms. The Ocala House provided a house orchestra for guest dancing. Like many hotels which featured some hunting and fishing, the hotel provided kennels for hunting dogs. The Ocala House survived until the early 1970s when it was demolished.

The Hotel Punta Gorda- opened in 1887 and was acquired by Plant in 1894 when he bought the Florida Southern Railway. The hotel contained 150 guestrooms in a relatively plain three-story structure but did provide steam heat, open fireplaces, call bells and a telegraph office. It operated only during the winter and provided dock facilities on Charlotte Harbor for guests arriving by yacht. Some of these included Andrew Mellon, W. K. Vanderbilt and John Wanamaker. In 1925, the hotel was acquired by Barron Collier and renamed it the Charlotte Harbor Inn. After various owners, the hotel burned to the ground on August 14, 1959.

The Fort Myers Hotel- was built in 1897 by Hugh O'Neill with Plant as a likely partner. O'Neill owned a famous New York City department store. O'Neill used the architectural firm of Miller and Kennard, the same company that designed the Hotel Belleview for Plant. The Fort Myers Hotel had forty-five guestrooms with separate bathroom facilities for men and women. The guestrooms were furnished with rocking chairs and white enameled head-boards and dressers. The Hotel operated a clubhouse on the Caloosahatchee River which contained a bowling alley, a billiard room, a shooting gallery and storage rooms for fishing gear and hunting guns. In 1907, Tootie McGregor, widow of Standard Oil executive Ambrose M. McGregor, bought the hotel, added fifty rooms and changed the name to the Royal Palm Hotel. Subsequent owners renovated and added rooms until World War II when the hotel was used as housing for U.S. Army soldiers. Finally, in 1948, the Royal Palm was demolished.

Plant and Flagler were friends who visited with each other on numerous occasions. A former mayor of Miami, John Sewell described them as, "best friends". They published each other's railroad schedules and advertised each other's hotels in their advertising and printed promotions. An apocryphal story illustrates their friendly rivalry. When the Tampa Bay Hotel opened in 1891, Plant invited Flagler to the opening events. When Flagler responded, "Where's Tampa?", Plant answered, "Follow the crowds". When Flagler built the Royal Poinciana in Palm Beach in 1894, Plant responded to the invitation, "Where's Palm Beach?" to which Flagler replied, "Follow the crowds." Most visitors to the Tampa Bay area eventually hear about nearby Plant City. This small city just east of Tampa styles itself as the "Winter Strawberry Capital," and backs up its claim with an annual strawberry festival. The city's name does not relate to agriculture, however, but to Henry B. Plant, the remarkable developer of Florida's Gulf Coast.

At the time of his death, Plant was a comparatively wealthy man and left a personal estate valued at $10,000,000. The Tampa Bay Hotel never achieved the results that Plant hoped for. The City of Tampa acquired it from the Plant estate for only $125,000 in 1905. They lost money until it was leased to W.F. Adams who operated it successfully during the Florida real estate boom. At the start of the Depression the City gave the hotel to the University of Tampa when it converted from a two-year community college to a four-year university. Some time later, the Henry Bradley Plant museum was created featuring a few of the old hotel rooms and many of the original Plant treasures.

SOURCE MATERIALS

1. Karl P. Abbott, *Open For The Season*, Doubleday & Company, Inc., Garden City, 1950

2. Susan R. Braden, *The Architecture of Leisure: The Florida Resort Hotels of Henry Flagler and Henry Plant,* University Press of Florida, Gainesville 2002

3. Dr. James W. Covington, *Plant's Palace: Henry B. Plant and the Tampa Bay Hotel*, Harmony House Publishers, Louisville 1999

4. Edward A. Mueller, *Steamships of the Two Henrys: Being An Account of the Maritime Activities of Henry Morrison Flagler and Henry Bradley Plant*, E.O. Painter Printing Co. De Leon Springs, Florida 1996

5. Kelly Reynolds, *Henry Plant: Pioneer Empire Builder,* The Florida Historical Society Press, Cocoa, Florida, 2003

6. G. Hutchinson Smyth, *The Life of Henry Bradley Plant: Founder and President of the Plant System of Railroads and Steamships*, G.P. Putnam's Sons, New York 1898; reprint

George Mortimer Pullman (1831-1897):
INVENTOR OF HOTEL ROOMS ON WHEELS

When young people ask their parents "What is a Pullman car?", they often receive a reply, "a railroad car you sit down in to have a meal on a train." Though a good reply, the full story of the invention and widespread usage of the Pullman car is much more interesting. You must go back to the development of the railroad sleeping cars by earlier pioneers than George Mortimer Pullman.

It seems that sleeping cars appeared on American railroads some twenty years before Pullman remodeled the two Chicago & Alton Railroad coaches into sleeping cars in 1858. The first two companies to introduce sleeping cars were the Cumberland Valley Railroad in 1836 and the New York & Erie Railroad in 1843. Twenty years later, such cars were in wide use but they were uncomfortable and difficult to convert from day coach use into sleeping cars for night travel.

George Mortimer Pullman was born on March 3, 1831 in Albion, N.Y., outside of Buffalo, the third of ten children of James Lewis and Emily Caroline (Minton) Pullman. James purchased the Budlong farm and built a small frame house where George was born. Lewis Pullman's skills as a carpenter enabled him to stay busy during the prosperous times of the 1830's. At that time, the major transportation facility in upstate New York was the Erie Canal which was utilized to move agricultural products to satisfy the country's increasing demand for food. The Erie Canal was completed in 1825 at a cost of $7 million by New York State. The 363 miles length between Albany and Buffalo became a popular waterway for passenger and freight traffic between the northeastern states and the new western territories. The building of the new Erie Canal required the relocating of structures along the right-of-way. Lewis Pullman worked as a building-mover and invented a machine for transporting buildings on wheels for which he received a patent in 1841. His sons followed in his footsteps and emulated his example.

George left formal education after the fourth grade and took a job in his uncle's general store, Buck and Minton's at a salary of $40 per year. He left his job after three years and joined his brother Albert in a cabinet-making business. During the following ten years, George expanded his woodworking and construction skills as factories, warehouses and other buildings were built adjacent to the newly-widened Erie Canal. After Lewis Pullman died on November 1, 1853, the twenty-two year old George, the eldest unmarried son, took over the responsibility to support the family. Soon thereafter, George decided to give up the cabinet-making business and concentrate on the building-moving business.

In 1854, George secured a contract with New York State to move twenty or more buildings back from the new right-of-way along the Erie Canal near Albion. However, by 1857, as a business recession occurred, he visited Chicago in search of new projects and ultimately secured the contract to raise the Matteson House, one of Chicago's better-known hotels and the largest building to be elevated to that time. This job was part of the project to raise portions of Chicago's business district by eight feet in order to build a sewage system. This was necessitated because Chicago had been built on the low land south of a sluggish river and suffered from a lack of proper drainage. Year after year, cellars became wells of water with mud choking the streets. Pullman was successful and built a solid reputation after raising a number of blocks of bricks and stone buildings including the massive Tremont House, a six-story brick hotel on an acre of ground.

Between 1855 and 1860, Chicago took steps to drain the thoroughfares, raise their grades, dig and install sewers, gas and water pipes. The process was difficult and fraught with potential accidents. Workmen inserted blocks, timber and thousands of jackscrews and heavyweight jacks. Then, at a signal, six hundred workers turned their screws a quarter turn, filled the gap with pilings and over a five day period lifted thirty five thousand tons of buildings nearly five feet.

Even before he left New York State, George Pullman showed enthusiasm for the fabrication of railroad sleeping cars. One of his close friends and neighbors in Albion, former State Senator Benjamin C. Field, had joined his partners in building and operating several sleeping cars.

In connection with both his cabinet shop and building–raising business, Pullman was familiar with uncomfortable sleeping accommodations on canal boats and railroad trains. Pullman and Field formed a partnership and secured a contract from the Chicago, Alton and St. Louis Railroad to develop a more comfortable sleeping car. Pullman hired a skilled Alton Railroad mechanic, Leonard Seibert, to implement his revolutionary ideas. Seibert later wrote,

> In 1858, Mr. Pullman came to Bloomington and engaged me to do the work of remodeling two Chicago & Alton Coaches into the first Pullman sleeping cars. The contract was that Mr. Pullman should make all necessary changes inside of the cars. After looking over the entire passenger car equipment of the road, which at that time constituted about a dozen cars, we selected Coaches Nos. 9 and 19. They were forty-four feet long, had flat roofs like box cars, single sash windows, of which there were fourteen on a side, the glass in each sash being only a little over one square foot. The roof was only a trifle over six feet from the floor of the car. Into this car we got ten sleeping–car sections, besides a linen locker and two washrooms- one at each end ..... The two cars cost Mr. Pullman not more than $2000, or $1000 each. They were upholstered in plush, lighted by oil lamps, heated with box stoves and mounted on four-wheel trucks with iron wheels. There was no porter in those days; the brakeman made up the beds.

While the two remodeled Chicago and Alton coaches were accepted by the public, the Civil War prevented more radical designs from being built. In 1864, Pullman had a new car built in Chicago at a cost of $20,178 and called it the "Pioneer." It was a vast improvement over any car then in service with springs reinforced by blocks of solid rubber. In order to gain a head start on his competition, George became a master of public relations with the following masterstrokes: a) used the word "palace" to describe his sleeping and dining cars b) invited kings and queens to use his personal car c) installed a printing press in the baggage compartment of the first all- Pullman transcontinental trip in order to publish dozens of self-praising newspapers. One of them featured this jingle:

> "Hurrah for a ride without a jostle or jar!
> Hurrah for a life on the iron bar!
> Hurrah for a ride in a Pullman car!
> Viva la compagnie"

The tycoon Andrew Carnegie was so intrigued by Pullman that he became his largest investor. History has recorded that the Pioneer was a foot wider and two and a half feet higher than any car then in service and therefore it could not pass over any existing railroad tracks. However, fate intervened.

In April 1865, after President Abraham Lincoln was assassinated, his body was being transported by the so-called "Lonesome Train" to Springfield, Illinois for burial. From Washington, D.C. the funeral train bearing his body started west by slow stages. Across the country, mourners lined the tracks and wept when given the opportunity to look upon "Father Abraham" for the last time. By the time the cortege reached Chicago, Mrs. Lincoln collapsed. When arrangements had to be made for her return directly to Springfield, Pullman offered his new Pioneer sleeper. The Chicago, Alton and St. Louis Railroad laborers worked day and night to widen viaducts, raise bridges and narrow platforms so that the Pioneer could pass. It was reported that they completed in two days a project that might otherwise have taken a year.

This apocryphal story is somewhat to be doubted in light of more recent research. George Pullman spun the story in later years but in 1865, there were no contemporary news stories that reported it. The first published reference to an oversized Pioneer car came some twenty-three years after Lincoln's death. The last such report appeared in the Pullman Company's final report in 1917, fifty-two years later.

In 1867, George Pullman went even further in his market penetration. He recognized that the typical meal on a train consisted of hard tack beef, stale coffee and doughnuts so hard that they were called "sinkers". Many travelers packed a portable lunch at home or purchased one at the station. One major exception was the Atchison, Topeka, & Santa Fe's association with the Fred Harvey Houses and the "Harvey Girls".

Pullman created and introduced his first hotel on wheels, the President, a sleeper with an attached kitchen and dining car. The food rivaled the best restaurants of the day and the service was impeccable. A year later in 1868, he launched the Delmonico, the world's first sleeping car devoted to fine cuisine. Both the President and the Demonico and subsequent Pullman sleeping cars offered first-rate service which was provided by recently-freed former house slaves who served as porters, waiters, chambermaids, entertainers, and valets all rolled into one person.

Pullman realized that if his sleeper cars were to be successful, he needed to provide a wide variety of services to travelers: collecting tickets, selling berths, dispatching wires, fetching sandwiches, mending torn trousers, converting day coaches into sleepers, etc. At first, Pullman hired whites but they were neither trained nor disposed to do the grunt work of janitor, shoe shiner, maid, waiter, porter, bellhop and valet. Pullman found that former house slaves has the right combination of training, acquiescence, size and color. He favored "the blackest man with the whitest teeth." Pullman was called a racist who "does more than any other organization in the world to make the negro a beggar and a grafter" wrote the New York Press in 1911. "More negroes are demoralized each year by the Pullman Company than are graduated by Tuskegee, Hampton and some other negro educational establishments."

Truth is that Pullman was way ahead of his time. He became the biggest single employer of blacks in the country and the job of Pullman porter was probably the very best job that a black man could get in the 101 year history of the Pullman Company. Later, Robert Todd Lincoln, son of President Lincoln who succeeded George M. Pullman as president (and served until 1911) had to appear before a Congressional Commission to explain their hiring policies. His representative, general manager L. S. Hungerford said, "the old southern colored man makes the best porter on the car. He is more adapted to waiting on passengers and gives them better attention and has a better manner."

The porters were carefully selected as a docile servant class always at the beck and call of white passengers. The porter lit the candles that illuminated the Pullman cars, stoked the pot-bellied coal stoves for heat and converted the day coach into an overnight sleeper compartment. He was part- chambermaid, part-butler and part-valet. He shined shoes, nursed hangovers and earned tips that gave him and his family middle class status. The wealthy white travelers called him "boy" or more often "George" like the practice of naming slaves after slavemasters. Porters were thought to be "owned" by George Pullman. Believe it or not, other men named George protested by forming a Society for the Prevention of Calling Sleeping Car Porters George or SPCSCPG which eventually attracted some 31,000 members including George M. Cohan and George Herman "Babe" Ruth.

Author Larry Tye said it best in his book, *Rising From The Rails*:

> Whether George Pullman knew his passengers were calling his porters "George" is unclear. That he would not have cared is certain. It was not that he was mean, or more coldhearted to black employees than to white. He believed he owed workers nothing more than a job, and when business slackened, even that was not ironclad. He hired more Negroes than any businessman in America, giving them a monopoly on the profession of Pullman porter and a chance to enter the cherished middle class. He did it not out of sentimentality, of which he had none, but because it made business sense. They came cheap, and men used to slave labor could be compelled to do whatever work they were asked, for as many hours as told.

Porters, meanwhile, created their own cultural superhero: Daddy Joe, a Bunyanesque figure. He was tall enough to pull down the upper berths on either side of the aisle at the same time, agile enough to service the uppers and lowers simultaneously, eloquent enough to talk a band of marauding Indians into accepting a pile of Pullman blankets in place of passenger scalps.

The Pioneer, President and Delmonico sleeping cars proved to be a huge success after a working test by the Michigan Central Railroad. Pullman suggested that both the new Pullman cars at $2 per night and old-style sleeping cars at $1.50 per night be operated on the same train. The decision apparently came immediately when the only travelers who rode in the old cars were those who couldn't get seats in the new cars. Within the next few days, the old cars were removed from service and the new Pullmans became the standard of service. The Chicago, Burlington and Quincy, a subsidiary of the New York Central and a Canadian line, the Great Western acquired and installed the new Pullman sleeping cars.

By the middle of 1869, Pullman's Palace Car Company owned more than seventy cars and soon thereafter acquired the Detroit Car and Manufacturing Company where they manufactured their own vehicles. Pullman continued to expand and struck leasing deals with the Pennsylvania Railroad company and the Hannibal and St. Joseph and North Missouri Railroad companies. By 1870, Pullman was manufacturing sleeping cars, drawing room cars, hotel cars and dining cars. The hotel car had two drawing rooms each furnished with a sofa and two large easy chairs that converted to two double and two single berths at night. Each hotel car had a large kitchen which prepared fine food that compared favorably with the best restaurants of the day. The wonderfully compact eight-foot square kitchen contained a specially-designed three-tiered range which permitted baking, broiling and boiling. Every inch of space was ingeniously designed for storage of kitchen equipment and supplies along with storage space for meats, vegetables, wines and condiments. From this kitchen, the cooks were able to produce 250 meals per day.

The Detroit Commercial Advertiser of June 1, 1867, commented:

> But the crowning glory of Mr. Pullman's invention is
> evinced in his success in supplying the car with a cuisine
> department containing a range where every variety of
> meats, vegetables and pastry may be cooked on the car,
> according to the best style of culinary art.

Hotel cars named "Western World" "City of Boston" and "City of New York" costing more than $30,000 each were put into service between Chicago and eastern points. However, in 1869 the Pullman Company received nationwide publicity when the Union Pacific and the Central Pacific track laying crews met. In May, 1870 the first through train from the Atlantic to the Pacific crossed the United States. The Pullman cars provided a level of comfort never before experienced. Magazines and newspapers extolled the marvels of the journey to the Pacific Ocean as "a six day's sojourn in a luxurious hotel, past the windows of which there constantly flowed a great panorama of the American continent; thousands of miles in length and as wide as the eye could reach." Illustrated magazine articles which appeared telling the story of a trip to California had as many pictures of Pullman interiors as they had of the big trees or the Yosemite valley. The effect of all this was far-reaching. The great Pennsylvania line abandoned its own service and adopted the Pullman, and many other lines made application for inclusion in the Pullman system.

On June 13, 1867, George Pullman married Harriett (Hattie) Amelia Sanger, the daughter of Mary Catherine McKibben and James Y. Sanger, a builder who helped construct railroads and the new State of Illinois penitentiary at Joliet. During the next eight years George and Hattie had four children: Florence (1868), Harriett (1869) and twin sons George Jr. and Walter (1875).

The Pullmans lived with an ostentatious display of wealth in the years that followed. They built a mansion on Prairie Avenue in Chicago which contained a bowling alley and billiard room. They made their first recorded visit to Long Branch, N.J. during the summer of 1871, where they visited with President Ulysses S. Grant and his wife, Julia. In 1874, they summered at their new house Fairlawn, just west of Long Branch, N.J. It was reported that the Pullmans traveled on a private train from Chicago to Long Branch carrying four children, twelve servants, three vehicles, and an assortment of trunks and other luggage. The train also contained a stable car which had space for five horses, carriages, berths for grooms and hostlers. Every summer, the family would visit Pullman's mother in the Thousand Islands in upper New York State. Subsequently, Pullman acquired an island (which, of course, he named Pullman Island) in Alexandria Bay and built several cabins on the property for his immediate family's use. In actual practice, Pullman traveled incessantly on business all over the United States and often to Europe.

In February, 1873, the Midland Railway Company announced that it had signed a contract with the Pullman Palace Car Company to provide Pullman equipment for Midland's routes in England. The business arrangement was unique: Pullman agreed to supply as many dining-room, drawing-room and sleeping cars as the demand required without charge. Pullman's compensation came from the extra fare paid by passengers for use of the cars and for the exclusive rights for fifteen years to furnish such cars. By 1875, Pullman established a factory in Turin, Italy to supply his cars throughout Europe.

In November 1, 1879 the Great Northern Railway put into service Pullman dining cars between Leeds and King's Cross Station, London. Genuine English food was served for luncheon and dinner including soups, fish entrees, roast joints, puddings and fruits. The London Telegraph wrote,

> If the British public can be brought to give this new refreshment-car system, just inaugurated by the Great Northern Railway, a fair trial, there will be another traveling infliction, besides Dyspepsia and Discontent, which will be speedily laid in the Red Sea…. Luncheon or dinner on board a Pullman palace-car will surely banish Boredom from railway journeys.

In 1880 Pullman purchased a site of 3500 acres near Lake Calumet some 14 miles south of Chicago on the Illinois Central Railroad. With demand exploding for his sleepers, Pullman decided to build the largest factory to mass produce them. With the vast influx of immigrants to the Chicago area came tuberculosis and cholera, crime, prostitution and drunkenness. George believed that if he built a company town without saloons and agitators, his workers would be forever loyal to the Pullman creed. Pullman designed and built a model town for his employees which grew to 12,000 inhabitants.

Pullman City had its own shopping center, a savings bank, theater, church, schools, parks and playgrounds. It also had a library of 8000 volumes and the luxurious Florence Hotel (named after Pullman's daughter). It attempted to furnish laborers with the best homes under the most healthful conditions and favorable surroundings in every respect.

The Hotel Florence in Pullman, Illinois was built in 1881 and named for George Pullman's daughter. Since 1991, it has been owned by the Illinois Historic Preservation Agency.

A reporter for <u>Harper's Magazine</u> in 1885 wrote,

> Very gratifying is the impression of the visitor who passes hurriedly through Pullman City and observes only the splendid provision for the present material comforts of its residents. What is seen in a walk or drive through the streets is so pleasing to the eye that a woman's first exclamation is certain to be, "Perfectly lovely!" It is indeed a sight as rare as it is delightful.... One of the most striking peculiarities of this place is the all-pervading air of thrift and providence... Contrary to what is seen ordinarily in laborers' quarters, not a dilapidated door-step nor a broken window, stuffed perhaps with old clothing is to be found in the city. The streets of Pullman, always kept in perfect condition,

are wide and finely macadamized, and the young shade trees on each side now ornament the town, and will in a few years afford refreshing protection from the rays of the summer sun!

The reporter continues,

> French roofs, square roofs, dormer-windows, turrets, sharp points, blunt points, triangles, irregular quadrangles are devices resorted to in the upper stories to avoid the appearance of unbroken uniformity.
>
> ...... The interior of the houses affords scarcely less gratification than their exterior. Even the humblest suite of rooms in the flats is provided with water, gas and closets and no requisite of cleanliness is omitted. Most of the cottages are two stories in height and contain five rooms, besides a cellar, closets and pantry. Quite a large number of houses contain seven rooms, and in these larger dwellings there is also a bath-room.

But as admirable as the physical qualities of Pullman City were, the shortcomings were so overwhelming as to plant the seeds of its destruction. For example, 1) the leases on all residences could be terminated on ten days notice 2) no resident could own their house 3) no independent newspapers were tolerated 4) the one church building was unoccupied because no denomination could pay the rent and no other congregation was allowed 5) no town meetings with free discussion of local affairs was allowed 6) strikes were regarded as the chief of social sins 7) mutual insurance associations or charitable organizations were discouraged because the Company feared that word would circulate that there were poor and needy people in Pullman City.

By 1889, Pullman had outlasted and acquired all his major competition including the Union Palace Car Company, the Marin Boudoir Car Company and the Woodruff Sleeping and Parlor Coach Company. In the same year, Pullman entered the second-class sleeping car field, (variously referred to as emigrant or tourist cars). Pullman had previously ignored this economy end of the business which furnished sleeping accommodations at $3 per night as opposed to the $13 paid by palace car users. To satisfy this market, Pullman acquired sixty tourist cars from the Atchison, Topeka and Sante Fe, twenty similar cars from the Atlantic and Pacific Railroad and a one-fourth interest in seventy second-class cars from the Union Pacific. These acquisitions enabled Pullman to provide moveable side-tracked sleeping cars in lieu of hotels to political delegates and convention attendees. For example, Pullman supplied 125 cars for the Grand Army of the Republic's reunion in San Francisco plus fifty-three cars for the GAR's event in Los Angeles. In addition, Pullman sent fifty-five cars to Boston for the Grand Sovereign Lodge of Odd Fellows and 200 cars for the Knights Templars Convention in St. Louis.

By 1890, the Pullman Palace Car Company reached the zenith of success:

- 2135 vehicles operating on 120,686 of the approximately 160,000 miles of railroad track in the United States

- Pullman sleepers accommodated 100,000 people a night, more than all the nation's top- notch hotels combined.

- 10,680 people living in Pullman City

- 12,367 workers on the payroll with earnings of more than $6.2 million per year

- 286 second-class cars in operation

- Fifteen to twenty-five year contracts with renewing railroad companies (up from ten years).

At age fifty-nine, George Mortimer Pullman was a great self-made success story, one of the nation's elite businessmen, a member of the "millionaires table" at the Chicago Club. His personal secretary for the last seven years of his life, was Edgar Mayer. Mayer described Pullman as "a difficult man, hard in business but always straight, scrupulously fair and most honorable in all his dealings."

By 1894, Pullman cars operated on three-fourths of all of the U.S. railroad mileage. Pullman manufactured and repaired his own Palace cars but also built many other kinds of railroad cars for the national market. These included freight and ordinary passenger cars, street and elevated cars. But trouble was brewing in the economy of the United States which was the prelude to trouble at the Pullman Company. In the spring of 1893, a financial panic signaled the start of a four-year recession which caused a severe decline in business activity. During the 1880's and 1890's many labor disputes occurred at various Pullman factories. Like other contemporary business executives, Pullman was adamantly opposed to labor unions and any form of collective bargaining. He used whatever means he could, including spies and spotters on the railroads, in the factories and in Pullman City. Union organizers and their supporters regularly lost their jobs and their homes. In August, 1893, Pullman cut costs throughout the company and reduced wages across the board by nearly a third. But he did not reduce the Pullman City rents thereby putting workers in an untenable situation. After a meeting on May 7, 1894 between American Railway Union and Thomas Wickes, Pullman Company's second vice president, three members of the grievance committee were fired. Workers were furious and under the guidance of the American Railway Union, declared a system-wide strike on May 11, 1894. In short order, the strike turned ugly and violent. Pullman used his political influence to get public officials to call up two thousand federal troops, four thousand Illinois militia, five thousand deputy marshals and the entire Chicago police force. The predictable outcome resulted in widespread violence and brickthrowing mobs overturning freight and Pullman cars which turned Chicago into a fiery inferno.

The Pullman strike finally ended after the summer of 1894 with the following consequences:

- Twelve people were killed

- The strikers were the big losers who had to end the strike with no concessions and no job security

- Eugene Debs, Clarence Darrow and Jane Addams emerged with enhanced reputations

- President Grover Cleveland gained a reputation as a strike breaker

- George Pullman's reputation was severely damaged

The strike revealed and heightened awareness of the racial intolerance in both the Pullman company and the American Railway Union. In Pullman City, only a handful of black factory workers were given leases but none to Pullman porters. Black men worked as waiters in the Florence Hotel but few at the Calumet, Illinois manufacturing facilities. The constitution of the American Railway Union started that members must be "born of white parents." No Pullman porters were invited to join the strike.

Later in 1894, President Cleveland appointed the United States Strike Commission which took testimony from 107 witnesses over a period of thirteen days. In its "Report and Testimony on the Chicago Strike of 1894", the Commission concluded:

- Pullman employees were denied the advantages and protection that they might have enjoyed as members of the union

- regarding the wage cuts instituted at Pullman, the company had placed a disproportionate amount of its losses on its laborers.

- salaries of officers, managers and superintendents should have been proportionately reduced.

- rents in Pullman City were 20 to 25% higher than those for similar accommodations in Chicago or surrounding towns.

- in spite of its threats, the Pullman Company never evicted a tenant during that period.

- that despite the company's protestations that it stayed in operation to help its labor force and to spare the public the annoyance of interrupted travel, its true purpose had been to benefit itself as a manufacturer.

- Employee demands for a return to the wage scale of June 1893 were unwarranted.

- Employee requests for lower rent were fair and reasonable under the circumstances and a slight concession in that regard might have averted the strike.

The image of a wealthy capitalist using the economic depression to browbeat his employees into submission was probably overstated. But this image stuck to Pullman for the rest of his life despite his extraordinary accomplishments as pioneer of the assembly line and mass production; his conception and creation of a model company town; his revolutionary creation of a "hotel on wheels" which revolutionized overnight travel.

As it turned out, Pullman won the strike but lost status, reputation and personal health. On October 19, 1897, George Pullman died of a massive heart attack at age sixty-six.

Pullman had earlier stipulated in detail exactly how he wanted to be buried in order to prevent possible desecration by disgruntled former employees. Author Liston Leyendecker in *Palace Car Prince* described Pullman's tomb as follows:

> His body lay in a lead-lined box that was wrapped in tar paper and coated it with an inch of asphalt. The casket, lowered into a pit thirteen feet long, nine feet wide, and eight feet deep, rested on a concrete flooring eighteen inches thick. Once it was properly positioned, workers filled the space surrounding the casket with concrete to its upper lid. They then built the enclosing walls up to one-half inch above the asphalt coating on the coffin and placed eight heavy T-rails transversely across the top. Resting on the concrete walls at either side, their lower surfaces cleared the asphalt covering by half an inch to allow for settling and to prevent the heavy steel from crushing the casket's top. After the rails were bolted together by two long rods, more tar paper was placed on top to prevent the flow of additional

concrete into the half-inch space between the rails and the asphalt surrounding the coffin. Covered by even more concrete, the rods lay like a "wall of stone and steel" between Pullman and would- be grave robbers.

SOURCE MATERIALS

1. Eric Arnesen, *Brotherhoods of Color: Black Railroad Workers and the Struggle for Equality*, Harvard University Press, Cambridge, 2001

2. Chicago Morning News, October 19, 1897, In Memoriam, George H. Pullman, Chicago Historical Society

3. Commission on Industrial Relations, Final Report and Testimony Submitted to Congress Washington, D.C., Government Printing Office, 1916 9553-54

4. Emmett Dedmon, *Fabulous Chicago* McClelland and Stewart, Toronto 1981

5. Joseph Husband, *The Story of the Pullman Car* A.C. McClurg & Co., Chicago 1917

6. Catherine Kirkland, *Chicago Yesterdays: A Sheaf of Reminiscences* Daughaday, 1919 Chicago, Illinois

7. Liston Edgington Leyendecker, *Palace Car Prince* University Press of Colorado 1992 pp. 23-26

8. Charles Long, "Pioneer and the Funeral Train: How 'Honest Abe' was Used to Create a Corporate Tall Tale." Railroad History Spring 2002

9. Julian Morel, *Pullman: The Pullman Car Company- Its services, cars and traditions* David & Charles, London 1983

10. Bessie Louise Pierce, *A History of Chicago* Vol. 2 1848-1871 Alfred A. Knopf, New York 1940

11. Bessie Louise Pierce, Editor, *As Others See Chicago: Impressions of Visitors*, 1673-1933 University of Chicago Press, 1939, Chicago, Illinois

12. Royal H. Pullman, D.D. "Dedication Sermon at the Pullman Memorial, Universalist Church, January 3, 1895, Albion NY

13. Jack Santino, *Miles of Smiles, Years of Struggles: Stories of Black Pullman Porters* University of Illinois Press, Chicago, 1989

14. Larry Tye, *Rising From The Rails* Henry Holt and Company, New York 2004

15. John H. White, *The American Railroad Passenger Car* Johns Hopkins Press, 1985

A. M. Sonnabend (1896-1964):

LEGENDARY FINANCIER, SQUASH CHAMPION AND HOTEL PIONEER

Abraham Malcolm Sonnabend was born in Boston on December 8, 1896, the son of Esther and Joseph Sonnabend. He graduated from the Boston Latin School in 1914 where he was the recipient of the Franklin Medal and several prizes in classical and modern studies, captain in the school regiment and business manager of the school paper. Entering Harvard University with the class of 1918, Mr. Sonnabend completed the four-year course in three years and graduated in 1917 in order to enlist. He was a member of the Harvard Reserve Officers Training Corps but upon completion of the course of training he was not old enough to be commissioned or to go to the Plattsburg Training Camp. He therefore enlisted in the United States Naval Flying Corps as a second-class seaman and was sent to the Massachusetts Institute of Technology for ground training. From there he was sent to Miami where he received his preliminary flight training and then to Pensacola where he completed his advanced flight training. He was commissioned an ensign and received his rating as a naval aviator. Early in November 1918, he was ordered to report in London for duty with the Northern Bombing Squadron but with the signing of the World War I armistice, these orders were rescinded. Ensign Sonnabend remained in Miami as instructor and flight qualification officer until he was released from active duty in March 1919.

Sonnabend was an excellent athlete and a high-ranking squash racquets player, ranked No. 6 in Massachusetts in 1936. He held the State doubles championship and represented the United States in international championship matches with Canada. He played regularly on the Harvard Club of Boston A team in the State league matches. In 1938, he won the U.S. National Veterans Squash championship.

At the end of World War I, Sonnabend joined his father's real estate organization. Itching to strike out on his own, the enterprising Bostonian borrowed $5000 from his father and took over the management of his father-in-law's real estate. One year later, he repaid the debt and still had $20,000 profit from his realty endeavors. He married Esther Lewitt in 1920. By 1927 he had increased his real estate holdings to a net worth of $350,000.

After the 1929 crash, Sonnabend concluded that economic conditions were going to get worse and he contrived a way to protect himself. He told every tenant that if they would sign a long-term lease, he would lower the rent. Few refused and in 1931 and 1932, Sonnabend's buildings remained occupied while those of many other owners slowly emptied. This impressed Boston's bankers, who by then owned much of the city's commercial real estate, and they began offering their foreclosed properties to Sonnabend. Again Sonnabend prospered and by the beginning of World War II, he was very likely the biggest apartment-house owner in Boston with ownership of 2,500 apartments. The well-known hotel and restaurant consultant Sumner Baye recalled that the Sonnabend Company was the landlord on his mother and father's apartment on Winthrop Road in Brookline, MA. Every month, young A.M. himself knocked on the door to collect the rent check.

In subsequent years, A.M. invested in Botany Mills, Consolidated Retail Stores, Studebaker-Packard Company, the Alleghany Corporation, Artistic Foundations, C.F. Hathaway, Seagrave Corporation, Premier Corporation of America, Lionel Corporation, etc. "Sonny" was an entrepreneur who purchased financially troubled companies for tax purposes, made them successful, and sold them at a profit. It was not until 1943, that A.M. Sonnabend at the age of 49 became involved with hotels as a real estate investment. The first hotel acquisition for A.M. (and six other partners) was the Preston Beach Hotel on the north shore of Boston. Because of his business acumen, A.M. took charge of the management of the Sonnabend-operated hotel division.

In 1944, Sonnabend (with seven partners) acquired a package of Palm Beach, Florida hotels for $2.4 million including the Biltmore, Whitehall and the Palm Beach Country Club. In little more than a year, Sonnabend's faith in Florida was vindicated when Conrad Hilton bought the Biltmore for almost as much as Sonnabend had paid for the whole package. Later on, he sold the country club alone for $1 million. Sonnabend continued to own and operate the Whitehall Hotel whose 300 rooms had been constructed in 1925 adjacent to Henry Morrison Flagler's mansion. Sonnabend acquired and operated the Sun and Surf Club to provide facilities where Jewish guests were welcome in contrast to the anti-semitic practices of some other Palm Beach clubs and hotels. HCA built a 50-room Charter House hotel in Annapolis, MD. as an overnight stopover for Jewish families driving from Boston to Florida.

Jim Cooke, a writer and historian in Quincy, Ma., has written a wonderful memoir of his experiences as a room service waiter at the Whitehall Hotel during the 1957-58 season. With his permission, here are some excerpted portions:

> Fifty years ago, the Whitehall Hotel in Palm Beach, Florida was owned and operated by the Sonnabend Corporation. The Samoset in Rockland, Maine was their "summer affiliate." I was a room service waiter at the Whitehall in the winter of 1957-58. The clientele was almost exclusively Jewish. In the last years of the Dwight Eisenhower Administration—Jews were not welcome at the Breakers- then and still the premiere, prestige Palm Beach establishment. The Whitehall Hotel was a ten-story, 300 room addition to the palatial mansion of southern railroad magnate Henry Flagler. It was very posh and grand. Today, the addition is gone and the Flagler Museum is a National Historic Landmark....

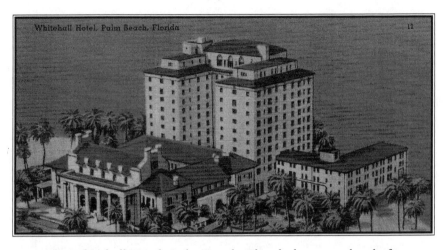

The Whitehall Hotel, Palm Beach, Florida became a hotel after Henry Flagler's death. The 300-room tower was built in 1925 behind Flagler's Whitehall mansion. It was owned and operated by the Hotel Corporation of America, an A.M. Sonnabend company.

Cooke describes how he and two friends read the want ads in Palm Beach and realized that they didn't qualify for many of the restaurants on Worth Avenue.

> Then, we applied at the Whitehall Hotel and they were glad to hire us; we were ready to go to work. The hotel supplied housing as well as meals. This benefit was deducted from the small salary—a pittance beyond pity—whether you used it or not. Anyway, we were all in it for the tips and there was a bonus if you stayed to the end of the season on April 15. The worker's accommodations were in an attractive residential house near beautiful white sandy beaches. Not bad? Wrong! It was very bad. For the first several nights we were crowded into a room with twenty or thirty beds. The rooms, with fireplace would have served a family as a living and dining room. Now, it was "the zoo" and was occupied by the youngest and newest employees. All through the night they wrestled, tossed balls, dirty socks or underwear and laughed, yelled and chattered. It was a zoo; sleep was an unlikely possibility.

After a week or so – we were no longer "new" and our situation improved. We graduated from the zoo to smaller rooms on the second or third floor shared with older workers. Still, it was three, four or five to a room but a great improvement over the zoo. A few senior workers, back for a second or third season, might have a double or even a single room. Nylon shirts were still new in 1957. We washed them in the bathroom sink and they would hang drying in the room. The rest of the uniform was black shoes, black trousers and a clip-on bow tie. The hotel provided a jacket. Some waiters worked in Maine and came to the Whitehall for the winter. As previously noted, the clientele was mainly Jewish. Without exception, the staff was Gentile. Looking back, among us, I recall none of the casual endemic anti-Semitism that had been a part of the culture at home and elsewhere. However, on New Years' Eve, just as 1957 was turning into 1958, Wally, boozing bellhop on a bet, passed through the main lobby: "Paging Mr. O'Brien!" "Phone call for Mr. O'Brien!" Wally was fired – as he had expected he would be and probably should have been....

Cooke characterizes the waiters as a various collection of musicians, misfits, college dropouts, drunkards and drifters with stories of past failures. Some were hard drinking gambling men who followed the greyhounds and lived for the daily double. A few professional waiters took pride in the work. Maurice, for example, owned a small hotel in Quebec. He spoke of his early training. "It was months before I was allowed to touch a dish- and then, I passed it to the waiter who set it down." Cooke said that Maurice was a study of seamless grace and movement causing food to happen in front of "his" people. Karl Wolf, on the other hand, was a red faced German with orange hair flaking dandruff—a parody of servile excess – all bustle and flourish as he tossed a salad at a table. Every move said, "Now: This is service."

Room service was available for all meals until eleven at night. The Whitehall, we were told, led all other hotels in number of breakfasts served in the room. While the dining room had waitresses as well as waiters—only men worked room service. We gathered in a holding area around the corner from the coffee station with its shining urns and a step or two up from the cement floor. Orders were phoned down to Mike Hart, a courtly coughing man who handed the order off through a cloud of cigarette smoke to the waiter next up. You got a tray table and put together your order. Then you got in line for the elevator. Emma, a kindly woman of sixty something, checked each tray against the order. "Where's your sugar?" "It says 'cream' with the flakes; you got milk." Mostly, we used lightweight tray tables with a handle to grasp on the underside. Occasionally, the order required a rolling table with a sterno-fired warming oven. Usually, but not always you got a better tip with the rolling tables. The average tip was a quarter for two people. I gained a reputation for patience and was assigned the most difficult, complaining or impossible guests. Invariably, they required prune juice, hardboiled eggs, or bran flakes along with a thermos carafe with hot, hot water—empty. Refill. Then run boiling water over the handle. It feels very hot and they are satisfied.

The waiters apparently worked a seven-day week in a variety of jobs, all involved with food and beverage. Cooke reported that,

> Jock and I often worked the hotel's Rib Room, a classy in-house restaurant with a limited menu of lamb, roast beef and steak. The average Rib Room tip, per person, was a dollar! Each waiter had a stash of steak knives that never went to the kitchen to be washed. (They were wiped clean on a napkin.)....

Cooke recalled that some famous people stayed at the Whitehall including the bandleader Sammy Kaye, novelist Taylor Caldwell and Mrs. Saks of Saks 5th Avenue. And, there was Marjorie Merriweather Post, heiress to the Post Cereal fortune, just then married to Herbert

A. May, Jr., heir to the May Department Stores. At one time, she was said to be the wealthiest woman in the world. The hotel had a supply of Post cereal flakes and had to remember not to serve her the usual Kellogg's.

> After work we might go to a bar in West Palm Beach. In Palm Beach, there was Merletto's with great pizza where two old black men strolled from table to table with an "Ink Spots" repertoire. One played guitar, both sang, one used a small megaphone ala Rudy Vallee. It was difficult to walk anywhere at night because the Palm Beach Police would pick you up to check your photo ID. Often, they would drive you to your destination.....
>
> The winter of 1957-58 was cold and Florida's citrus froze on the trees. They said that it was the coldest winter since 1890. Tourists stayed home or cut their vacations short. People envied Jock's Chevy with its car heater. They would see the New Hampshire plates and yell, "Got the heater on?"

A.M. later negotiated unsuccessfully to acquire the Boca Raton Resort from the Mizener family. Sonnabend bought the Edgewater Beach Hotel in Chicago for only $5000 per room at eight times earnings. According to his son Roger Sonnabend, A.M. was never in competition with Ernest Henderson at the Sheraton Corporation or Conrad Hilton to build a chain of hotels. In 1948 and 1949 Sonnabend almost acquired the Waldorf-Astoria Hotel in New York but lost out to Conrad Hilton. A.M.'s major interest was making money through a variety of strategic investments.

Sonnabend (with partner Royal Little) beat out Hilton two years later when he acquired the Van Sweringen properties in Cleveland including the fifty-two story Terminal Tower, three other office buildings and the 1000 room Hotel Cleveland. Later, Sonnabend's bid to acquire the Statler Hotels Corporation lost out again to Hilton.

In 1953, Hilton sold Sonnabend the Plaza Hotel in New York City for $15 million and immediately leased it back for two and half years and upon expiration for an additional four years. Subsequently, in face of the U.S. Department of Justice charge that Hilton was monopolizing the convention business, Hilton sold the Mayflower Hotel in Washington and leased the Roosevelt in New York to Sonnabend.

In 1956, Sonnabend created the Hotel Corporation of America (HCA) and used it to leverage tax losses from the Childs Restaurant Corporation. Finally, in January 1960, HCA assumed management of the Plaza Hotel. In turn, HCA hired some of the most famous General Managers in the industry: Neil Lang, Al Salamone, Jack Craver and George DeKornfeld.

Jim Burr is president of the Burr Company which offers consulting services in hotel asset management strategy development and due diligence. Jim has more than 40 years of industry experience including this wonderful recollection of the Hotel Corporation of America (which I reprint with his permission):

> .... I worked at The Plaza, fresh out of the Cornell Hotel School, from 1963 until 1965. Al Salomone was the GM and George DeKornfeld was his assistant. I was in a department known as "Budget and Control," which was set up in all the HCA hotels by Carl Albers, who later directed all hotel operations. I have always regarded my experience there as being akin to a post-graduate course in hotel management. With 40+ years of perspective, I now realize that some of what we were doing was a precursor to internal asset management.
>
> Albers pioneered the industrial engineering and systems approaches to hotel management. HCA was among the first companies to use staffing guides that were established on the basis of achieved work hour productivity. At the time, Hilton and others were still trying to work with percentages. I recall hearing often: "Control the hours and you control the dollars. And you also control the "burden." The Company was heavily into food and beverage control and emphasized yield testing and food

and beverage potential costs. Several of the HCA hotels featured Rib Rooms, and the Company did extensive testing of the roasting temperature and the configuration of the rib that provided the best yield. They developed a metal tool for measuring ribs at the receiving point so they could be quickly accepted or rejected....

With these new techniques, HCA revolutionized work sampling and work simplification in the hotel kitchen. HCA flow-charted the path of a room service order through the original Plaza Hotel kitchen (which had 105 white-jacket cooks) and helping to create new and more effective staging.

> Budget & Control developed the concept of a "ditto master" for the monthly financial report, so someone (with handwriting far better than mine) could quickly fill in the actual results for the month vs. budget and last year and get the report circulated so department heads could review variances and quickly react to them. The formal report, which the Controller's office released a couple of weeks later, after it was typed, checked, corrected, run and collated, became a "for the record" document that had little utility.

> Budget & Control undertook, and I was involved in the development of a five-year strategic plan that, at the Plaza, identified the need for additional function space that was eventually created on the second floor and the plan to create another restaurant (which eventually happened, and was called the Oyster Bar) in an underutilized area then occupied by the Hitchcock Gift Shop.

Jim Burr continued with these pertinent memories:

> It was definitely Roger Sonnabend, with his Harvard Business School background, who championed these approaches. Paul was probably a force behind the scenes, but although he had the title of President of

the Plaza at the time, and occasionally came in for meetings, his close involvement with the hotel was not evident to me.

I had intended to include in my list of pioneering efforts the use of Industrial Psychologists. Every key manager was subjected to interview and testing by RH&R- Rohr, Hibler & Replogle. I believe they did some counseling of upper management as well. My session with them took the better part of a day. Before I started it, I commented to the Corporate Employment Manager, "We'll see if this guy determines that I'm some kind of nut." His response: "I guarantee he will; the question is if you are our kind of nut." HCA was also big on the understanding and application of "The Management Grid." We were taught the importance of the 9-9 management style, where everyone wins, with a 9-1 backup for critical or emergency situations, where the manager must control. And were cautioned about the "country club" style, 5-5, where little gets accomplished and employees aren't happy.....

Burr reports that Sheraton Boston Hotel began life as one of several new prototype hotels being developed by HCA as the "Hotel America." Before completion, the Sonnabends found the opportunity to sell it at a substantial profit, so it opened as a Sheraton.

Sonnabend also pioneered a presence in Europe. The Carlton Tower in London was built and opened as an HCA hotel. It later became a Hyatt and is now run by Jumeirah......

Of course, it was The Plaza where the Beatles stayed when they came to the States for the first time to be on the Ed Sullivan show. A few days before their arrival, one of the reservationists picked up on the fact that G. Harrison, R. Starr, J. Lennon and P. McCartney had booked accommodations and knew who they were.

Security arrangements were quickly made. I was there at the time and it was a real zoo.

The famous Plaza Hotel reopened at the beginning of 2008 with a 100 year anniversary celebration. The $350 million renovation contains 130 rooms and 152 condo-hotel units. Prices for the 152 condominium suites range from $1.6 million to more than $9 million which works out to $3800 to $6000 per square foot. The hotel portion is managed by Fairmont Hotels & Resorts.

In addition, the completely-renovated Plaza contains 182 unfurnished private residence condominiums starting at $2.5 million and high-end retail stores. The fabled food and beverage outlets: the Palm Court, the Oak Bar and Oak Room and the Edwardian Room will be restored including a replica of the original stained glass ceiling in the Palm Court. A 1921 addition to the hotel blocked the natural light and the skylight itself was removed during World War II to prevent it from being a beacon during air raids. The new plan calls for artificial lights above the glass ceiling to create the impression of sunlight.

The Plaza Hotel was designed by Henry Janeway Hardenbergh, who was already well known for the Dakota Apartments, one of the first luxury apartment buildings in New York and the original Waldorf Hotel which preceded the Empire State building at 33rd Street and Fifth Avenue. The Plaza had 800 rooms, 500 bathrooms, large private suites, 10 elevators a two-story ballroom and the Palm Court with a Tiffany leaded glass-domed ceiling. On this same site, an earlier Plaza Hotel opened in 1890 with 400 rooms but was demolished 17 years later for the 18-story current Plaza Hotel.

The New York Landmarks Preservation Commission also bestowed landmark status on eight of the Plaza's famous public rooms, adjacent corridors and vestibules, including murals, chandeliers and decorative metalwork. The rooms include the Palm Court, the setting for a scene from the movie "The Great Gatsby"; the Terrace Room, where Marilyn Monroe's dress strap once slipped off her shoulder during an interview; the Oak Bar, where Cary Grant's character was kidnapped in Alfred Hitchcock's "North by Northwest". Walter Matthau in "Plaza Suite" and Barbra Streisand in "The Way We Were" used the Plaza as a stage set. The Plaza in 1930 was the backdrop in a scene for "No Limit", the first talking picture filmed on location in New York City. Its star was the famous "It Girl", Clara Bow.

Of all the show people who have been part of the Plaza's history, only one had a permanent monument there. He's an American theatrical icon named George M. Cohan who was an actor, composer, playwright, producer, theater owner and a legend; the only person ever awarded the Congressional Medal of Honor for a song, the World War I favorite "Over There". The Plaza is the only 10 minutes away from Broadway and it was a convenient place for him to unwind before the curtain went up on the evening performance. From 4 PM to 7 PM each day, he had pre-theater cocktails in the Oak Room where his reserved table was a booth in the northwest corner. After he died in the early '40's, the Lambs Club put a bronze plaque on the wall above his booth which reads, "Here in this corner where he spent many happy hours, the Lambs have placed this tablet in honor of the most brilliant and versatile gentleman in the theatre of his day, George M. Cohan". The Plaza, then owned by Conrad Hilton, officially named the Oak Room's northwest corner, "The Cohan Corner". In 1959, the municipal statue of Cohan was finally erected in Duffy Square on Broadway between forty-sixth and forty-seventh streets- the same site that had earlier been proposed for General William Tecumsah Sherman's monument which now stands in Grand Army Plaza opposite the Plaza Hotel. Will "The Cohan Corner" survive the current renovation?

For nearly 40 years, the Persian Room, a legendary nightclub at the Plaza, presented the most talented live performers. It opened on April 1, 1934, four months after the repeal of Prohibition, in the southern half of the Fifth Avenue dining room. It was designed in Art Deco style by the Viennese designer Joseph Urban with murals by Lillian Gaertner Palmedo. Until it closed in 1975, the Persian Room featured such stars as Liberace, Carol Channing, Burl Ives, Eddy Duchin, Kitty Carlisle, the Mills Brothers, Bob Fosse, Victor Borge, Marge and Gower Champion, Eddie Fisher, Xavier Cugat, the McGuire Sisters, Dinah Shore, Vic Damone, Bob Hope, Robert Goulet, Frankie Laine, Ethel Merman, Eartha Kitt, Henny Youngman and Hildegarde, among others.

In 1943, the Plaza was sold to Conrad Hilton for $7.4 million after thirty-six years of continuous original ownership. Hilton made important physical changes:

- removed the brokerage firm of E. F. Hutton from its ground-floor office (monthly rent $416) and converted it to the Oak Bar

- converted a basement storage area (once the Grill Room) into the Rendez-vous supper club

- mezzanine writing rooms overlooking the lobby were converted into private meeting rooms

- vitrines were installed throughout the lobby.

- The leaded-glass dome over the Palm Court was removed.

Hilton sold the Plaza to the Boston industrialist A.M. Sonnabend for $15 million in 1953 whose Hotel Corporation of America (HCA) kept the legend alive for 22 years until 1975.

Long before the name Sonesta became synonymous with quality hotels, a prize-winning dairy farm in Holliston, Massachusetts proudly proclaimed that it was "Sonesta Farms", named after its owners, Abraham (nicknamed "Sonny") and Esther Sonnabend.

However, according to the famous hotelier Jack Craver, the name "Sonesta" was first used in the Rib Room restaurant at the Roosevelt Hotel in New York City by Resident Manager Charles Meredith White. He named the baked potato with sour cream and chives as the "Sonesta potato". Later, when HCA built the Royal Sonesta Hotel in New Orleans, it was known as the "baked potato" hotel by local owners.

When A.M.'s three sons reached young adulthood, he handed them responsibility at several HCA hotels. Roger, the eldest, graduated from MIT and the Harvard Business School and was only 21 when he took the helm at the Nautilus Hotel and Beach Club, in Atlantic Beach, Long Island, NY. Paul Sonnabend became General Manager of Boston's Hotel Shelton, immediately after graduating from Cornell's School of Hotel Administration in 1950. Stephen, Sonny's youngest son, graduated from Harvard and assumed an executive position with the Childs Restaurant Corporation.

By the time A.M. Sonnabend passed away in the early 60's (at age 68), his three sons were managing a rather large and diverse business. However, Roger, Paul and Stephen preferred their role as hoteliers rather than financiers or real estate investors. As a result, they decided to sell their unprofitable properties and keep the hotel company relatively small. This decision gave them the opportunity to develop a hotel management company and maintain their hands-on approach in the operation of their hotels.

In 1977, the Loews Corporation almost purchased Sonesta International Hotels including the stock owned by members of the Reuben Gryzmish family, friends of A.M. Sonnabend. A third generation of Sonnabends has now joined the executive ranks to manage the company:

- Stephanie Sonnabend, CEO and President

- Peter Sonnabend, CEO and Vice Chairman

- Jacqueline Sonnabend, Executive Vice President

- Alan Sonnabend, Vice President Development

- Kathy Sonnabend Rowe, Senior Vice President, Food & Beverage

- Tom Sonnabend, Regional Sales Director New England

- Patti Sonnabend Wagner, Director of Corporate Accounting

The Sonnabend family has endeavored to transition from the second generation to the third generation and keep Sonesta successful. Their harmony as a family has translated into a company-wide commitment to manage upscale hotels that deliver uncompromising personal service and reflect the history and culture of their locations.

For over 60 years, Sonesta has owned, managed, designed, built and marketed hotels throughout the world. There are presently 28 Sonesta hotels and resorts, including 5 Nile cruise ships. The properties are located in the Boston, Miami, New Orleans, Orlando (2007), St. Maarten, Peru, Brazil and Egypt.

By consolidating assets and positioning the company for opportunities to expand with more hotels and resorts, Sonesta has emerged as a stronger company over the past five years. While growth will be continuous, it will likely be at a pace that preserves the character that distinguishes each Sonesta property.

A.M. Sonnabend's civic and charitable interest were extraordinary. He was Vice President of the American Jewish Committee and served as National Chairman for the AJC's Institute of Human Relations. In Palm Beach, he was active in the Community Chest and Red Cross and was a governor of the Good Samaritan Hospital.

SOURCE MATERIALS

1. Collection of newspaper articles and columns and magazine articles:

>   Brookline Chronicle June 4, 1936
>   Time Magazine October 16, 1950
>   Time Magazine December 27, 1954
>   New York Times April 10, 1955
>   Time Magazine August 18, 1958
>   Boston Sunday Globe August 24, 1958
>   New York Journal American September 7, 1958
>   Fortune Magazine September 1958
>   Palm Beach Daily News April 5, 1959
>   New York Journal American November 17, 1959
>   New York Journal American November 18, 1959
>   New York Journal American November 20, 1959
>   New York Journal American December 2, 1959
>   New York Journal American April 28, 1960
>   Boston Traveler January 4, 1962
>   New York Herald Tribune February 12, 1964
>   Boston Evening Globe October 13, 1972
>   Courier- Gazette October 1972

2. First-hand recollection of Jim Burr (jburr@jimburr.com). Hotel Executive and Consultant

3. Reminiscence by Jim Cooke (crankyyankees@aol.com), Writer and Historian

Ellsworth Milton Statler (1863-1928):

HOTEL MAN OF THE HALF CENTURY

In 1950, the hotel industry picked the late E. M. Statler as the "Hotel Man of the Half Century." By then, Statler had been dead for 22 years, but his impact on the art and science of innkeeping was so great that no one else even came close. In order to make this selection official, the magazine *Southern Hotel Journal* held a contest. Out of one hundred and four hotel executives polled, one hundred and two named E.M. Statler as the "Hotel Man of the Half Century."

While Ellsworth Milton Statler was considered by many to be the premier hotel man in the industry, he did not look or sound like a successful executive. He was a plain, rugged self-made man who started to work at the age of nine. Even after he became successful, he still wore twenty dollar suits and four dollar shoes. Someone said that Statler looked more like Will Rogers than Rudolph Valentino.

Statler, therefore, was more interested in plain vanilla comfort in his hotels than fancy trimmings. He said, "A shoe salesman and a traveling prince want essentially the same thing when they are on the road- namely, good food and a comfortable bed- and that is what I propose to give them." In response to criticism that Statler hotels were not luxurious enough, Statler said, "Look, if I wanted to, I could run a so-called luxury hotel or a resort hotel that would beat any damn thing those frizzly-headed foreigners are doing, but I just don't operate in that field. To hell with it; I'm not interested in it. All I want to do is to have more comforts and conveniences and serve better food than any of them have or do, and mine will be at a price ordinary people can afford." Stephen Rushmore, President and Founder of HVS International reports that his favorite E.M. Statler quote is "Life is service. The one who progresses is the one who gives his fellow human being a little more, a little better service."

Ellsworth M. Statler was born on October 26, 1863, the son of William Jackson Statler and Mary Ann McKinney. The Statlers moved from a farm near Gettysburg, Pa. to Bridgeport, Ohio which is across the Ohio River from Wheeling, West Virginia. Ellsworth worked for a short time at age nine at the La Belle Glass Factory in Kirkwood, Ohio alongside his older brothers, ages 11 and 13. The work, that of a glory hole tender, was hard and hot. Glory holes were small furnaces used in glass factories to heat and soften glass so that it could be formed into bottles or other glass products. At age 13, Ellsworth got a job as a night-time bellboy at the McLure House Hotel in Wheeling, West Virginia.

Statler's father died when Ellsworth had been working for two years as a bellboy at the McLure House Hotel. Statler was paid six dollars a month, plus his board, a place to sleep and whatever he could earn in tips. In 1878, the McLure House had an elevator but it was reserved for guests and the manager. Bellboys carried luggage up and down the stairs and did the same with ice and water, kindling for fires and hot water for guest baths. Guest rooms at the McLure House were barely adequate with a bed, one chair, a large hook on the back of the entry door for hanging clothes. Plumbing consisted of a pitcher of water, a large bowl, a spittoon and shared toilets down the corridor. Apparently, the McLure's saloon was more in tune with guest needs. It offered free lunch with a buffet consisting of cold meats, hard-boiled eggs and rye bread. A large painting of a nude female hung over the bar.

At age 15, Ellsworth became head bellman with the nickname of "Colonel". By the time he was 16, he learned how to keep the accounting records and at 19 years of age became the hotel manager. The McLure lobby had marble floors, brass spittoons, heavy oak chairs and tables and mounted heads of bison and mountain sheep on the walls. Baseball scores were posted in the lobby and the atmosphere was charged with talk about cockfighting, prize fighting, gambling and steamboat races on the Ohio River. Enterprising and innovative, Statler leased the McLure Hotel's billiard room and railroad ticket concession and made them into profitable ventures. He got help from an unexpected source when he realized that his younger brother Osceola had developed an amazing talent for billiards. Osceola's fame spread all over town which brought people into the hotel to watch the local champion defeat all comers from out-of-town. Statler bought out the company that had been operating the nearby four-lane Musee Bowling Lanes, added four additional lanes and installed eight pool and billiard tables. Statler then organized a city-wide bowling tournament with a grand prize of $300 for the winning team.

To accommodate the crowds, Statler started the "The Pie House" in the Musee building where his mother's pies and minced chicken and minced ham sandwiches were served on egg-shell china and quadruple-plated table silver. In anticipation of the Starbucks phenomenon, Statler used the best coffee he could get not only for pleasing his customers' taste but for attracting them with delicious aromas. The place was so busy that the pin boys in the bowling alleys had to spend their spare time turning cranks on the ice-cream freezers. However, the *piece de resistance*, from which the restaurant derived its name, were the delicious home made lemon meringue, fruit and custard pies which were baked by Statler's mother and sister.

The entire Statler family was involved in business in Wheeling: Ellsworth's brother Osceola was partner and manager of the billiard room. Another brother, Bill, had charge of the Musee bowling lanes. Mother Statler and sister Alabama were turning out sandwiches and pies. As for Ellsworth, he was enjoying an income of $10,000 per year which made him affluent and eager to own and operate his own large hotel.

His oft-expressed wish at that time was to own and operate a 1000-room hotel in New York City. Ultimately, Statler fulfilled his dream but not until he followed a standard vaudeville performer's line that "to get to New York City, you had to go by way of Buffalo."

After his success in Wheeling, Statler used to go fishing each summer with a couple of friends in the St. Clair River at Star Island in Canada. In 1894, on one of his trips, Statler stopped in Buffalo where he observed the new Ellicott Square building under construction and billed as the "largest office building in the world". He learned that the building's management was looking for someone to operate a large restaurant in part of the main floor and basement for $8,500 per year rental. Statler struck a verbal agreement with the renting agent to lease this space provided he could raise enough money to furnish a large restaurant. That same summer, Statler married Mary Manderbach whom he had met in Akron eight years earlier. They moved to Buffalo where on July 4, 1895, Statler's Restaurant opened amidst a blaze of fireworks and an outpouring of patriotic oratory. But, Buffalo had never been noted as a festive place or a center of fine dining. Despite heavy promotion and efficient operation, Statler's creditors closed in after he changed the name from Statler's Restaurant to George E. House's Restaurant (House was one of Statler's Wheeling friends who had underwritten his lease). Statler then rushed to Wheeling to change title to his mother's house to prevent it from being foreclosed.

Statler staked everything on the coming encampment of the Grand Army of the Republic which was about to bring thousands of Union Army veterans and their families to Buffalo. Statler advertised widely the most amazing menu ever offered at "All you can eat for 25¢." For just a quarter, patrons could eat the following: bisque of oysters, olives, radishes, fried smelts with tartar sauce and potatoes, lamb sauté Bordelaise with green peas, roast young duck with applesauce and mashed potatoes, Roman punch, fruit or vegetable salad with Russian dressing, cream layer cake, Metropolitan ice cream, coffee, tea or milk. What's more, you could eat as much as you liked! The veterans and their families loved Statler's menu and made the restaurant profitable.

Statler's dream was to have his own hotel and in 1907, that dream became a reality. He opened the 300-room Buffalo Statler and advertised "a room and a bath for a dollar and a half." The architectural firm Esenwein and Johnson designed the building which was built by Mosier and Summers Construction Company.

On October 18, 1912, the second Statler Hotel opened in Cleveland, Ohio. The architectural firm was George B. Post, a prominent New York architect and Louis Rorimer as the interior decorator (Rorimer also decorated the other Statler Hotels as well). This hotel was 16 stories tall with 800 rooms. An expansion wing of 300 additional rooms was added for traveling men. Today, this hotel has been converted into 295 apartment suites called the *Statler Arms*.

The Statler Hotel located at 1539 Washington Blvd. Detroit, Michigan was built in 1914 and opened on Feb. 6, 1915. The building is fifteen stories tall and originally had eight hundred guestrooms, each with a bath, thus creating a new standard of excellence in the hotel industry. The building was designed by George B. Post using subtle Italian and Adamesque architectural detailing. In 1958, it became known as the Statler Hilton after the Hilton bought out the chain. Later the hotel was renamed the Detroit Heritage Hotel and it closed its doors in 1975.

On December 11, 1916, Statler acquired the operating lease of the Hotel Pennsylvania in New York. He paid $1,000,000 a year for the lease. It was the largest hotel at the time with 2,200 rooms each with a bath.

The Statler Hotel located at 822 Washington Ave. in St. Louis was opened on November 4, 1917. It was the fourth Statler Hotel built and was designed by George B. Post & Sons of New York with Mauran, Russell & Crowell of St. Louis. The 650-room, twenty-story Statler featured lavish public rooms and an arcaded lobby on the first floor with a stunning, two-story ballroom at the top.

Seeking a competitive edge, Statler designed a common shaft known as the "Statler plumbing shaft" that permitted bathrooms to be built back to back, providing two baths for little more than the price of one, and allowing him to offer many private rooms with adjoining baths. These shafts, besides carrying water and waste lines, also contained heating pipes and the electrical conduits for each room.

Starting in 1908, Statler's preoccupation with guest comfort and operational efficiency brought about the following innovations, among others; ice water circulating to every bathroom, a telephone in every room, a full-size closet with a light, a towel hook beside every bathroom mirror, a free newspaper each morning, and a pin-cushion with needle and thread. In 1922, at the Pennsylvania Statler in New York City, Statler introduced the Servidor, a bulging panel in the guest-room door where the guest hung clothes needing cleaning or pressing. The valet could pick up the clothes and return them without ever entering the room. The Pennsylvania Statler was the first hotel to offer complete medical services including an x-ray and surgical room, a night physician and a dentist.

Later, as he built more hotels, Statler made certain that they operated on the same principle. He wrote: "Statler Hotels are operated primarily for the comfort and convenience of their guests. Without guests there could be no Statler Hotels. These are simple facts, easily understood. It behooves every and woman employed here to remember this always, and the treat all guests with courtesy and careful consideration."

In his instructions to managers about what sort of people to hire for hotel service, he wrote in 1917:

> From this date you are instructed to employ only good-natured people, cheerful and pleasant, who smile easily and often. This ought to go for every job in the house, but at present I'll insist on it only for people that come in contact with guests… If it's necessary to clean house, do it. Don't protest. Get rid of the grouches, and the people that can't keep their tempers and the people who act as if they were always under a burden of trouble and feeling sorry for themselves. You can't make that sort of a person over; you can't do anything with them profitably, but get rid of him. Let the other fellow have him and you hire a man that can be taught.

Statler's precepts eventually became the "Statler Service Code," which outlined for employees the founder's ideals. The code aroused so much interest that it was made available to guests and became a Statler tradition. New employees learned from it what was meant by "Statler Service" and guests gained a better understanding of the kind of service they could expect in a Statler Hotel.

The Statler Service Code reflects Ellsworth M. Statler's precepts: "Statler Hotels are operated primarily for the comfort and convenience of their guests. Without guests there could be no Statler Hotels... It behooves every man and woman employed here to remember this always, and to treat all guest with courtesy and careful consideration." This 22 page booklet was distributed to employees and guests.

The 61st edition of the Code published in 1955 began with this introduction:

> The late E.M. Statler founded his business on the simple precept that "the guest must be pleased." When he established the first Hotel Statler, in Buffalo in 1908, he said it this way:
>
> "A hotel has just one thing to sell. That one thing is service. The hotel that sells poor service is a poor hotel. The hotel that sells good service is a good hotel. It is the object of the Hotel Statler to sell its guests the very best service in the world."

And later as he built more hotels, always on this same principle, he said:

"Statler Hotels are operated primarily for the comfort and convenience of their guests. Without guests there could be no Statler hotels. These are simple facts, easily understood. It behooves every man and woman employed here to remember this always, and to treat all guests with courtesy and careful consideration.

The Code aroused so much interest that years ago it was made available to guests and it has now become a Statler tradition. Here's an excerpt:

<u>What is Statler Service?</u>

Perfect hotel service is not the accomplishment of any single employee to any single guest. Service, as interpreted by Statler, means the maximum of courteous and efficient attention given by each employee to each individual guest.

This is the kind of service a Statler guest pays for- the kind to which he is entitled, whatever the size of the bill.

<u>Little Things That Make A Big Difference</u>

The first Statler employee the guest sees is the doorman. He can swing the door in a way that bids the traveler welcome, or he can do it in a way that arouses resentment in the guest and makes him expect a cold, impersonal reception at the room desk.

It is the total of many such little things that prompts guests to say later, "I stopped at the Statler!" rather than to yawn, "I put up at the hotel last night."

You cannot afford to be superior or impolite to guest- they're all important, and they're all paying for the same service.

Old and new customers

New customers are just as important as the old customers you recognize. Remember that each new customer is an old customer in the making. Do your part to give him the desire to come back to us bringing his family and friends.

Satisfied guests

Statler guests should be made to feel that we want to give them more sincere service for their money than they ever before received at any hotel. The employee who helps to foster this feeling in our guests is never out of a job, nor does he escape the eyes of his department head or the manager. Make the guest feel the fine good-fellowship of the hotel; the "No-trouble-to-help-you" spirit. Never be perky, pungent or fresh. Remember: the guest pays your salary.

Yardsticks of Service

Statler Service, beginning in Buffalo, can now be obtained in seven other great American cities and has become synonymous with good service—the yardstick of hotel service everywhere. We want these words, Statler Service, to mean even more than that. We hope to make them mean not only good service, but the best service, always. You can help us to realize this hope. Your opportunity with the Statler organization will be measured by your ability to make that part of Statler Service for which you are responsible the tops of its kinds to be found in any hotel, anywhere.

Statler Success Didn't Just Happen

The Statlers are successful hotels. Why? Because men and women of good judgment from all parts of the world make the Statler their home—when away from home. Why? Because every waiter, bellman, clerk, the chef and manager, himself, is working all the time to make them feel at home.

Each member of the organization is valuable to us only in direct proportion to his contribution toward that end.

Money Saved, More Service- Better Jobs

The department head who can so improve the system of his division to save time or labor can make more money for the Statler—and more for himself. Every dollar saved in any department means we can sell more service for the same price. Every item of extra courtesy makes for a more contented guest and every contented guest makes for a better, bigger Statler. And this means better, bigger jobs.

Particularly To Our Guests

In the interest of improving our opportunity to give our guests the utmost in hotel service, we should like to include in this booklet some excerpts from another publication of ours: Tips For Travelers. In the following paragraphs we repeat some of the questions guests ask us most frequently—and give the answers.

1. Why Make Reservations in Advance?

It is still very difficult in many cities to secure a hotel room without advance notice. You take a chance when you travel without reservations, as the hotel may be filled by travelers who took the trouble to make a reservation. Sending a wire just before you leave home does not give us sufficient time to tell you that a room can be reserved. The wise traveler makes his reservation as far in advance as possible.

2. Why Can't I Get A Hotel Room?

Any hotel manager would much rather give you a room than tell you why he can't. Many travelers think that hotel managers hold out rooms. This is not so. Many people think that knowing someone will produce a room. Short-sighted, indeed, would be the hotel man who reserved a room because someone knew someone, at the expense of the traveler who didn't know someone.

There are many times when a hotel is filled to the point where it cannot accommodate a single additional guest.

If two men from the same company occupy a room with twin beds, that means an extra for someone else. That someone may be you on your next trip.

3. Why Do Hotels Book Conventions?

Sometimes when people can't get accommodations in a hotel and they find a convention in the hotel, they ask, "Why do you book conventions?" Even when Statler is host to a convention, we reserve a substantial proportion of rooms for non-convention guests. But we do book conventions:

Because they fulfill a necessary function in the American way of doing things—industries, associations, organizations hold meetings to exchange information, develop programs, plans courses of action;

Because conventions stimulate business in the cities where they are held, benefiting merchants, restaurants, theaters, transportation companies and others as well as hotels:

Because it is our business and our duty to do the best job we can in accommodating all travelers and visitors.

Stanley Turkel

Incidentally, without this group business now and then, the fine metropolitan hotels of today would not have been possible. It takes more than day-to-day patronage of individual travelers to support the facilities that distinguish the modern American big-city hotel.

4. Why Can I Walk Into Another Hotel And Get A Room?

Our competitor reaches a point where he cannot take any more reservations. So do we. If every guest who had a reservation picked it up, and if every guest left on the day he promised, there would be no problem.

5. Why Should I Cancel If My Plans Change?

A hotel can accept only so many reservations. If your reservation has been accepted and your plans change, it helps us if you notify us. If you do not, it means that some other traveler must be told that he cannot have a room.

6. Why Do You Sometimes Keep Me Waiting For My Room?

We don't like to but we can't help it! Here's why: In many cities most guests arrive in the morning and most guests leave in the evening. If the hotel was filled the night before, arriving guests must check their baggage and wait for a room to become vacant. Incoming guests could be roomed much more promptly if those holding the rooms would release them early and check their baggage until the time of their departure.

Any Suggestions?

We have emphasized that Statler hotels pride themselves on their ability to please the discriminating guest— the one who says he is hard to please. If the service you received is not thoroughly satisfactory—and satisfying—in every detail, we want to know it so we can do something about it.

Our basic policy is built upon:

The recognition of your right to courteous, interested, helpful service from every Statler employee, with satisfaction guaranteed- even if it become necessary for you to refer the transaction to the Executive Offices in Hotel Statler, New York, N.Y.

We would welcome, too, any suggestions you may have as to how we can improve our way of running a hotel. Many of the best-liked Statler innovations resulted from ideas expressed by our guests. If something comes to mind, please let us know!

Your suggestions will help us to accomplish that goal toward which we are always striving- the very best in hotel service.

In the days before the word "empowerment" became a cliché, every Statler employee signed off on the following pledge:

1. To treat our patrons and fellow employees in an interested, helpful, and gracious manner, as we would want to be treated if positions were reversed;

2. To judge fairly–to know both sides before taking action;

3. To learn and practice self-control;

4. To keep our properties—buildings and equipment—in excellent condition at all times;

5. To know our job and to become skillful in its performance;

6. To acquire the habit of advance planning;

7. To do our duties promptly; and

8. To satisfy all patrons or to take them to our superior.

Statler's greatest contribution may have been forgotten: his formula for planning hotels so that smaller staffs could deliver services conveniently and efficiently. Statler departed from the customary practice of locating the kitchens in the less valuable basement area. Rather, he positioned a three-sided kitchen to simultaneously serve the restaurants, ballroom and meeting areas. Statler could be seen on the top floor of a new hotel, stop watch in hand, timing to the second how long it took the toilet to flush or a bath to fill.

The Statler Hotel, Buffalo, New York, Statler's first hotel opened in 1908 with 300 rooms. It advertised "a room with a bath for a dollar and a half." It contained such unheard-of-in-room luxuries as telephones, running ice-water and a morning newspaper under the door.

I've just acquired an old book with the words "Hotel Statler" embossed on the cover. It is entitled "Heart Throbs in Prose and Verse" published by the Chapple Publishing Company, Boston, 1905. While it contains 840 items of inspirational poems, anecdotes and stories, it is the frontispiece that caught my attention. Here it is verbatim:

To the Guests of this Hotel: This book is part of the permanent room equipment and is for the pleasure and convenience of our guests. We believe you will enjoy reading it and hope you will find in it a favorite poem or bit of prose which will awaken pleasant memories.

If this book suggests further reading, visit the well-selected Library on the Mezzanine floor, as it may have just the volume you wish; or choose from the catalog in your room and the Librarian will gladly send books at your request.

Apparently, operating genius ran in the family. His widow, Alice Seidler Statler, managed to stay solvent during the Depression, the only major hotel company to do so. She operated Statler Hotel Co. until 1954, when she sold it to Hilton Hotels for $111 million, merging Statler's 10,400 rooms with Hilton's 16,200 units. It was the greatest hotel merger and largest private real estate transaction in history.

An insight into his character is revealed in an account of a trip Ellsworth Statler made in the middle 20's to visit the newly-formed Hotel Administration Program at Cornell University. Although he was originally not in favor of college education for hotelmen, he made the trip as a favor to an old friend. Seeing what was being done, he liked it and said: "Give Professor Meek anything he wants". Later, he set aside one-sixth of the Statler stock as an educational trust fund.

The Statler Foundation today has assets of many millions and has made grants totaling well over $12 million. The School of Hotel Administration at Cornell has received more than $10 million for teaching facilities—Statler Hall and the Statler Inn and for scholarships, faculty salaries and research. San Francisco City College has a Statler Library. To this day, The Statler Foundation matches funds raised by regional hotel and restaurant educational foundations.

SOURCE MATERIALS

1. Donald E. Lundberg, *The Hotel and Restaurant Business*, Institutions/ Volume Feeding Management Magazine, Chicago, 1971

2. Floyd Miller, *Statler: America's Extraordinary Hotelman*, The Statler Foundation, New York 1968.

3. Jefferson Willamson, *The American Hotel*, Alfred A. Knopf, New York 1930.

4. Statler Service Code- 61st Edition, Published in 1955.

Juan Terry Trippe (1899-1981):

FOUNDER OF PAN AMERICAN WORLD AIRWAYS AND THE INTERCONTINENTAL HOTELS COMPANY

Juan Trippe was the founder and guiding hand behind Pan American Airways, one of the most successful and famous airlines in U.S. aviation history. What is less well known, he also developed the InterContinental Hotel Company which operated 222 hotels from 1946 to 1996. Only 18 of these hotels were in the United States.

Among all the pioneers of commercial flight, Juan Trippe was Wall Street's own child. Born a commuter's ride away in North Branch, New Jersey, he was the son of William Trippe, senior partner in the Wall Street investment house of White, Weld and Company. Trippe's association with flying went back to his earliest years. In 1903, two bicycle-shop owners and brothers, Orville and Wilbur Wright, built a glider with two propellers mounted on the rear. On December 17th they made the first controlled flight of an airplane at Kitty Hawk, North Carolina. While this event was scarcely noticed, the Wright Brothers gave exhibitions in the next five years in the United States and Europe. In 1909, ten-year old Juan Trippe saw an airplane competition on Governor's Island in New York harbor between Wilbur Wright and Glenn Curtiss. Curtiss' machine was caught in crosscurrents of wind and wouldn't stay aloft more than 45 seconds. Wright's first flight over water crossed the mile of Bedloe's Island where he overtook a sea gull and circled the Statue of Liberty before flying a figure-8 to his starting point. The New York Times reported that "New Yorkers had seen balloons but never the captain of the real aeroplane lift himself into the air high enough for millions to see and applaud him." Trippe's father took him to watch the country's first air race from the field at Mineola, Long Island around the Statue of Liberty and back. With his father he saw Glenn Curtiss triumphantly complete his sensational long-distance flight down the Hudson Valley from Albany in 1910. As a boy he watched Arch Hoxey and Lincoln Beachey fly upside down in front of the reviewing stand at Mineola. He met both of the Wright brothers. When he went to Yale in the war years it was foreordained that he would join the Navy and learn to fly with his classmate John Hambleton in Florida. Returning to Yale for a fourth year, he organized a flying club and took transportation as his chief classroom subject. He also found time to edit the Yale Graphic and he hired Sam Pryor, later a Pan Am vice president, as ad salesman and made a profit.

There was no question that Trippe would go to Wall Street. But when he went to work for the investment house of Lee, Higginson and Company, whatever his fathers expectations were, his own notion was clear. The work would give him access to cost figures for such transportation industries as railroads shipping lines and bus lines, there being no airlines yet. Even in college, Trippe could see far. Before long, Trippe heard from some friends that the Navy was disposing of some mint-fresh planes from World War I surplus stock. Calling on some Yale friends to join in and putting up some of the Yale Graphic profits for a starter, Trippe bought nine trainers and started New York Airways to fly to Southampton on the weekends. Trippe never piloted the planes himself, but he learned a good deal about what it cost to keep planes flying.

Congressman Clyde Kelly, a Yale friend of Trippe's, introduced the Kelly Act in 1925. The bill allowing private contractors to fly airmail was passed and Trippe and his "Yalie" friends were awarded Air Mail Route No. 1, New York-Boston. Eventually, Trippe's endeavor, Easter Air Transport, joined forces with another route from Connecticut, the Bee Line to become Colonial Air Transport. Colonial was awarded a contract to deliver mail from Boston to New York via Hartford on October 7, 1925. Trippe was the vice president of Colonial and managed operations for $7,500 per year.

During a publicity flight to Cuba to show-off Colonial's new Fokkertrimoter airplane, Trippe obtained an appointment with Cuban president Gerardo Machado. During their meeting Machado agreed to give Trippe exclusive rights to land at Camp Columbia, Havana's army airport. The conservative directors often did not agree with Trippe's unorthodox and speculative business ventures. On October 19, 1927 La Nina, a Fairchild FC-2 floatplane piloted by Cy Caldwell, took off from Key West bound for Camp Columbia carrying 30,000 letters and landed one hour and 20 minutes later.

Pan American Airways Incorporated was founded on March 14, 1927, by Major Henry H. "Hap" Arnold who would later head the U.S. Army Air Force during World War II. Their shell company was able to obtain the U.S. mail delivery contract to Cuba, but lacked the physical assets to do the job. On June 2, 1927, Juan Trippe formed the Aviation Corporation of America with the backing of powerful and politically-connected financiers William A. Rockefeller and Cornelius Vanderbilt Whitney. Trippe became the operational head of the new Pan American Airways Incorporated, created as the primary operating subsidiary of Aviation Corporation of the Americas. The U.S. government had approved the original Pan Am's mail delivery contract with little objection, out of fears that the German-owned Colombian carrier SCADTA would have no competition in bidding for routes between Latin America and the United States. Trippe and his associates planned to extend Pan Am's network through all of Central and South America. During the late 1920s and early 1930s, Pan Am purchased a number of ailing or defunct airlines in Central and South America, and negotiated with postal officials to win most of the government's airmail contracts to the region.

Miami Terminal of Pan American Airways, Miami, Florida. Thousands of passengers and tons of international air mail passed through this air terminal each year starting in 1929. Pan Am's great "Clipper Ships" brought Miami within a few days travel of 32 countries in South and Central America and the West Indies. At the time, Miami was the world's largest International Airport.

Pan Am's holding company, the Aviation Corporation of the Americas, was one of the hottest stocks on the New York Curb Exchange in 1929, and flurries of speculation surrounded each of its new route awards. On a single day in March, its stock rose 50% in value. Trippe and his associates had to fight off a takeover attempt by the United Aircraft and Transport Corporation to keep their control over Pan Am (UATC was the parent company of what are now Boeing, Pratt & Whitney and United Airlines).

In the history of American commercial aviation, there was no airline more influential, important, and better known than Pan American World Airways. It was not the first American passenger airline, nor did it ever meet with much success in the domestic market, but Pan Am (as it was more commonly known), represented a new adventurous image of the United States to the world. When filmmaker Stanley Kubrick produced his landmark vision of the future in the 1968 movie "2001: A Space Odyssey," he envisioned Pan Am as the space carrier that would take men and women regularly into space. Pan Am's history is inseparable from the life and career of Juan Trippe, the company's founder and guiding visionary for five decades.

The U.S. government strongly supported a mail service between North and South America. Congress passed the Foreign Air Mail Act on March 8, 1928, to regulate such international service, and later that month, the postmaster general advertised bids for a wide-ranging network of mail routes all across Latin America and the Caribbean. The Act provided impetus for the three companies to unite. Under Trippe's firm guiding hand, Atlantic, Pan American, and the Aviation Corporation united on June 23, 1928. Trippe's group at the time held 40 percent stock in the new holding company. A new Pan American Airways entity was set up as the main operating subsidiary of the new corporation.

The U.S. government looked very favorably at Pan Am, and viewed it as its "chosen instrument" for foreign policy by using Pan Am to facilitate economic expansion into Latin America and the Caribbean. The U.S. government, in fact, awarded Pan Am every foreign airmail route for which bids were invited. These included flights to Havana, Cuba; San Juan, Puerto Rico; Nassau in the Bahamas; Mexico City; and Santiago, Chile.

On May 21, 1927, Charles A. Lindbergh completed one of the most famous flights of all time- the first solo non-stop transatlantic flight in history. Lindbergh piloted his plane, the Spirit of St Louis, 3,610 miles between Roosevelt Field on Long Island, New York and Paris, France in 33.5 hours. With that flight, Lindbergh won the $25,000 prize offered by a practically unknown New York City hotel owner, Raymond Orteig.

In 1919, Orteig, issued an extraordinary challenge to the fledging flying world. Enthralled by tales of pioneer aviators, the French-born Orteig, who owned the Brevoort and Lafayette Hotels in New York City, offered a purse of $25,000 to be awarded to "the first aviator who shall cross the Atlantic in a land or water aircraft (heavier than air) from Paris or the shores of France to New York, or from New York to Paris without a stop."

Orteig said his offer would be good for five years, but five years came and went without anyone accomplishing this feat. No one even tried. In 1926, Orteig extended the term of his offer for another five years. This time around, however, aviation technology had advanced to a point where some thought that it might, indeed, be possible to fly non-stop across the Atlantic Ocean. Charles A. Lindbergh was one who thought it could happen, but few people believed that this obscure mail pilot had any chance of collecting Orteig's $25,000 prize.

Born in France, Raymond Orteig emigrated to the United States in 1882. He began a career in the hotel and restaurant business and eventually became the maitre d' at the Lafayette Hotel in New York City, which was located not far from the Brevoort Hotel in Greenwich Village. In 1902 he purchased the Brevoort, which was known for its basement café. Comprising three adjoining houses on Fifth Avenue between 8th and 9th Street, the Brevoort had gained a reputation in the late 19th century as a stopping place for titled Europeans. The Brevoort Café's French character, enriched by Orteig's yearly wine-buying trips to France attracted an illustrious crowd of Greenwich Village artists and writers. Among them was Mark Twain, lonely but popular, who took up residence between 1904 and 1908 in the Gothic-revival town house located on the southeast corner of Fifth Avenue and East 9th Street. (That house had been built in 1870 by James Renwick, architect of nearby Grace Church, built in 1845, and St. Patrick's Cathedral, completed in 1878.) In 1954, the entire block, including the hotel and Mark Twain's townhouse, was razed to make way for the 19-story Brevoort apartment building.

As a youth, Lindbergh studied with fascination the flying exhibits of the French ace Rene Fonck, who shot down 75 German planes during World War I. In September 1926, Fonck set his sights on claiming Orteig's prize by crossing the Atlantic from New York to Paris. Fonck's attempt failed before it ever got off the ground, when his luxurious silver biplane burst into flames on takeoff. Fonck survived the crash, but two crew members were killed. By this time Lindbergh had gained a reputation as a talented barnstormer, although he had not achieved the widespread acclaim of some of his fellow fliers. Nevertheless, his experience as daredevil, mechanic, and intrepid airmail pilot drew the notice of what was then a small community of fliers. Just as important was the fact that Lindbergh had the confidence necessary to undertake such a bold adventure as a transatlantic flight.

Lindbergh recalled that confidence in his autobiography, the *Spirit of St. Louis*: "Why shouldn't I fly from New York to Paris? … I have more than four years of aviation behind me, and close to 2,000 hours in the air. I've barnstormed over half of the 48 states. Why am I not qualified for such a flight?" Convinced that he was qualified, Lindbergh set out to convince others too. He found his partners in February 1927. Less than 24 hours after hearing of Lindbergh's search for a long range, single-engine plane, the Ryan Airlines Corporation of San Diego, offered to build such a craft. The airplane that Lindbergh would fly, dubbed the Spirit of St. Louis, was designed and built with the single purpose of transatlantic flight. Compared to a typical plane, extra fuel tanks were added and its wing span increased to accommodate the additional weight. The plane would have a maximum range of 4,000 miles, more than enough to reach Paris from New York. One innovative design decision put the main fuel tank in front of the pilot, rather than behind. Lindbergh didn't want to be caught between the tank and the engine if the plane was forced into an emergency landing.

This configuration meant that Lindbergh would not be able to see directly ahead as he flew. That did not seem to trouble him much, as he later wrote: "There's not much need to see ahead in normal flight. I won't be following any airways. When I'm near a flying field, I can watch the sky ahead by making shallow banks. All I need is a window on each side to see through." If he needed to see ahead, Lindbergh would use a periscope attached to the plane's port side. The plane's overall weight was crucial, so every ounce mattered. In his efforts to pare down the plane's weight, Lindbergh considered every detail. He left behind any item considered too heavy or unnecessary, including a radio, parachute, gas gauges, and navigation lights. He designed special, lightweight boots for the flight and went so far as to cut his maps down to include only the reference points that he would need. Upon its completion on April 28, 1927, the Spirit of St. Louis weighed in empty at 2,150 pounds. Still on view at the Smithsonian Museum of Air and Space, the plane stands nine feet, eight inches high, and extends

27 feet, eight inches in length, with a wingspan of 46 feet. The craft was powered by a 220-hoursepower, air cooled, nine-cylinder Wright J-5C "Whirlwind" engine that was designed to perform flawlessly for over 9,000 hours. This engine was outfitted with a special mechanism designed to keep it lubricated during the entire transatlantic flight.

Two days before Lindbergh's scheduled departure from San Diego on May 10, 1927, the news broke that the French pilots Charles Nungesser and Francois Coli had taken off from Paris bound for New York. It appeared as though all of Lindbergh's and Ryan Airline's efforts would be in vain. Despite a radio report claiming that Nungesser and Coli had been spotted over the Atlantic, the two were never heard from again. Thus, the loss Nungesser and Coli meant that Lindbergh's chance for glory was still within reach.

"Lucky Lindy" and the Spirit of St. Louis flew from San Diego to Curtis Field on Long Island (New York) on May 12, 1927. En route, pilot and plane set a new record for the fastest United States transcontinental flight. Eight days later, Lindbergh took off for Paris from New York's Roosevelt Field. Fighting fog, icing, and sleep deprivation, Lindbergh landed safely at Le Bourget Field in Paris at 10:22 PM on May 20, 1927 – and a new aviation hero was born. The plane had carried him over 3,600 miles in less than 34 hours.

The first trans-Atlantic flight heralded the "Lindbergh Boom" in aviation. Aircraft industry stocks rose in value, and interest in flying skyrocketed. During Lindbergh's subsequent U.S. tour and goodwill flight to Central and South America, the flags of the nations he visited were painted on the cowling of his plane. At the invitation of Juan Trippe, he then joined Pan Am World Airways. Trippe recalled that he was present at Roosevelt Field when Lindbergh started his history-making flight.

Conversely, Raymond Orteig is all but forgotten. His Lafayette Hotel (known as the Hotel Martin from 1863 to 1902, when Orteig acquired and rechristened it) was patronized by international celebrities who were drawn by its French food and service. When the Brevoort faltered in 1932 during the Great Depression (as did so many other hotels) Orteig sold it and nurtured the Lafayette through the depression. In 1953 the

Lafayette was demolished for a modern apartment building, the six-story Lafayette Apartments at University Place and 9th Street.

After establishing a Caribbean mail network, Pan Am began to acquire several other key airlines that had tried to compete with Pan Am in the area. These included the West Indian Aerial Express (acquired in December 1928) and the Campañia Mexicana de Aviación (CMA), a Mexican-American airline (acquired in January 1929). Trippe's ultimate target in the early 1930s was Buenos Aires, Argentina, the largest city in the southern hemisphere. Pan Am, however, faced stiff resistance from the Grace shipping company. Eventually, the two companies reached a compromise and on January 25, 1929, formed Pan American-Grace Airways, Inc. (PANAGRA), with each side contributing 50 percent of the capital.

Pan Am's heyday was in the 1930s when it operated its famous Clipper Ships in an ocean-wide network with a fleet of 25 flying boats that crisscrossed both the Pacific and the Atlantic oceans. The service flourished in the late 1930's delivering mail and passengers, and gained a reputation as one of the most dependable and elegant air services in the world. The "Clippers," a name of 19th century ocean- crossing ships, were the only American passenger aircraft capable of international travel. To compete with ocean liners, the airline offered first-class seats on such flights, and the style of flight crews became more formal. Instead of being leather-jacketed, silk-scarved airmail pilots, the crews of the "Clippers" wore naval-style uniforms and adopted a set procession when boarding the aircraft. However, during World War II most of the Clippers were pressed into the military, with Pan Am flight crews operating the aircraft under contract. During this era, Pan Am pioneered a new air route across western and central Africa to Iran, and in early 1942, the airline became the first to operate a route circumnavigating the globe. Another first was in January 1943, when Franklin Roosevelt became the first U.S. president to fly abroad, in the Dixie Clipper. It was also during the period that *Star Trek* creator Gene Roddenberry was a Clipper pilot. He was aboard the Clipper Eclipse when it crashed in Syria on June 19, 1947.

In its 19th Annual Report covering the year 1946, Pan American World Airways reported that it was diversifying into the hotel business: "Anticipating the need for additional hotel accommodations, particularly clean, modern accommodations for travelers of modest means, your company immediately after V-J Day undertook to sponsor that development of such facilities in all Latin American countries. A subsidiary was organized to assist in raising capital for the design and construction and ultimately the management and operation of individual hotels in important traffic centers." With an Export-Import Bank credit of $25 million for hotel financing, Trippe tried to interest hotel companies like the Statler Hotels Corporation to undertake hotel development in Latin America. Statler's chief executive, H.B. Callis, after a detailed study, concluded that the project would put too great a strain on Statler's limited financial and personnel resources. When no other hotel company could be found, a reluctant Pan Am agreed to take up the challenge, reserving the right to assign the package to an existing U.S. hotel company if an interested one could be found, a search which continued to prove fruitless. Nevertheless, Juan Trippe was eager to commence hotel development because he realized that many hotels were needed if his vision of mass civilian, business and pleasure air travel was to become a reality. At the time, he served as a director of New York's Waldorf-Astoria Corporation and was a good friend of its chief executive, Lucius Boomer. Boomer had an impressive hotel-keeping career behind him as chief executive of the McAlpin Hotel in New York and the original Waldorf-Astoria in New York (on the site of the Empire State Building), the Bellevue Stratford in Philadelphia, the Willard in Washington, the Windsor in Montreal, the New York Sherry-Netherland and the Lennox in Boston.

By 1947, the board concluded that the Pan American name did not reflect a worldwide hotel company and selected "InterContinental" over "International". Unfortunately, Boomer was killed in an air crash on June 26, 1947 while vacationing in Norway. He was succeeded by Byron Calhoun, who had worked his way to the top over a thirty-five year hotel career in the Midwest, focused attention on employee training, guest room design and, most important of all, the utilization of InterContinental Hotel Corporation's (IHC) management services to owners of existing hotels. The first two hotels operated by InterContinental were the eighty-five room Grande in Belem, Brazil (1949) and the 400 room Hotel Carrera in Santiago, Chile (1950).

Next was a management agreement for the 220 room Hotel El Prado in Baranquilla, Colombia (1950).

Past president of the American Hotel & Lodging Association Kirby Payne told me that his father Phyl Paine was the second general manager of InterContinental's Grande Hotel in Belem, Brazil which was built at the turn of the century. Each of the four floors had a single telephone which was under the supervision of a phone attendant who would run to summon guests from their rooms when a call arrived. Kirby said that floor attendants were also responsible for keeping the GM's son from hitting guests with his tricycle. The hotel's laundry was in the building's colonial-style central courtyard where twenty laundresses washed by hand. They also used hand irons heated with hot charcoal embers in them. The hotel had its own ice plant where big containers were lowered into brine. Rooms were cooled by window fans as was the bar. A very popular sidewalk café gave the place a vaguely European feeling despite the heat and humidity which went with an oceanfront city one degree south of the equator. Kirby said that the maintenance department built a tree house with electricity and running water for him. The hotel's losses were turned to profit in the first year and this was doubled in the second year of IHC operation. The hotel was run by IHC for 17 years during which time it served as the first posting for many young GM's who went on to important careers with the company. In 1951, IHC purchased the 270-room Reforma Hotel in Mexico City, Mexico. InterContinental grew along Pan Am's routes becoming the first international hotel company to operate in Asia/Pacific, Africa and the Middle East.

During the prohibition years when the sale of alcoholic beverages was forbidden in the United States, hotelkeepers had to learn how to make a profit from selling rooms and food without wine and liquor sales. Many accounting innovations were introduced by three Hungarian immigrants, the Horwath brothers and Louis Toth. Horwath and Horwath ultimately had offices in all principal U.S. cities. When InterContinental turned to them for help, they assigned William Busquets as senior auditor. Busquets converted the books to the Uniform System of Accounts for Hotels which had recently been developed for the American Hotel Association by Horwath and Horwath and Harris, Kerr & Forster.

Before anyone else, Trippe believed in airline travel as something to be enjoyed by ordinary mortals not just a globe-trotting elite. In 1945 other airlines didn't think or act that way. Trippe decided to introduce a "tourist class" fare from New York to London. He cut the round-trip fare more than half to $275 ($1,684 in today's dollars which makes current pricing a bargain). This went over like a lead balloon in the industry where air fares were fixed by a cartel, the International Air Transport Association (IATA), who didn't want to hear about the tourist class. Incredibly, Britain closed its airports to Pan Am flights that had tourist seats. Pan Am was forced to switch to remote Shannon, Ireland. The industry's aversion to competition and making travel affordable was to have a long life as Sir Freddie Laker would discover in the 1970's and Virgin Atlantic nearly a decade later.

By 1953 IHC had doubled in size with hotels in Bermuda, Montevideo, Bogota, Maracaibo and Caracas. Perhaps the most spectacular hotel was the 400-room Tamanaco in Caracas which opened in 1954. The V-shaped Tamanaco featured tiered garden terraces at the ends of each floor, an indoor/outdoor restaurant and bar, a free-form swimming pool surrounded by a ring of cabanas overlooking views of the city below and the nearby mountains.

The Hotel Tamanaco, Caracas, Venezuela opened in 1954 with 400 rooms. The V-shaped hotel featured tiered garden terraces at the ends of each floor, an indoor-outdoor restaurant and bar, a free-form swimming pool surrounded by a ring of cabanas overlooking views of the city below and the nearby mountains.

Finally, in 1952, Trippe's relentless attacks on IATA forced all airlines to accept the inevitability of tourist class. However, flying the oceans was still mostly for the rich and famous. Trippe saw that the new jets being introduced by Boeing and Douglas could mark the end of that demographic and he ordered many new jets. In October 1958, a Pan Am Boeing 707 left New York for its first scheduled flight to Paris. The jet age had begun and the transformation was dramatic. The 707 flew almost twice as fast at 605 MPH as the Stratocruiser, the civilian version of the B29 it had replaced.

In 1955, IHC became the major owner of the 550-room Hotel Nacional in Havana, Cuba (still in operation) and was generally considered to be one of the top ten hotels in the world. Their partners were the United Fruit Company (35%) and Cuban interests (18%) which purchased an option covering the thirty-four year unexpired term of a lease which had belonged to the Kirkeby Hotel group, a U.S. company specializing in resort operations. The hotel's casino was subleased to a group headed by Meyer Lansky, a Florida entrepreneur with close ties to organized crime.

In 1964 Juan Terry Trippe was the chairman and founder of a billion-dollar conglomerate including the mightiest international airline, hotels, missile ranges, business jets and a massive New York City office building. Pan Am was flying jets to Europe 214 times a week, up from 170 flights in 1958 in propeller planes carrying half as many passengers. In 1966, traffic increased by 25 percent with service to 118 cities and a net profit of $132 million. By 1970, InterContinental Hotels Corporation, a completely-owned subsidiary, was operating sixty hotels in some fifty countries, a total of approximately 20,000 rooms.

Pan American also played a key role in shaping the economics and eventual design of a new generation of wide-bodied jets. By defining requirements for size and passenger capacity, Trippe influenced the shape of Boeing's new aircraft- called the 747- which was capable of carrying as many as 490 passengers. Pan Am also built "Worldport", a terminal building at John F. Kennedy International Airport that was the world's largest airline terminal for many years. It was distinguished by its elliptical, four-acre roof, suspended far from the outside columns of the terminal below by 32 sets of steel posts and cables. The terminal was designed to allow passengers to board and disembark via stairs without getting wet by parking the nose of the aircraft under the overhang. The introduction of the jetbridge made this feature obsolete.

By the time Trippe retired in 1968, Pan Am was flying to 85 nations on six continents. When Trippe died in 1981, his vision of a world where more people flew for less money had become a reality. After a steady and sustained rise as the most important American airline, Pan American's fortunes began to dip in the 1970's. Economic problems related to over-expansion and recession forced the company into debt. Deregulation and its consequences only added to Pan Am's woes. Although the company attempted to break into the domestic market by acquiring National Airlines (in October 1980), its problems only grew. Pan Am's iconic image also made it a target for terrorists. The airline finally began to fall apart following the 1986 hijacking of Pan Am Flight 73 in Pakistan, in which over 140 passengers and crew were killed or injured, and the 1988 bombing of Pan Am Flight 103 (*Clipper Maid of the Seas*) above Lockerbie, Scotland, which resulted in 270 fatalities. Many travelers avoided booking on Pan Am as they had begun to associate the airline with danger. Faced with a $300 million lawsuit filed by more than 100 families of the PA103 victims, the airlines subpoenaed records of six U.S. government agencies, including the CIA, the Drug Enforcement Administration, and the State Department. Though the records suggested that the U.S. government was aware of warnings of a bombing and failed to pass the information to the airline, the families claimed that Pan Am was attempting to shift the blame. Through the 1980s, it slowly sold off all its assets and was operating at a huge loss. In 1990, Pan Am sold off its major hub in London and the routes that it served to United Airlines. Although the airline operated for a very short while on emergency funding from Delta Air Lines, it collapsed into bankruptcy in December 1991.

Despite a dramatic fall from grace, Pan American left behind a legacy unmatched by any other airline in the history of U.S. aviation. Pan Am's China Clipper services, its expansion into South America, its pioneering partnership with Boeing, its ambitious routes such as its round-the-world jet service inaugurated in October 1959 and its development of an unprecedented worldwide hotel company, all made Pan Am one of the greatest U.S. companies.

The airline appeared in many movies, notably in several James Bond films. The company's Boeings 707s were featured in *Dr. No, From Russia with Love*, and the well-known parody *Casino Royale*, while a Pan Am 747 and the Worldport appeared in *Live and Let Die*. The airline's logo was featured in *License to Kill*, where James Bond checks in for a Pan Am flight that he ultimately doesn't board.

Other mentions include:

- The 1969 film *Bullitt* features a chase scene at San Francisco International Airport, where Steve McQueen's character runs after the villain on the tarmac while dodging several Pan Am 707s.

- Also in 1969, Argentinean actress Isabel Sarli checks in and boards a Pan Am 707 flight from Panama City, Panama, to Buenos Aires, Argentina, in Armando Bo's *Desnuda en la arena*.

- The airline's logo was also seen in the film *Blade Runner*. Subsequently, Pan Am became one of the victims of the supposed Blade Runner curse on large corporations whose logos were featured in scenes from the film.

- Pan Am also figured prominently in *Scarface* (set in the city of Miami, one of Pan Am's major hubs), where the airline's logo and slogan were adopted by criminal overlord Tony Montana.

- In the 1988 film *High Spirits*, a family of American tourists travels to Peter Plunkett's (Peter O'Toole) Irish castle on a Pan Am 747. The film was one of the last in which an audience would see a 747 in Pan Am's new colors.

- The airline was also featured in an opening scene of the Robin Williams's film *Hook*, in which the family is aboard a Pan Am 747-100 to London. Ironically, the movie opened just a week after the airline ceased operations.

- The airline's logo was also featured in the opening sequence of *The Family Man*, where Nicholas Cage checks in at the Worldport for a Pan Am 747 flight from New York to London. Some years later his character finds the old Pan Am boarding passes.

- The battle between Juan Trippe and TWA owner Howard Hughes over Pan Am's transatlantic monopoly was featured prominently in *The Aviator*.

During the fifty-year period from 1946 to 1996 under Trippe's direction, InterContinental Hotels developed and managed hotels all over the world:

	No. of Hotels
South America	17
Caribbean	13
Central America	10
Mideast	32
Africa	18
Europe	80
Far East	31
Canada	3
United States of America	18

THE INTER-CONTINENTAL GROUP HOTEL PORTFOLIO 1946-1996

Hotel	Location	IHC Affiliation Commenced	Terminated
Grande	Belém, Brazil	1949	1966
Carrera	Santiago, Chile	1950	1960
El Prado Inter-Continental	Barranquilla, Columbia	1950	1977
Reforma Inter-Continental	Mexico City, Mexico	1952	1970
Victoria Plaza	Montevideo, Uruguay	1953	1968
Princess	Hamilton, Bermuda	1953	1955
Tequendama	Bogotá, Columbia	1963	---
Del Lago Inter- Continental	Maracaibo, Venezuela	1969	---
Tamanaco Inter-Continental	Caracas, Venezuela	1953	---
Nacional de Cuba	Havana, Cuba	1956	1960
Jaragua Inter-Continental	Santo Domingo, Dominican Republic	1957	1960
Embajador Inter-Continental	Santo Domingo, Dominican Republic	1957	1977
Curacao Inter-Continental	Curacao, Netherlands Antilles	1957	1977
Varadero Oasis	Varadero Beach, Cuba	1957	1959
El Salvador Inter-Continental	San Salvador, El Salvador	1958	1975
El San Juan Inter-Continental	San Juan, Puerto Rico	1958	1961
El Ponce Inter- Continental	Ponce, Puerto Rico	1960	1975
Phoenicia Inter-Continental	Beirut, Lebanon	1961	1976
Ducor Inter-Continental	Monrovia, Liberia	1962	1987
Hotel Indonesia	Jakarta, Indonesia	1962	1974
Southern Cross Inter- Continental	Melbourne, Australia	1962	1977
Dublin Inter-Continental	Dublin, Ireland	1963	1972
Cork Inter-Continental	Cork, Ireland	1963	1972
Limerick Inter-Continental	Limerick, Ireland	1963	1972
Frankfurt Intercontinental	Frankfurt, Germany	1963	---
Ivoire Inter-Continental	Abidjan, Ivory Coast	1963	---
Singapura Inter-Continental/Forum	Singapore	1963	1983

Mandarin	Hong Kong	1963	1974
Inter-Continental Jordan	Amman, Jordan	1964	---
Inter-Continental Wien	Vienna, Austria	1964	---
Inter-Continental Geneve	Geneva, Switzerland	1964	---
Inter-Continental Jerusalem	Jerusalem	1964	1988
Karachi Inter-Continental	Karachi, Pakistan	1964	1985
Okura	Tokyo, Japan	1964	1972
Esplanade Inter-Continental	Zagreb, Yugoslavia	1964	1975
Inter-Continental Hannover	Hanover, Germany	1965	1994
Oberoi Inter-Continental	New Delhi, India	1965	1985
Pago Pago Inter-Continental	Pago Pago, American Samoa	1965	1973
Siam Inter-Continental	Bangkok, Thailand	1965	---
Inter-Continental Dacca	Dacca, Bangladesh	1966	1983
Bali Beach	Saour, Bali, Indonesia	1966	1983
Continental	Accra, Ghano	1967	1969
Ambassador Inter-Continental	Accra, Ghann	1967	1969
Inter-Continental Quito	Quito, Ecuador	1967	1988
Inter-Continental Lahore	Lahore, Pakistan	1967	1985
Inter-Continental Rawalpindi	Rawalpindi, Pakistan	1967	1985
Inter-Continental Auckland	Auckland, New Zealand	1968	1983
Inter-Continental Lusaka	Lusaka, Zambia	1968	---
Musi-o-Tunya Inter-Continental	Livingstone, Zambia	1968	---
Tahara's Inter-Continental	Papè éte, Tahiti,		
	French Polynesia	1968	1974
Delmon Inter-Continental	Manama, Bahrain	1969	1970
Inter-Continental Dusseldorf	Dusseldorf, Germany	1969	1992
Inter-Continental Manila	Makati, Philippines	1969	---
Inter-Continental Paris	Paris, France	1969	---
Bristol Kempinski	Berlin, Germany	1969	1974
Inter-Continental Nairobi	Nairobi, Kenya	1969	---
Inter-Continental Kabul	Kabul, Afghanistan	1969	1984
Duna Inter-Continental	Budapest, Hungary	1969	1993
Inter-Continental Medellín	Medellín, Colombia	1970	---

Vier Jahreszeiten Kempinski	Munich, Germany	1970	1994
Inter-Continental Cali	Cali, Columbia	1971	---
Inter-Continental Teheran	Teheran, Iran	1971	1980
Okura Inter-Continental Amsterdam	Amsterdam, The Netherlands	1971	1982
Inter-Continental Kinshasa	Kinshasa, Zaire	1971	---
Cyrus Inter-Continental	Shiraz, Iran	1971	1973
Darius Inter-Continental	Persepolis, Iran	1971	1973
Portman Inter-Continental	London, United Kingdom	1971	1992
Inter-Continental Cologne	Cologne, Germany	1971	1992
Inter-Continental Valencia	Valencia, Venezuela	1971	---
Inter-Continental Guyana	Ciudad Guyana, Venezuela	1971	---
Inter-Continental Bucharest	Bucharest, Romania	1971	---
Inter-Continental Helsinki	Helsinki, Finland	1972	---
Keio Plaza Inter-Continental	Tokyo, Japan	1972	---
Inter-Continental Hamburg	Hamburg, Germany	1972	---
Taj Mahal Inter-Continental	Bombay, India	1972	1995
Lee Gardens Forum	Hong Kong	1972	1976
Okoume Palace Inter-Continental	Libreville, Gabon	1972	---
Ceylon Inter-Continental	Colombo, Sri Lanka	1973	---
Munich Penta Forum	Munich, Germany	1973	---
Forum Jamaica	Kingston, Jamaica	1973	1975
Mark Hopkins Inter-Continental	San Francisco, Ca., U.S.A.	1973	---
Furama Inter-Continental	Hong Kong	1974	1990
Inter-Continental Prague	Prague, Czech Republic	1974	---
Borobudur Inter-Continental	Jakarta, Indonesia	1974	---
Forum Wiesbaden	Wiesbaden, Germany	1974	1991
Rose Hall Inter-Continental Hotel/			
Country Club	Montego Bay, Jamaica	1974	1982
Inter-Continental Rio	Rio de Janeiro, Brazil	1974	---
Emir du Liban	Beit-ed-Din, Lebanon	1974	1976
Forum Warsaw	Warsaw, Poland	1974	---
Inter-Continental Dubai	Dubai, United Arab Emigrates	1975	---
Inter-Continental Ocho Rios	Ocho Rios, Jamaica	1975	1982

Inter-Continental London	London, United Kingdom	1975	---
Riyadh Inter-Continental	Riyadh, Saudi Arabia	1975	---
Makkah, Inter-Continental	Makkah, Saudi Arabia	1975	---
Inter-Continental Zagreb	Zagreb, Croatia	1975	---
Khyber Inter-Continental	Peshawar, Pakistan	1975	1985
Port Vila Inter-Continental			
Island Inn	Vila, Vanuatu	1975	1989
Victoria Inter-Continental	Warsaw, Poland	1976	---
Inter-Continental Maui	Maui, Hawaii, U.S.A.	1976	1996
Golf Forum/Inter-Continental	Abidjan, Ivory Coast	1976	---
Inter-Continental Istanbul	Istanbul, Turkey	1976	1979
Saipan Beach Inter-Continental Inn	Saipan, Marianas	1976	1984
Muscat Inter-Continental	Muscat, Oman	1977	---
Inter-Continental Kingston	Kingston, Jamaica	1977	1982
Ritz Carlton	Montreal, Quebec, Canada	1977	1991
Le Vendome	Beirut, Lebanon	1977	1978
Davao Insular Inter-Continental Inn	Davao, Philippines	1977	1992
Punta Baluarte Inter-Continental	Calatagan, Philippines	1977	1989
Massarah Inter-Continental	Taif, Saudi Arabia	1977	---
Montfleury Inter-Continental	Cannes, France	1977	1982
Inter-Continental New York	New York, New York, U.S.A.	1978	---
Four Ambassadors Inter-Continental	Miami, Florida, U.S.A.	1978	1981
Forum Tel Aviv	Tel Aviv, Israel	1978	1979
Inter-Continental Berlin	Berlin, Germany	1978	---
Ritz Inter-Continental Lisbon	Lisbon, Portugal	1979	---
Inter-Continental Beograd	Belgrade, Serbia	1979	---
Regency Inter-Continental Bahrain	Manama, Bahrain	1980	---
Abu Dhabi Inter-Continental	Abu Dhabi, United		
	Arab Emirates	1980	---
Mount Kenya Safari Club	Nanyuki, Kenya	1980	1986
Bonaventure Inter-Continental			
Hotel & Spa	Fort Lauderdale, Florida U.S.A.	1981	1984
Plaza Inter-Continental	Buenos Aires, Argentina	1981	1982

St. Anthony Inter-Continental	San Antonio, Texas, U.S.A.	1981	1988
Forum Budapest	Budapest, Hungary	1981	---
Al Ain Inter-Continental	Al Ain, Abu Dahabi		
	United Arab Emirates	1981	---
Pavilion Inter-Continental			
Singapore	Singapore	1982	1988
Athenaeum Inter-Continental			
Athens	Athens, Greece	1982	---
Britannia Inter-Continental			
London	London, United Kingdom	1982	---
Forum London	London, United Kingdom	1982	---
May Fair Inter-Continental	London, United Kingdom	1982	---
Amstel Inter-Continental	Amsterdam, The Netherlands	1982	---
American	Amsterdam, The Netherlands	1982	---
Europa Belfast	Belfast, Northern Ireland,		
	United Kingdom	1982	1986
Brussels Europa	Brussels, Belgium	1982	---
Le Grand Hotel Inter-Continental	Paris, France	1982	---
Prince des Galles	Paris, France	1982	1984
Meurice Inter-Continental	Paris, France	1982	1988
Lotti	Paris, France	1982	1984
Paris Penta	Paris, France	1982	1983
Europa Inter-Continental	London, United Kingdom	1982	1983
Carlton Inter-Continental	Cannes, France	1982	---
George Forum/Inter-Continental	Edinburgh, Scotland	1982	---
	United Kingdom		
Castellana Madrid	Madrid, Spain	1982	---
De La Ville Forum/			
Inter-Continental	Rome, Italy	1982	---
D'Angleterre Inter-Continental	Copenhagen, Denmark	1982	1984
Dhahran Algosaibi	Dhahran, Saudi Arabia	1982	1985
Victoria	Amsterdam, The Netherlands	1982	1985
Mount Royal	London, United Kingdom	1982	1983

Piccadilly	London, United Kingdom	1982	1983
Kennedy	London, United Kingdom	1982	1983
St. Ermin's	London, United Kingdom	1982	1983
Chesterfield	London, United Kingdom	1982	1984
Clifton-Ford	London, United Kingdom	1982	1983
Savoy	Rome, Italy	1982	1984
Amra Forum	Amman, Jordan	1982	---
Scanticon Princeton	Princeton, New Jersey, U.S.A.	1982	1991
Drury Lane	London, United Kingdom	1983	1983
Petra Forum	Petra, Jordan	1983	---
Inter-Continental New Orleans	New Orleans, Louisiana, U.S.A.	1983	---
Inter-Continental Houston	Houston, Texas, U.S.A.	1984	1988
Inter-Continental San Diego	San Diego, California, U.S.A.	1984	1987
Nairobi Safari Club	Nairobi, Kenya	1984	1991
Inter-Continental Luxembourg	Grand Duchy of Luxembourg	1985	---
Abha Inter-Continental	Abha, Saudi Arabia	1985	---
Inter-Continental Hilton Head	Hilton Head, South Carolina, U.S.A.	1985	1988
Inter-Continental Sydney	Sydney, Australia	1985	---
Inter-Continental Miami	Miami, Florida, U.S.A.	1985	---
Leconi Palace Inter-Continental	Franceville, Gabon	1985	---
Inter-Continental Mombasa	Mombasa, Kenya	1985	---
Al Bustan Palace Inter-Continental	Muscat, Oman	1985	---
Inter-Continental Miami	Miami, Florida U.S.A.	1986	---
Willard Inter-Continental	Washington, D.C., U.S.A.	1986	---
Sorrento Palace	Sorrento, Italy	1986	---
Ancira Sierra Inter-Continental	Monterrey, Mexico	1986	1991
Semiramis Inter-Continental	Cairo, Egypt	1987	---
Scanticon Minneapolis	Minneapolis, Minnesota, U.S.A.	1987	1991
Strand Inter-Continental	Helsinki, Finland	1988	---
Forum Cracow	Cracow, Poland	1988	---
Taj Palace Inter-Continental	New Delhi, India	1988	---
Forum Prague	Prague, Czech Republic	1988	---
Inter-Continental Stuttgart	Stuttgart, Germany	1988	---

Inter-Continental Cancun	Cancun, Mexico	1988	1991
Inter-Continental Seoul	Seoul, Korea	1988	---
Schweizerhof Inter-Continental	Berlin, Germany	1989	---
Scanticon Denver	Denver, Colorado, U.S.A.	1989	1992
Forum Glasgow	Glasgow, Scotland, United Kingdom	1989	1990
Inter-Continental Chicago	Chicago, Illinois, U.S.A.	1989	---
Forum Bratislava	Bratislava, Slovakia	1989	---
Forum Shenzen	Shenzen, China	1990	---
Des Indes Inter-Continental	The Hague, The Netherlands	1990	---
Inter-Continental Toronto	Toronto, Ontario, Canada	1990	---
Hotel Metropol Moscow	Moscow, Russia	1991	---
Yokohama Grand			
Inter-Continental	Yokohama, Japan	1991	---
Forum Berlin,	Berlin, Germany	1992	---
Inter-Continental Montreal	Montreal, Quebec, Canada	1992	---
Forum Geneve	Geneva, Switzerland	1992	---
Inter-Continental Los Angeles	Los Angeles, California, U.S.A.	1992	---
Jeddah Inter-Continental	Jeddah, Saudi Arabia	1992	---
Inter-Continental Leipzig	Leipzig, Germany	1992	---
Yamoussoukro, Palace	Yamoussoukro, Ivory Coast	1992	---
Las Lomas Forum	Rionegro, Columbia	1993	---
Churchill Inter-Continental	London, United Kingdom	1993	---
Bali Inter-Continental Resort	Jimbaran, Bali, Indonesia	1993	---
Terrace Inter-Continental	Adelaide, Australia	1993	1996
Hurghada Inter-Continental			
Resort & Casino	Hurghada, Egypt	1994	---
V Centenario Inter-Continental	Santo Domingo,		
	Dominican Republic	1994	---
Presidente Los Cabos			
Forum Resort	San Jose del Cabo, Mexico	1994	---
Presidente Inter-Continental			
Cancun	Cancun, Mexico	1994	---
Presidente Inter-Continental	Cozumel, Mexico	1994	---

Cozumel			
Presidente Inter-Continental	Mexico City, Mexico	1994	---
Mexico City	·		
Preisdente Ixtapa Forum Resort	Ixtapa, Guerrero, Mexico	1994	---
Presidente Inter-Continental			
Puerto Vallarta	Puerto Vallarta, Mexico	1994	---
Inter-Continental Buenos Aires	Buenos Aires, Argentina	1995	---
Royal Plaza Inter-Continental			
Montreux	Montreux, Switzerland	1995	---
Forum Hamburg	Hamburg, Germany	1995	---
Inter-Continental Singapore	Singapore	1995	---
Inter-Continental Tokyo Bay	Tokyo, Japan	1995	---
Cape Sun Inter-Continental			
Cape Town	Cape Town, South Africa	1995	---
Sandton Sun & Towers			
Inter-Continental Johannesburg	Johannesburg, South Africa	1995	---
Beverly Hills Sun			
Inter-Continental Durban	Durban, South Africa	1995	---
Forum Schwiezerhof Hannover	Hanover, Germany	1995	---
Inter-Continental Sofia	Sofia, Bulgaria	1995	---
Forum Nicosia	Nicosia, Cyprus	1995	---
Lev Inter-Continental Ljubljana	Ljubljana, Slovenia	1995	---
Ceylan Inter-Continental Istanbul	Istanbul, Turkey	1996	---
Le Vendome Inter-Continental			
Beirut	Beirut, Lebanon	1996	---

SOURCE MATERIALS

1. Marilyn Bender and Selig Altschul, *The Chosen Instrument*, Simon and Schuster, New York, 1982

2. Robert Daley, *An American Saga: Juan Trippe and His Pan Am Empire*, Random House, New York, 1980

3. Desmond Fairbairn, *Pan Am: Gone But Not Forgotten*, Transportation Trails, Illinois, 1996

4. Max Hampton, *Throw Away The Key*, The Bobbs-Merrill Company, Inc., Indianapolis, 1966

5. Matthew Josephson, *Empire of the Air*, Ayer Company Publishers, Inc., North Stratford, 1999

6. Lawrence Mahoney, *The Early Birds: A History of Pan Am's Clipper Ships*, The Pickering Press, Miami, 1987.

7. James E. Potter, *A Room With a World View: 50 Years of Inter-Continental Hotels and its People*, 1946-1996, George Weidenfeld & Nicolson Ltd., London, 1996

Kemmons Wilson (1913-2003):

FOUNDER OF HOLIDAY INNS AND THE WORLD'S INNKEEPER

In the early 1900s motels were the epitome of modernism- the civilized evolution from tents to tourist cabins to auto courts to motor hotels. The writer James Agee wrote in Fortune magazine in 1934,

> In the two-dollar cabin you find a small, clean room, perhaps ten by twelve, Typically its furniture is a double bed-a sign may have told you it is Simmons with Beautyrest mattress- a table, two kitchen chairs, a small mirror, a row of hooks. In one corner a washbasin with cold running water; in another the half opened door to a toilet. There is a bit of chintz curtaining over the screened windows, through which a breeze is blowing... Inside you have just what you need for a night rest, neither more or less. And you have it with a privacy your hotel could not furnish- for this night this house is your own.

With the vast improvement in roads spurred on by the visionary Carl G. Fisher's building of the Lincoln Highway from New York to San Francisco in 1917, the tourist cabin business grew into a large industry. By 1925, Florida had 175 of the new roadside motor courts. In the United States, the number grew from 1000 to 2000 from 1920 to 1926. By the 1930's, despite the Depression, motor courts increased from 9800 in 1935 to 13,500 by 1939 with total guest registrations pre- Pearl Harbor at some 225 million. By the early 1940's there were 25 million cars registered and new motor courts being built at the rate of 800 per year. 87% of these rooms had private baths, 89% had heating, 14% had air conditioning, 72% provided innerspring mattresses, 60% had rugs or carpeting, and 16% had room phones.

It is believed that the first use of the term "motel" happened at the Milestone Motor Hotel in 1925 in San Luis Obispo, California. The owner, Charles Hamilton, hired architect Arthur Heinman to design an elaborate motor lodge complete with a bell tower and clay tile roof. When GM Harry Eliot couldn't fit the words "Motor hotel" on his sign, he fused them to form the unique acronym "motel". Since the law didn't allow for names and titles to be copyrighted, Arthur Heinman registered "Milestone Mo-tel" with the Library of Congress as a trademark in December 1925. The American motel was born.

After World War II, many veterans decided to open roadside motels. A Veteran's Administration 1946 manual warned, "The operation of a successful motor court takes hard work, 7 days a week, the year round. This endeavor should not be viewed as one where it is possible to sit in the sun by the side of the road and ring a cash register." Nevertheless, the statistical data about the postwar motel boom is staggering. There were some 20,000 motels in 1940, 30,000 in 1948, and 61,000 by 1960. By the late 1940s more than 86 percent of travelers were behind the wheels of their cars, and thus potential motel customers. By 1950 there were 22 million vacationers, and more than half of them stayed in motels. And by 1951 motels had surpassed hotels as the leading suppliers of rooms.

As the federal government implemented a new system of highway destinations in the late 1920s, the Automobile Association of America started to publish travel guides and maps. In turn, various owners of tourists camps and cabins produced a great variety of competing guides: Official OK Auto Courts, Rainbow Cottage Camp System, Yellow Octagon Guide, Approved Wayside Stations recommending "Inns, Tea Rooms Lunches, Camps and Tourist Houses," Travelers Motor Court Service with a Guide to Better Courts, Trailways of the Northland, At the Sign of the Red Arrow, etc. However, since there were no universal standards or inspections, the amenities and cleanliness varied widely from shabby to satisfactory. In the 1930s the first referral chains began which were a beneficial arrangement for mom-and-pop motel owners. Some of the more successful associations were the United Motor Courts, Quality Courts United, Alamo Plaza Courts and the National Autohaven Company.

On January 3, 1920 in the <u>Saturday Evening Post</u>, Sinclair Lewis wrote,

> Somewhere in these states there is a young man who is going to become rich. He may be washing milk bottles in a dairy lunch. He is going to start a chain of small, clean, pleasant hotels, standardized and nationally advertised, along every important motor route in the country. He is not going to waste money on gilt and onyx, but he is going to have agreeable clerks, good coffee, endurable mattresses and good lighting; and in every hotel he will have at least one suite which, however small, will be as good as the average room in a great modern city hotel. He will invade every town which hasn't a good hotel already...

As most of you know, the young man who fulfilled Sinclair Lewis' prediction was Kemmons Wilson who in 1952 opened his first Holiday Inn in Memphis. Kemmons Wilson did for the motel business what Ellsworth Statler did for the hotel business. He brought relative luxury to the middle class at prices they could afford. He standardized motel-keeping just as Howard Johnson standardized the roadside restaurant. All three men Wilson, Statler and Howard Johnson, insisted on cleanliness, relative uniformity and careful attention to maintenance. Such practices endeared a product or service to the middle class who want, above all else, predictability and safety in lodging and food.

When the first Holiday Inn opened in Memphis, TN, founder Kemmons Wilson commissioned his designer, Eddie Bluestein to design and build a huge green, orange and yellow billboard of never-before-seen proportions that would attract motorists whizzing by to the Holiday Inns located adjacent to the highway.

Kemmons Wilson was born in 1913 in Osceola, Arkansas. A year later, his father died and his mother Ruby brought him to Memphis where she took a job as a dental assistant at $11 a week. When she lost her job during the Depression, Wilson quit high school and went to work for good. At fourteen, he was a delivery boy for a Memphis drug firm and at seventeen set himself up in the popcorn business- with a popcorn popper bought on $50 credit- nothing down, $1 a week. As he recalled, "I was soon making more than the theater manager, so he threw me out and took over the popcorn concession himself." Wilson sold him the machine for $50 and then invested the money in five used pinball machines. (He later bought the popper back and displayed it in his office.)

Later, Wilson bought an old airplane, prevailed on the seller to teach him to fly and sold dollar rides around country towns. Dorothy, his future wife, sold tickets while his mother sold popcorn. By 1933 he had saved $1700 which he used to build a house on which he was able to borrow $6500 from a bank. "Right then", he said, "I decided to go into the building business". He went on to build more houses, buy apartments and acquire the regional Wurlitzer juke box distributorship. By World War II, Wilson was rich and in 1943 he sold his business for a quarter of a million dollars. He then enlisted in the Air Transport Command at age 30, went to flight training school and ultimately piloted C47s over the Himalayan hump during World War II.

Following the World War I, when new automobile sales skyrocketed, American motorists looked for roadside facilities which offered convenience, informality and affordability. A wide variety of sleeping facilities was born: tourist cabins, motor courts and roadside inns of every imaginable shape, design and color. Often these facilities were detached cabins operated by a family whose home was the registration office. Different from downtown urban hotels, these cabins provided the convenience of payment-in-advance, adjacent free parking, no tipping and easy coming and going. There were wigwams, igloos, log cabins, shotgun shacks, auto park camps, etc.

By the end of the 1930s automobiles were faster, roads were better and neon signs advertised the roadside motels. America's first neon sign advertised Earl Anthony's automobile dealership in Los Angeles. But neon proved to be the perfect material for motor lodges and tourist courts. Sign markers were able to use electrified gases trapped inside glass tubing which was bent, twisted and shaped to spell out motel names, vacancy signs and recreational amenities. Some owners outlined their buildings with long stands of colorful tubing.

By the mid 1930s many roadside properties were known as "hot sheet motels" which were rented by the hour. In a 1940 article "Camps of Crime", FBI chief J. Edgar Hoover, in a flight of typical hyperbole, declared that many roadside motels were vice dens which harbored corrupt gangs of thugs who terrorized the surrounding neighborhoods.

In 1951, Wilson took his family on a driving vacation from Memphis, TN. to Washington, D.C. They stayed in motels along the way which were cramped, costly and uncomfortable. For poor accommodations he was charged $10 a day plus $2 for each of his three children. Wilson said "it was the most miserable vacation trip of my life." Wilson remembered that "as soon as I got back to Memphis, I decided to build a motel that had all the things that we missed." The draftsman who designed it, Eddie Bluestein, scrawled a title across the bottom of the plans: "Holiday Inn" which he copied from the Fred Astaire/ Bing Crosby movie which he had recently seen.

Wilson borrowed $300,000 from a bank and in 1952 the first 120-room Holiday Inn opened on Summer Avenue, one of the roads leading into Memphis. It was so successful, that he built three more Holiday Inns within 20 months on other approach roads into Memphis. Each of the Holidays Inns had an in-ground swimming pool, an on-site restaurant, refrigerated air-conditioning, telephones in every room and free ice. As World War II ended, Holiday Inn founder Kemmons Wilson commissioned his designer, Eddie Bluestein to design and build a huge green, orange and yellow billboard of never-before-seen proportions that would attract automobiles whizzing by. This entrance sign looked more like a movie marquee than any motel sign before it. It was complete with an arrow that swooped up from the ground and pointed to the building; it had space to announce functions, restaurant specials, events and banquet announcements. These Las Vegas-style signs were 50 feet high, had 1,500 feet of neon tubing, 500 light bulbs and 10,000 pounds of steel. Some motel operators and franchisors copied the Holiday Inn sign while others commissioned massive signs of their own design.

Wilson's mother, Ruby 'Doll' Wilson, decorated the rooms of the first 50 Holiday Inns with bright colors and warm tones. Each Holiday Inn featured free parking, kennels to board the family pup and a list of baby sitters on call. In years to come, dentists and physicians were made available to those in need.

While Wilson was pleased with the startup of Holiday Inns, he dreamed of building a national franchised chain of 400 motels. To meet that lofty goal, he approached Wallace Johnson, one of the country's biggest real estate developers and a man the *Saturday Evening Post* called "the Henry Ford of the home building industry." Johnson was a director of the National Association of Home Builders whose network of contacts with home builders all over the United States helped to recruit franchisees. In 1954, Holiday Inns of America Inc. was born and the first franchise opened in Clarksdale, Mississippi paying a $500 fee plus 5¢ per night for each occupied room as a royalty. In return, the franchisee received Holiday Inns' plans, national advertising and reservations from the referral system. It turned out that building developers weren't the best market to sell the idea of a service-oriented motel.

Wilson and Johnson shifted their attention to wealthy lawyers, doctors, dentists and other professionals. Meanwhile the start of the $76 billion federal interstate highway-building program in 1956 gave a great lift to Holiday Inns. The first 75 Inns were one-story clones of the first one. But by the late 1950s, the cheaper-to-build and larger two-story Holiday Inns became the standard. These new Holiday Inns were much more like the hotels that the original motor courts replaced, and they were much larger, often with 150 to 300 rooms. The rooms were in multistory buildings often arranged back-to-back along a central utility core. This was an efficient and economical way to build, but noisy for the guests who knew when another guest on the other side of the bathroom wall was flushing the toilet at five in the morning. Often the motor inns were located near the new interstates- the very same highways that were a major factor in wiping out many of the smaller mom-and-pop operations of the past. The Holiday Inn empire exploded in size. The 50th Inn was opened in Dyersburg, Tennessee in 1958; the 100th in Tallahassee, Florida in 1959; the 500th in Johnstown, Pennsylvania in 1964; and the 1,000th in San Antonio, Texas. During those halcyon years, Wilson estimated that a new Inn was being opened every three days and a new room was being built every 20 minutes. By 1970, Holiday Inn reported a total of 175,000 rooms worldwide.

Just three years after the founding of the Holiday Inn brand, Kemmons Wilson created a franchise advisory council of Holiday Inn franchisees which was charged with reviewing issues important to the Holiday Inn system. The original name "National Association of Holiday Inns" was changed in 1963 to the International Association of Holiday Inns, Inc. (IAHI). In 1976, the Association was incorporated to reflect itself as a partially independent Association organized to represent the views and objectives of Holiday Inn hotel owners worldwide. At present, the IAHI reflects the interests of the owners of InterContinental Hotels Group brands including: Crowne Plaza Hotels and Resorts, Holiday Inn Hotels and Resorts, Holiday Inn Express, Staybridge Suites and Candlewood Suites. While it bills itself as a separate/ independent organization with close access to the leadership of Holiday Inns Worldwide, it nevertheless is essentially a franchise advisory council not an independent owners association. IAHI corporate offices are located in the Holiday Inn Worldwide Headquarters in Atlanta, Georgia. IAHI is funded by a combination of Association annual membership dues, system funds and expense allocations from Holiday Inns Worldwide.

The mission of the IAHI is admirable in its stated intent: to operate an association of hotel owners and operators that create a multi-level forum for exchange of information, ideas and best practices between franchisees and IHG company executives:

- Review and agree on IHG hotel brand standards and hallmarks.

- Review and agree on the optimum use of marketing and advertising funds that deliver each brands consumer message in a clear concise manner consistent with the approved standards and hallmarks.

- Assist in creating long-term brand and hotel asset value through excellent brands, quality operations, superior marketing and team member development.

- The IAHI will also work to effectively represent members' interests as a part of the broader hotel industry, on legislative and economic issues that impact their businesses.

The exchange of ideas, recommendations, advice and counsel between the IAHI and Holiday Inn Worldwide is mainly through a Committee

System designed to utilize the knowledge and expertise of Association members. Standing committees of Information Technology/Reservations and Advertising/Marketing monitor the recommended spending of more than $100 million of assessment funds paid to Holiday Inn Worldwide by Holiday Inn owners. Many other committees of owners review and make recommendations on Rules of Operation, Standards, Product and Design, Food and Beverage, Human Resources, Education and Training, Governmental Affairs, Technology and many other subjects that have impact on their hotels.

The IAHI also has regional committees in North America and International Committees in Europe, Middle East and Africa and Latin America. An advisory group is being developed in Asia Pacific. These groups consider regional opinions and recommendations that are forwarded to the IAHI Board of Directors for consideration and then to Holiday Inn Worldwide.

The Association has an active Political Action Committee named "INN-PAC." This activity financially supports Federal congressional candidates who consistently support and strengthen the free enterprise system and the importance of the Lodging and Hospitality industry. IAHI members voluntarily contribute to the "INN-PAC" fund on a calendar year basis.

By the early 1960s, a whole new generation of "budget" motels began to enter the marketplace with names like Howard Johnson, Ramada Inn, and TraveLodge. One of these new brands was Motel 6 founded by William Becker (1921-2007), a painting contractor in Santa Barbara, California. In 1960, Becker, his wife and son took a month long automobile trip to upstate New York to his family's farm outside of Saratoga Springs, N.Y. Like Kemmons Wilson, Becker experienced high prices and poor lodging conditions. With his friend Paul Green, a building contractor, the partners built the first Motel 6 in Santa Barbara in 1962. It had 54 rooms with no closets, hanging bars and open shelves, shower stalls with rounded corners to reduce cleaning time; no-iron sheets, plastic drinking cups; and coin-operated TVs (25 cents for six hours). Today Motel 6 is owned by Accor North America and has about 800 motels in the United States and Canada.

Motel 6 was founded by William Becker in 1962 in Santa Barbara with 54 rooms, no closets, open shelves, shower stalls, no-iron sheets, plastic drinking cups and coin-operated TVs (25 cents for six hours). Motel 6 is now owned by Accor North America and has about 800 motor inns in the United States and Canada.

Another motel owner named Merile Guertin from Long Beach, California had a dream of finding a group of quality motels. In 1947, he drove 5000 miles in 29 days (as the story is told) and inspected some 507 motels. He picked the best 66 properties and started Best Western. In the following year, he published five million copies of the Best Western guide and distributed them from West to East. In the next 60 years, Best Western has become "The World's Largest Hotel Chain" with 4200 properties in 80 countries. Best Western is a membership organization and all member hotels are independently owned.

Still another motel pioneer was Cecil Day, a devout Christian entrepreneur from Atlanta, who said that "no one was looking out for the middle American, the guy with two, three or four children traveling on a limited budget." He opened his first Days Inns of America in 1970 offering "luxury" rooms at $8 a night. Day tithed 10% of his profits to religious institutions and took pride in giving away a 700-page modern version of the Bible. On the book's yellow and black cover was printed

"Take With You for Spiritual Uplift" (in place of the words "Steal This Book" which was originally considered).

The design of all these new motel rooms were barely distinguishable one from the other. Ada Louise Huxtable, the architectural critic for the *New York Times,* wrote a scathing and critical article entitled "Hospitality and the Plastic Esthetic" (October 14, 1973):

> And yet I never approach a trip requiring an overnight stay without a sinking heart. It's not that I won't be reasonably comfortable.... it is that one is forced into a banal, standardized, multi-billion-dollar world of bad colors, bad fabrics, bad prints, bad pictures, bad furniture, bad lamps, bad ice-buckets and bad wastebaskets of such totally uniform and cheap consistency of taste and manufacture that borax or camp would be an exhilarating change of pace.

Part of Kemmons Wilson's success may be attributed to his work ethic. He was known for this advice: "Only work half a day. It doesn't matter which half you work- the first 12 hours or the second 12 hours." The evolution of Holiday Inn may be studied in its changing slogans. During the 1960s "The Nation's Innkeeper" and "Your Host from Coast to Coast" became "The World's Innkeeper." In 1975 Holiday Inn advertised "the best surprise is no surprise" as their slogan, thereby promising that a night in one Holiday Inn was like a night in all others. Unfortunately, Wilson did not know about the famous architect Frank Lloyd Wright who, in his autobiography, described a new type of American architecture related to and dependent on the roadway: "The great highway is becoming, and rapidly, the new horizontal line of Freedom extending from ocean to ocean." Wright designed two motels in 1956:

- The Bramlett Motor Hotel designed for a site in Holiday Inn's backyard in Memphis. It had three circular nine-story towers joined at the base with lobby, front desk and a garage. It was linked at the roof by a restaurant with spectacular views of the Memphis skyline.

- The Wieland Motel had ten bilevel circular guestroom pods joined on a shallow crescent with parking located under the second levels.

In 1969, the Sunday Times of London listed Kemmons Wilson among the 1,000 most important men of the 20th century, along with Winston Churchill and Franklin Roosevelt.

Time Magazine (June 12, 1972) with a picture of Innkeeper Kemmons Wilson on the cover described "The Man with 300,000 Beds," as follows,

> Charles Kemmons Wilson, 59, founder and chairman of Holiday Inns Inc., was doing what he like best, scouting new locations for the world's largest and fastest-growing lodging chain. Wherever he may be-paddling down the Amazon in a canoe, riding along the Riviera in a Mercedes or poring over maps in his computer- crammed headquarters at Memphis- Kemmons Wilson is always seeking new sites. "Looking for land," he says, "is like going on an Easter egg hunt, and sometimes you find the golden egg."
>
> Wilson has been finding so many of them lately that he seems to have a patent on the golden goose. On the average, a new Holiday Inn is opened every three days- or one new room every 36 minutes. The inns are a catalyst and a reflection of the age of mass travel, last year alone they served 72 million guests. The Holiday Inn sign, a 43-ft tall tower in screaming green, orange and yellow, is almost inescapable on American highways and it is well on its way to becoming a Pop symbol of U.S. enterprise abroad.....
>
> Indeed, few corporations dominate their industries the way that Holiday Inns dominates the fast-growing business of lodging. Its success has lured a host of imitators into the motor-inn field: Howard Johnson's, ITT Sheraton, Marriott. Despite this competition,

Holiday Inns has more than four times as many rooms as its closest rival in the hotel or motel field, Ramada Inns. Right now Wilson's company counts 208,939 rooms with a total of more than 300,000 double beds…..

Time Magazine reported that Holiday Inns was the first national chain to put up children at no cost when they share a room with parents, the first to offer free cribs for babies, as well as free TV sets and telephones in every room, a swimming pool at every motel and a kennel for traveling dogs. It was also the first to place ice machines and soft drink machines in hallways, thus sparing the traveler the cost of room service. Today every Holiday Inn has a local doctor and dentist on call to treat guests at almost any hour.

The originator and chief executive of the chain is a bluff, zesty man who believes absolutely in the company motto that is imprinted on the necktie that he wears, "It's a wonderful world….." A high school dropout, he is also fond of remarking with put-on bad grammar, "When you ain't got no education, you just got to use your brains." Like many visionaries, he takes an uncomplicated view of the world that leaves little room for doubt. "When you get an idea." He says, "you've got to think of a reason for doing it, not of a reason for not doing it."….

His main diversion is tennis, and he plays as often as he can at home or on business trips round the world. "Just call me an international tennis player," he quips. Despite an old leg injury, which has left him with a slight limp, he plays a strong, fast game and above all loves to win……

Keeping this global enterprise running smoothly is an exquisite exercise in managing millions of minute details simultaneously-something like building an Eiffel Tower out of matchsticks, without glue. Success is measured in holding costs to a minimum while seeming to stint on nothing and guaranteeing about the same level of service at all inns. The standards are maintained by 40 full-time investigators who make surprise calls at most inns four times a year.

There is one other thing keeping Wilson from retirement. Inside the dynamic, socially committed tycoon lurks a youngster who never quite got over his love affair with land. "There's no one who loves land more than me," he admits. For that kind of man, no job in the world could offer more a chance to chase daylight round the world, clambering over hills, slogging through rain forests, stalking through prairie grass in a never-ending hunt for the perfect motel site, Kemmons Wilson's ultimate golden egg.

However, the roadside Holiday Inns that became fixtures in towns across the USA beginning in the 1950s are disappearing. London-based InterContinental Hotels Group, current owner of the brand that pioneered franchised motor hotels, is in the process of shedding roughly half the nearly 1,100 properties that it had in 2004, mainly by ending franchise agreements with operators of substandard properties.

Among the first to go are those two-story low-rises with exterior corridors that defined the early years of Holiday Inn. In their place: multistory, contemporary-style hotels with fewer rooms and smaller restaurants. The multiyear campaign to remove the brand from outdated hotels – the largest cutback of its undertaken by a single chain- is expected to be complete in 2009. By the time the campaign ends, Holiday Inn will have removed about 100,000 rooms and opened about 35,000 new ones in the United States. With this effort, management hopes to revive the aging chain's image, which has suffered as newer competitions have cashed in on Holiday Inns traditional strength: consistent quality at an affordable price.

One reason the Holiday Inn brand holds such potential is that millions of baby boomers who stayed in Holiday Inns, as kids still have a deep fascination with the hotel chain. People loved the chain's clean pools, free ice, predictable architecture and its four-story tall garish green road signs. Guests were so enamored of it that they made a tradition of stealing the green-and-white-striped logo towel from rooms. Holiday Inn poked fun at the tradition by holding "towel amnesty" days, and in 2005 released a coffee-table book containing stories of guests and their "borrowed" towels, says Andrew Wood, a San Jose State University associate professor who writes about early roadside hotels.

Before the hotel-closure campaign, Holiday Inn franchisees for years had complained about a lack of direction. Many felt that InterContinental, the owner of the brand since 2003, and its predecessor, Six Continents, lavished more attention on the higher-end Crowne Plaza chain and the high-growth, limited-service brand, Holiday Inn Express.

As the new hotel designs (with interior corridors) are rolled out, there is a quiet but potentially explosive controversy simmering just below the surface of the hotel franchising industry. Some hotel franchisors like Holiday Inns have concluded that exterior corridor properties are obsolete and detrimental to their brands image. As a result, they're defranchising these motels to take advantage of current market conditions and the possibility of franchising newer and more modern properties. Unfortunately, there is a dearth of reliable data regarding many of the questions involved in this controversy:

- How many exterior-corridor properties are in operation in the U.S.?

- What do travelers think about exterior-corridor properties?

- Are these properties considered outdated and undesirable?

- How many guests still would rather park close to their rooms so they can

  - see their SUVs and their possessions

  - have a short walk with their luggage

  - have the privacy and convenience of avoiding hotel lobbies, elevators and long interior corridors?

- Do women guests believe that interior corridor hotels are safer?

There are an estimated 500,000 brand-affiliated, exterior-corridor hotel rooms now operating in the United States. If you add in independent properties, there are probably 750,000 rooms, or 40 percent of all domestic hotel rooms. At a 50 percent occupancy and $50 Average Daily Rate, these hotels generate nearly $6 billion in annual room revenues and pay $180 million in royalty fees (using a conservative three-percent franchise fee).

The hotel industry badly needs primary research on consumer preferences for exterior corridor hotels. Franchisors and franchisees should sponsor such research under the aegis of one or more of the following: the American Hotel & Lodging Association, The Cornell Center for Hospitality Research, the Asian American Hotel Owners Association, the NYU Tisch Center for Hospitality, Tourism and Sports Management and/or other hotel graduate schools at major universities.

The InterContinental group began to recognize how much the brand had slipped after travel began rebounding in 2003 from the post 9/11 doldrums. It was the start of a hotel boom, and the new owners of the iconic brand were unwilling to allow it to underperform. It became clear to brand executives and hotel franchisees that nostalgia alone couldn't support an older chain with strong ambitions of growing worldwide.

That year, InterContinental decided to stop renewing franchise agreements with operators of inferior or outdated sites, beef up Holiday Inn quality inspections and develop a prototype for future hotels. The chain mainly franchises hotels, it owns just five in the USA. While lax management played a role, Holiday Inn primarily fell victim to a confluence of changes in life styles, travelers' expectations, hotel economics and an influx of new competition.

Factors that forced InterContinental to act:

- Outdated hotels.

    In 2002, the average age of a Holiday Inn was 20.2 years. Many in the Southeast where the chain, got started – were more than 30 years old. Because of their age, many were in declining commercial districts.

- Consumer expectations.

  Holiday Inn had to react to changing customer expectations that evolved at a pace after 9/11. Customers began demanding more from hotels, even those charging about $100 a night. Limited-service brand hotel chains such as Courtyard by Marriott, Hampton Inns and InterContinentals own Holiday Inn Express began offering free breakfast, Internet access and better fitness centers.

- Less demand for full service.

  Holiday Inn, long categorized by the industry as having midprice, full-service hotels, was the biggest player in that shrinking category. Of those 534,000 rooms, Holiday Inn's share is about 26% and exceeds the number of rooms controlled by rivals such as Ramada, Quality and Howard Johnson. The category declined earlier this decade as more travelers opted for limited-service chains that served free breakfast buffets. It's not only customers who turned away from Holiday Inns. Developers, the people who finance and build hotels, spurned Holiday Inn and other brands in the midprice, full-service segment in search of greater profits in other types of lodging. Running a restaurant and room service as Holiday Inns do, for instance, began to drain profits once it became easier for customers to find chain restaurants such as T.G.I. Fridays and Denny's near their hotels.

  Fueling more worries about the brand, big owners such as FelCor Lodging Trust, a publicly traded real estate holding company in Dallas, started selling off hotels. As part of a broader repositioning of FelCor, the company sold two-thirds of its 50 Holiday Inns in smaller markets such as Knoxville, Tenn; Waco, Texas; and Montgomery, Ala. The hotels "were performing poorly" and getting trounced by new, limited-service rivals, says FelCor Chairman Tom Corcoran.

In newly built Holiday Inns, customers are seeing nothing that resembles the kitschy roadside hotels that had become the chain stereotype. The lobby in a new BattleCreek, Mich., Holiday Inn for example boasts rich cherry wood, black-and-white marble and large, highly polished tiles. Each of the 120 rooms in the five-story hotel has a flat-screen television and high-speed wireless Internet throughout the hotel. It has a black marble bar with glass pendant lamps and modern bar stools, and a restaurant with a high-end menu. It also offers room service, which continues to be a chain requirement. The hotel's fitness center is about three times the size of a guest room, bigger than average for Holiday Inns.

Kemmons Wilson, Jr. son of the founder, is building a Holiday Inn after years of reducing the number his company owns and operates. His company, which he operates with his two brothers will soon break ground on Holiday Inn in downtown Memphis. It's similar to the Battle Creek hotel in design and its not far from where his father built the first Holiday Inn 55 years ago. They decided to build a Holiday Inn instead of a rival brand partly to honor their father, but "also hopefully have a nice, solid investment," he says. When it opens in a year and a half, the hotel will be stocked full of reminders of the glory days, including a display of a bed and nightstand from the original hotel, borrowed from a local museum.

Wilson says InterContinental management is "restoring the great legacy my father, and others worked so hard to establish. They're doing the right thing. That's why we're back."

SOURCE MATERIALS

Alan Anderson and John Tompkins, *The Man with 300,000 Beds, Innkeeper Kemmons Wilson of Holiday Inn*, Time Magazine, June 12, 1972

Donald E. Lundberg, *The Hotel and Restaurant Business, Institutions/* Volume Feeding Management Magazine, Chicago, 1971

John Margolies, *Home Away From Home*, Little, Brown and Company, Boston, 1995

Walter A. Rutes, Richard H. Penner, Lawrence Adams, *Hotel Design, Planning and Development*, W.W. Norton & Company, New York, 2001

Michael Karl Witzel, *The American Motel*, MBI Publishing Company, Wisconsin, 2000

BIBLIOGRAPHY

Karl P. Abbott, *Open For The Season*, Doubleday & Company, Inc., Garden City, 1950

Edward N. Akin, *Flagler: Rockefeller Partner and Florida Baron*, Kent State University Press, Kent, 1988

Donald Albrecht, *New Hotels For Global Nomads*, Cooper-Hewitt, National Design Museum, New York, 2002

Alan Anderson and John Tompkins, *The Man with 300,000 Beds, Innkeeper Kemmons Wilson of Holiday Inn*, Time Magazine, June 12, 1972

Eric Arnesen, *Brotherhoods of Color: Black Railroad Workers and the Struggle for Equality*, Harvard University Press, Cambridge, 2001

Marilyn Bender and Selig Altschul, *The Chosen Instrument*, Simon and Schuster, New York, 1982

Susan R. Braden, *The Architecture of Leisure: The Florida Resort Hotels of Henry Flagler and Henry Plant*, University Press of Florida, Gainesville, 2002

Whitney Bolton, *The Silver Spade: The Conrad Hilton Story*, Farrar Strauss and Young, New York, 1954

Arnold Berke, *Mary Colter: Architect of the Southwest*, Princeton Architectural Press, New York, 2002

Eve Brown, *The Plaza*: 1907-1967, Duell, Sloan and Pearce, New York, 1967

Collection of newspaper articles and columns and magazine articles:

> Brookline Chronicle June 4, 1936
> Time Magazine October 16, 1950
> Time Magazine December 27, 1954
> New York Times April 10, 1955
> Time Magazine August 18, 1958

Boston Sunday Globe August 24, 1958
New York Journal American September 7, 1958
Fortune Magazine September 1958
Palm Beach Daily News April 5, 1959
New York Journal American November 17, 1959
New York Journal American November 18, 1959
New York Journal American November 20, 1959
New York Journal American December 2, 1959
New York Journal American April 28, 1960
Boston Traveler January 4, 1962
New York Herald Tribune February 12, 1964
Boston Evening Globe October 13, 1972
Courier- Gazette October 1972

David Leon Chandler, *Henry Flagler*, Macmillan Publishing Company, New York, 1986

Chicago Morning News, October 19, 1897, In Memoriam, George H. Pullman, Chicago Historical Society

Commission on Industrial Relations, Final Report and Testimony Submitted to Congress Washington, D.C., Government Printing Office, 1916 9553-54

Dr. James W. Covington, *Plant's Palace: Henry B. Plant and the Tampa Bay Hotel*, Harmony House Publishers, Louisville 1999

Albert Stevens Crockett, *Peacocks on Parade*, Sears Publishing Company, Inc. New York, 1931.

Thomas Ewing Dabney, *The Man Who Bought The Waldorf: The Life of Conrad N. Hilton*, Duell, Sloan and Pearce, New York, 1950

Robert Daley, *An American Saga: Juan Trippe and His Pan Am Empire*, Random House, New York, 1980

Albin Pasteur Dearing, *The Elegant Inn: The Waldorf-Astoria Hotel*, 1893-1929, Lyle Stuart Inc. Secaucus, 1986

Emmett Dedmon, *Fabulous Chicago*, McClelland and Stewart, Toronto 1981

Charles Dickens, *American Notes For General Circulation*, Penguin Classics, New York, 1842

Leslie Dorsey and Janice Devine, *Fare Thee Well: A Backward Look at Two Centuries of Historic American Hostelries, Fashionable Spas & Seaside Resorts*, Crown Publishers, Inc., New York, 1964

Susan M. Drake, *They Call Him John Q: A Hotel Legend*, Black Parts Publishing, LLC, Memphis, 2002

Marvin Dunn, *Black Miami in the Twentieth Century*, University Press of Florida, Gainesville, 1997

Desmond Fairbairn, *Pan Am: Gone But Not Forgotten*, Transportation Trails, Illinois, 1996

Jane Fisher, *Fabulous Hoosier: A Story of American Achievement*, Robert M. McBride & Company, New York, 1947

Jerry M. Fisher, *The Pacesetter: The Untold Story of Carl G. Fisher*, Lost Coast Press, Fort Bragg, California, 1998

Flagler Museum, *An Illustrated Guide*, Palm Beach, Florida 1998

Mark S. Foster, *Castles in the Sand: The Life and Times of Carl Graham Fisher*, University Press of Florida, Gainesville, 2000

Curtis Gathje, *At the Plaza: An Illustrated History of the World's Most Famous Hotel*, St. Martin's Press, New York, 2000

Harold Geneen with Alvin Moscow, *Managing*, Avon Books, New York, 1984

Gerald W. Glover, Scott R. Morrison, Jr., and Alfred C. Briggs, Jr., *"Making Quality Count: Boca Raton's Approach to Quality Assurance."* Cornell Hotel and Restaurant Administration Quarterly, Vol. 25, No. 1 (May 1984)

Thomas Graham, *Flagler's Grand Hotel Alcazar*, St. Augustine Historical Society, 1989

Thomas Graham, *Flagler's Magnificent Hotel Ponce De Leon*, St. Augustine Historical Society, 1990

John Q. Hammons: *"A Passionate Commitment To His Work,"* Celebrate Magazine, July 2006

Max Hampton, *Throw Away The Key*, The Bobbs-Merrill Company, Inc., Indianapolis, 1966

Ernest Henderson, *The World of "Mr. Sheraton"*, David McKay Company, Inc., New York, 1960

Reiko Hillyer, *The New South in the Ancient City: Flagler's St. Augustine Hotels and Sectional Reconciliation*, The American Hotel Journal of Decorative and Propaganda Arts, The Wolfsonian- Florida International University, Miami Beach, 2005

Conrad Hilton, *Be My Guest*, Prentice-Hall, Englewood Cliffs, 1957

Edward Hungerford, *The Story of the Waldorf-Astoria*, G.P. Putnam's Sons, New York, 1925

Joseph Husband, *The Story of the Pullman Car*, A.C. McClurg & Co., Chicago 1917

Matthew Josephson, *Empire of the Air*, Ayer Company Publishers, Inc., North Stratford, 1999

Lesley Poling-Kempes, *The Harvey Girls: Women Who Opened the West*, Marlowe & Company, New York 1991

Catherine Kirkland, *Chicago Yesterdays: A Sheaf of Reminiscences* (Daughaday, 1919 Chicago, Illinois)

Howard Kleinberg, *Woggles and Cheese Holes: The History of Miami Beach's Hotels*, The Greater Miami & The Beaches Hotel Association, Miami Beach, 2005

Sonny Kleinfield, *The Hotel: A Week in the Life of the Plaza*, Simon and Schuster, 1989

Marianne Lamonaca and Jonathan Mogul, Editors, *Grand Hotels of the Jazz Age: The Architecture of Schultze & Weaver*, The Wolfsonian-Florida International University, Princeton Architectural Press, New York, 2005

Samuel D. Laroue, Jr. and Ellen J. Uguccioni, *The Biltmore Hotel: An Enduring Legacy*, Arva Parks & Company and Centennial Press, Miami, 2002

Sinclair Lewis, *Work of Art*, Doubleday, New York, 1934

Liston Edgington Leyendecker, *Palace Car Prince*, University Press of Colorado 1992

"Accidental No More" by Harry Lister, Lodging, December 1996

"Born to Last" by Harry Lister, Lodging, January 1999

Rochelle Logan and Julie Halverstadt, *100 Most Popular Business Leaders For Young Adults: Biographical Sketches and Professional Paths*, Libraries Unlimited, Greenwood Village, Colorado, 2002

Charles Long, "Pioneer and the Funeral Train: How 'Honest Abe' was Used to Create a Corporate Tall Tale." Railroad History (Spring 2002)

Donald E. Lundberg, *The Hotel and Restaurant Business*, Institutions/Volume Feeding Management Magazine, Chicago, 1971

Lawrence Mahoney, *The Early Birds: A History of Pan Am's Clipper Ships*, The Pickering Press, Miami, 1987

Making People Feel At Home For 75 Years, Howard Johnson Company Booklet

John Margolies, *Home Away From Home*, Little, Brown and Company, Boston, 1995

J. Willard Marriott, Jr. and Kathi Ann Brown, *The Spirit to Serve: Marriott's Way*, HarperCollins, Publishers, New York, 1997

Sidney Walter Martin, *Florida's Flagler,* The University of Georgia Press, Athens 1949

James Remington McCarthy, *Peacock Alley*, Harper & Brothers, New York, 1931

Brian McGinty, *The Palace Inns: A Connoisseur's Guide to Historic American Hotels*, Stackpole Books, Harrisburg, 1978

Bill McMillon, *Old Lodges and Hotels of Our National Parks*, Icarus Press, South Bend, 1983

Floyd Miller, *Statler: America's Extraordinary Hotelman*, The Statler Foundation, New York 1968

Joel Millman, *The Other Americans*, Viking Penguin, New York, 1997

Julian Morel, *Pullman: The Pullman Car Company: Its services, cars and traditions* David & Charles, London 1983

Edward A. Mueller, *Steamships of the Two Henrys: Being an Account of the Maritime Activities of Henry Morrison Flagler and Henry Bradley Plant*, E.O. Painter Printing Co., DeLeon Springs, FL. 1996

Robert O'Brien, *Marriott: The J. Willard Marriott Story*, Deseret Book Company, Salt Lake City, 1979

Pat Parks, *The Railroad That Died At Sea*, The Stephen Greene Press, Brattleboro, Vt., 1968

Bessie Louise Pierce, *A History of Chicago* Vol. 2 1848-1871, Alfred A. Knopf, New York 1940

Bessie Louise Pierce, Editor, *As Others See Chicago: Impressions of Visitors, 1673-1933*, University of Chicago Press, 1939, Chicago, Illinois

James E. Potter, *A Room With a World View: 50 Years of Inter-Continental Hotels and Its People*, 1946-1996, George Weidenfeld & Nicolson Ltd., London, 1996

Royal H. Pullman, D.D. "Dedication Sermon at the Pullman Memorial, Universalist Church, January 3, 1895, Albion NY

Dolly Redford, *Billion-Dollar Sandbar: A Biography of Miami Beach*, E. P. Dutton & Co., New York, 1970

Charles A. Reynolds, *Tribute: The Architecture of the Hotel Ponce de Leon in Its Relation to the History of St. Augustine*, Brochure 1890.

Kelly Reynolds, *Henry Plant: Pioneer Empire Builder*, The Florida Historical Society Press, Cocoa, Florida, 2003

Walter A. Rutes, Richard H. Penner, Lawrence Adams, *Hotel Design, Planning and Development*, W.W. Norton & Company, New York, 2001

Anthony Sampson, *The Sovereign State of ITT*, Stein and Day, New York, 1973

Jack Santino, *Miles of Smiles, Years of Struggle: Stories of Black Pullman Porters*, University of Illinois Press, Chicago, 1989

Robert J. Schoenberg, *Geneen*, W.W. Norton & Company, New York, 1985

G. Hutchinson Smyth, *The Life of Henry Bradley Plant: Founder and President of the Plant System of Railroads and Steamships*, G.P. Putnam's Sons, New York 1898; reprint

"*The Complete John Q.: The Man, His Gifts, His Legacy,*" Signature Magazine, Spring 2006

Ida M. Tarbell, *The History of the Standard Oil Company*, 2 Vols. Macmillan, New York, 1925

The American Hotel: The Journal of Decorative and Propaganda Arts, The Wolfsonian- Florida International University Miami Beach, Issue 25, 2005

J. W. Travers, *History of Beautiful Palm Beach*, Palm Beach Press, West Palm Beach, 1931

Larry Tye, *Rising From The Rails*, Henry Holt and Company, New York 2004

Jerome J. Vallen, *The Art and Science of Modern Innkeeping*, Ahrens Publishing Company, New York, 1968

"A Patel Motel Cartel?" by Tunku Varadarajan, New York Times Magazine, July 4, 1999

Marta Weigle and Barbara A. Babcock, Editors, *The Great Southwest of the Fred Harvey Company and the Santa Fe Railway*, The Heard Museum, Phoenix, 1996

Arthur White, *Palaces of the People: A Social History of Commercial Hospitality*, Taplinger Publishing Company, New York, 1970

John H. White, *The American Railroad Passenger Car*, Johns Hopkins Press, 1985

Jefferson Willamson, *The American Hotel*, Alfred A. Knopf, New York 1930

"Vested Interests" by Anne Willoughby, Lodging, September 2001

Michael Karl Witzel, *The American Motel*, MBI Publishing Company, Wisconsin, 2000

"All in the Family: AAHOA Comes of Age", Lodging Hospitality, by Carlo Wolff, February 2001

INDEX

Brevoort Hotel, New York, N.Y. 293
Brickyard 29
Bright Angel Lodge, Grand Canyon, Arizona 101-103
Brown Hotel, Louisville, Ky. xxi
Brown Palace Hotel, Denver, Co. xxi
Brown, Dee 90
Brunswick Hotel, New York, N.Y. 136
Buckingham Hotel, New York, N.Y. 136
Buggsi Hospitality Group 213
Burger King 161
Burlington Railroad 89, 90
Burr, Jim 260
Busquets, William 299

Caldwell, Cy 291
Calhoun, Byron 298
California School of Design, San Francisco, Ca. 95
Camelback Inn, Scottsdale, Arizona 175
Camp Columbia, Havana, Cuba 290
Candler, William 7
Caribe Hilton Hotel, San Juan, Puerto Rico 130
Carlton Tower, London, England 262
Carnegie, Andrew 238
Carrera Hotel, Santiago, Chile 298
Carrere and Hastings 50, 51

Carrere, John M. 47
Casa del Desierto Harvey House, Barstow, Ca. 97
Casa Marina Hotel 63
Casa Monica Hotel, St. Augustine, Fl. 52, 54
Cendant Corporation162, 195
Central Hotel, Boscobel, Wis. 5
Chapman, Harkness and Company 43
Chapman, Dana Dorsey 59
Charter House Hotel, Annapolis, Md. 255
Chateau on the Lake, Branson, Mo. 74, 75, 76, 80
Chicago, Alton & St. Louis Railroad 235, 237
Chicago, Burlington and Quincy Railroad 241
Childs Restaurant Corporation 260
Church of Jesus Christ of Latter-Day Saints 170
City Hotel, Baltimore, Md. xviii
City Hotel, New York, N.Y. xviii
Cleveland Hotel, Cleveland, Ohio 260
Cleveland, President Grover 248
Clifton Hotel, Florence, Kansas 96
CNL Hotels and Resorts 9
Cohan, George M. 264
Collins, John 31
Colonial Hotel, Nassau 59
Colored Town, Miami, Fl. 59
Colter, Mary Elizabeth Jane 94, 98, 99, 100-103

Hokanson, Drake 29
Holiday Inn Roadside Sign 320
Holiday Inns of America 71, 72, 320
Holland House, New York, N.Y. 1, 136
Homewood Suites 146
Hoover, J. Edgar 139, 140, 321
Hopi House 89, 98-102
Horwath and Horwath 299
Hospitality Franchise Systems Inc. 162
Host Marriott Corporation 178, 182
Hot Shoppes 152, 159, 173, 174, 175
Hotel Corporation of America (HCA) 256, 260, 265
Hotel Man of the Half Century 271
Hotel World Magazine 4
House, George E. Restaurant 273
Howard Johnson Bible 153
Howard Johnson Motor Lodges 154, 155, 158
Hoxey, Arch 290
Hubbard, Elbert 29
Huckel, Minnie Harvey 97, 98
Hughes, Howard 304
Huxtable, Ada Louise 327
Hyatt Regency Hotel, Atlanta, Ga. xxi

Indian Building 95
Indianapolis Speedway 28-29

INDO American Hospitality Association 194
In-Flite Service 175
Ingraham, James E. 53
Inn at Port Tampa, Tampa Fl. 230
INN-PAC 325
Inter-Continental Group Hotel Portfolio For 1946-1996 306-313
InterContinental Hotel Company 133, 289, 298
International Air Transport Association (IATA) 300
International Association of Holiday Inns, Inc. (IAHI) 85, 324, 325
International Harvester Company 54
International Society of Hospitality Consultants 213
International Telephone & Telegraph Co. xii, 119
Interstate Highway System 72, 155

James, Henry 48
James, Howard 'Bud' 121
JHM Hotels 213
Jim Crow racism 49
Johnson, Howard Brennan 151, 159
Johnson, Howard Dearing (1896-1972) 151-166, 317
Johnson, Reginald 14
Johnson, Wallace 323

DATE DUE